KENT
DISASTERS

KENT
DISASTERS

ROY INGLETON

Wharncliffe Books

First published in Great Britain in 2010 by
Wharncliffe Local History
An imprint of
Pen & Sword Books Ltd
47 Church Street
Barnsley
South Yorkshire
S70 2AS

Copyright © Roy Ingleton, 2010

ISBN 978 1 84563 116 1

The right of Roy Ingleton to be identified as the
author of this work has been asserted by him in accordance
with the Copyright, Designs and Patents Act 1988

A CIP catalogue record for this book is
available from the British Library

Typeset in Ehrhardt
by S L Menzies-Earl

Printed and bound in England
by CPI UK

Pen & Sword Books Ltd incorporates the imprints of
Pen & Sword Aviation, Pen & Sword Maritime,
Pen & Sword Military, Wharncliffe Local History, Pen & Sword Select,
Pen & Sword Military Classics, Leo Cooper, Remember When,
Seaforth Publishing and Frontline Publishing

For a complete list of Pen & Sword titles please contact
PEN & SWORD BOOKS LIMITED
47 Church Street, Barnsley, South Yorkshire, S70 2AS, England
E-mail: enquiries@pen-and-sword.co.uk
Website: www.pen-and-sword.co.uk

Contents

List of Plates

Introduction
and Acknowledgements

disaster; *n* an adverse or unfortunate event;
a great and sudden misfortune; a calamity.
(*Chambers Dictionary*)

As 'The Garden of England', Kent is usually regarded as a peaceful, largely rural and agricultural county and it may therefore come as something of a surprise to learn that it has seen more than its fair share of death and destruction. As will be seen, fire and flood, war and terrorism, plague and pestilence, industrial and transportation accidents have all been experienced in the county and this book merely covers some of the more important, unusual or interesting examples.

In some cases, the incident involved a significant loss of life – sometimes hundreds of victims. In others, the fatalities may have been fewer but the damage incurred or certain other effects make them noteworthy. In any event, they were all misfortunes or calamities and certainly fall within the dictionary definition given above.

No work of this nature can be compiled without the assistance, encouragement and support of numerous people and bodies. It is not possible to list them all but particular thanks are extended to Martin Easdown, the Kent Fire & Rescue Services Museum (John Meakins), the Faversham Heritage Centre (Arthur Percival), the Kent Police Museum (John Endicott), the Marden Heritage Centre, Kent Arts & Libraries Service, Medway Archives, the *Kent Messenger* and various town museums, to name but a few. To the many others who have helped me in my research, I offer my grateful thanks.

Some of the photographs are my own and with regard to the others, acknowledgement has been given or permission sought wherever it has been possible to trace the copyright holders. I apologise in advance to those concerned if there has been any unintentional oversight and assure them that this will be corrected in future editions.

Roy Ingleton
Maidstone
November 2009

Chapter 1

Fire

Ever since man discovered how to make and harness fire, it has been both a boon and a bane. On the one hand, it provided warmth, a means of cooking food and discouraged predators but it could also maim and kill people and destroy property. It is not surprising therefore that many of the disasters and catastrophes that have occurred in Kent have been associated with this element.

The Statute of Westminster, which Edward I promulgated in 1285, laid down that every town should provide a system of 'watch and ward' with watchmen to patrol the streets at night. Although largely a crime-prevention measure, the intention was also to give early warning of any fire that might break out as, with buildings largely constructed of timber, wattle and daub and with thatched roofs, any fire that got out of control would rapidly destroy the building concerned and could spread to others before anyone was sufficiently awake to appreciate what was happening.

In a matter of minutes, rather than hours, a whole town could be destroyed. Despite the presence of watchmen (who perhaps were not always as wide awake as they might have been), the town of Gravesend, for example, was virtually totally destroyed on more than one occasion, as was mediaeval Hythe.

Although the formation of fire brigades and the provision of real firefighting equipment would have to wait a further two centuries, some steps were taken by many of the borough corporations in the late sixteenth century. In the county town of Maidstone, for example, in 1591, chains, buckets and hooks were provided '. . . for the better defence of the town against any sudden fier [sic]'. Some thirty years later, two long ladders and twelve leather buckets were supplied for the general use of the town and brewers, innkeepers and maltmen were asked to keep suitable ladders on their premises. Ratepayers were required to provide one or two leather fire buckets, depending on the value of their property.

As time went on, more premises began to be built of robust materials, such as brick and stone, and the potential for destruction was lessened. Fire prevention was still encouraged, however, and Maidstone Corporation laid down in 1604 that no flax was to be dressed except in: '. . . shops and other fit roomes open towards the streete and severe close without riftes and chinks with lyme or lome from other roome of the houses'.

At about the end of the eighteenth century, fire brigades began to be formed, by insurance companies to begin with, but later on by the various municipalities. In 1802 the Kent Fire Insurance Company was formed, with the white horse of Kent as its symbol.

The First Fire Brigades

In the same year (1802), the first fire brigade in Kent was formed in Hythe, equipped with a wooden fire engine. The fire engine was no doubt an excellent one for its day, although it was unable to prevent the death of three fine black horses belonging to the Archbishop of Canterbury which were in the stables at the White Hart Inn. These, with three other horses that survived, had brought the Archbishop's coach to Hythe that day in June 1806.

Some years later the Hythe fire brigade was split into two under the names of the Corporation Fire Engine Brigade and the Scot & Lot Fire Engine Association (scot and lot being an old municipal tax, which suggests how the association was funded). In 1860 the two brigades were reunited and later took the name of the Hythe Volunteer Fire Brigade, being provided with a brand-new Paxton engine, made by Merryweather and Sons and costing £173 3s 0d, this sum being raised by public subscription. Well-known names among the subscribers included Mr H B Mackeson (the local brewer), Colonel Deedes and Baron Rothschild, the latter being Hythe's Member of Parliament.

The new, horse-drawn fire engine was quickly put to use when a serious fire broke out in Stade Street, Hythe in 1866. William Hole, described as a fisherman but evidently rather more prosperous than most who followed this calling, owned a house there with stabling and a herring-hang attached, together with a large wooden shed. One night, he awoke to find the whole of the premises well alight and sent for the fire brigade. With a great clattering of hooves, the engine arrived with eight firemen and three officers – probably the whole of the brigade. Such was the conflagration that even the fire engine from the nearby Army School of Musketry attended with a further forty men. The engines were however hampered by the lack of mains water pressure and, despite taking water from the sea and nearby wells, it proved impossible to save the buildings, although all the adjacent houses were preserved. Mr Hole lost the outbuildings and everything in them: nets, farm equipment, a van and a cart and the black mare that used to pull them. He was not fully insured.

Just behind the Swan Hotel, in Bartholemew Street, there stood three wooden cottages and, in the early hours of one Sunday morning in 1884, Grace Riddington, who lived in the middle cottage with her husband, their three children and her elderly father, awoke to hear an unfamiliar noise. On investigation, she found the front room well alight. Racing up the stairs she called to her father and, her husband having climbed out of the window, she passed the children to him. She went back to check on her father but the flames were too fierce and she, too, had to leave by the window.

The next-door neighbour tried to force the door to reach the old man but was driven back by the heat and went back to make sure his own family (he had six sons and a daughter) was safe. He then retrieved his doe rabbit and her litter and tried to salvage some clothing and possessions.

The town fire brigade was quickly on the scene, as was the engine from the nearby brewery but, despite their best efforts, all three cottages were destroyed. Grace's father, Hammonden Vidgeon, was found dead in his attic room, still clutching the remains of a candlestick which he had evidently used in his bid to escape. The cause of the fire was never established.

Lack of water and poor communications were major drawbacks, especially where the larger houses on the outskirts of the town were concerned. In 1902, a sizeable house in the course of construction in Saltwood for Mr A C Leney, the Dover brewer, was badly damaged by fire and the interior completely burnt out. The total cost of the damage was estimated at the enormous sum of £4,000.

At the beginning of of the twentieth century, the barrister W H Upjohn KC, who owned a newly completed mansion in Lympne, was also to discover the disadvantages of having a house in rural parts. Early one Sunday morning the building caught fire and the site foreman had to cycle to Hythe to call out the fire brigade. When the brigade arrived they found the only water was in an inaccessible well and this magnificent house, of mainly oak construction, was burnt to the ground. On this occasion arson was suspected, although no one was ever arrested for the crime.

The dearth of telephones and lack of an adequate water supply were to figure in another Hythe fire in 1913. The meter house at the Hythe Gasworks had caught alight and the flames were threatening the nearby gasholders but, although there was a telephone at the gasworks, there was no one at the fire station and no member of the fire brigade was on the phone. There was not even a telephone in the newly opened county police station in Hythe as it had been decided that, as there was already one in the Seabrook Police Station, one was not needed in Hythe.

In fact, the stokers at the gasworks had rung the telephone exchange and the young female operator, entirely on her own and 'in such attire as she would be at that time of night, and with her hair down at the back', had to leave her post and go out into the street to try to find a policemen or somebody else to whom she could impart this important information. (In fact, it was not uncommon at this time for fire brigades to be called to a fire by the sending of a telegram.)

So far as the essential water supply was concerned, the nearest hydrant to the gasworks was at the extreme end of the town's water supply and the pressure was insufficient. It should have been possible to increase the pressure by obtaining supplementary supplies from the Saltwood Reservoir, but the man whose job it was to open the valve was asleep and failed to hear the maroon that was set off to call out the fire brigade. It was later discovered that there was another hydrant nearer the scene of the fire but this was hidden under soil and accumulated rubbish.

Fortunately the fire did not reach the gasholders and there were no injuries, but what could have been a night of great drama took on the aspect of a Keystone Cops film.

The delays occasioned by the lack of means of communication were aggravated by the fact that, until around the time of the First World War, all fire engines were horse-drawn. In Maidstone, for example, the town's fire brigade had no horses of its own and was obliged to use those on the nearby cab rank, which were often not in the best of condition and were very tired by the evening. One horse in fact dropped dead from heart failure on its way to attend a fire at Maidstone Prison. The introduction of motorised fire engines, while a great advance in the way of efficiency, nevertheless deprived the public of the great thrill of seeing a 'steamer' pump appliance drawn by horses at full gallop as they raced to a fire.

Gravesend Razed to the Ground

Around 1790, a particularly fierce conflagration destroyed 250 dwellings in the town of Gravesend. Although there was a fire engine available for use, it was in such poor condition as to be useless and the fire just spread from house to house and from shop to shop until a building was blown up to provide a fire break.

A committee of 'gentlemen of the town' was set up to collect money for those poor residents who had lost their homes and all their possessions in the conflagration. The treasurer to this committee, one William Jefferys, described the blaze in the following terms:

> It began in a building on the river bank in which was deposited a great deal of cordage and oakum. In a few minutes, the shed, the adjoining forge and warehouses and a hoy, with her mast and sail which lay close to the side of the wharf, were one general blaze. The men employed on the wharf, endeavouring to extinguish the fire, exposed themselves to great danger and were scarcely able to effect their escape. The strength of the fire was so great that on the falling of the houses large flakes of fire were thrown up to a prodigious height and carried to a considerable distance, burning haystacks in fields to the south of the town. To describe this calamitous scene is impossible; parents searching after their children, whole families roofless and penniless and such like spectacles were everywhere to be seen. But the most dreadful catastrophe was the fatal burning of William Bassett, . . . and the death of Mrs Dunk and her infant child who incautiously ventured too near a burning home and were struck by a falling chimney.

Tudor Home Destroyed

On another occasion, poor communications resulted in a building being severely damaged by fire – this time with the loss of four lives.

At about midnight on 17 October 1927 a fire broke out in the gas-lit study of The Hall, Wateringbury, where the owner, Captain Richard Booth Leslie Bazley-White DSO, of the Royal West Kent Regiment and the Egyptian Army, had been reading before going to bed. The Hall was a large, rambling, rather isolated Tudor building, not far from Mereworth Castle, and the family had been living there for some eighteen months.

The fire was first noticed by the Captain's wife, Katherine, who woke the cook, Edith Whitfield, by her cries of 'Fire! Fire!' before rushing to save her 4-year-old son John and the boy's nurse, 55-year-old Rose Weekes, who were both asleep in the night nursery.

Hastily slipping on a dressing gown, Mrs Whitfield opened the door of her room, intending to go down to the study and use the telephone to call the fire brigade, but saw smoke and flames coming from the door to the study. She therefore went back into her room, closed the door and, clambering out of the window, sat on the ledge and shouted, 'Fire!' before bravely launching herself from this first-floor window onto the gravel path below. Fortunately, she was uninjured and she ran round the house, still calling 'Fire!'. Marjorie Sharp, the parlour maid, also heard Mrs Bazley-White's cries and, slipping on a coat, she managed to escape down the back stairs before these were cut off by the flames. The other two servants also managed to get out of the building before the flames engulfed it.

Meanwhile, Mrs Whitfield decided to go and get help and so she hurried to her father's house in the village to raise the alarm, arriving there in a state of collapse. She managed to wake her father and three brothers, one of whom set off for The Hall on his motor cycle, taking with him some sheets. Her father, Stephen Butcher, was running towards The Hall when he saw a taxi coming towards him from the direction of Mereworth. He waved the vehicle down and the driver, Frank Franklin, agreed to telephone for the fire brigade. In the village of Wateringbury he stopped at the police house and tried to wake the local sergeant but without success. In fact, the sergeant was not at home at the time.

While the young taxi driver was hammering on the door of the police house, he was joined by an acquaintance, Charles Pearce, who, when he heard the news, offered to help. Pointing across the nearby railway line he said, 'I'll try the signal-box' and he scrambled over the fence dividing the railway from the road and ran up to the signal-box. Charles called up to the signalman, 'There's a fire at The Hall. Call the fire brigade, quick!' But the railway employee was apparently something of a 'jobsworth': 'I'm not authorised to make phone calls just like that. You'll have to go to the police house,' he responded. Exasperated, Charles tried to explain: 'We've already tried the sergeant's house. We can't get any reply.'

But the signalman was not to be moved. 'Well, I can't make the call from here. On whose authority would it be? And who would pay for the call? Anyway, the fire brigade wouldn't turn out even if I did call them.'

By this time, Frank Franklin had joined Charles Pearce and they decided they were wasting their time. Franklin ran across the road to the pub, leaving his friend to tell the railwayman what he thought of him. 'You're a silly old fool!' he shouted, in disgust – a comment that the Coroner was later to describe as 'not an overstatement'.

Meanwhile, Frank Franklin was having no success in rousing the landlord of the pub and moved on to the home of Doctor Severne. Not unaccustomed to being called out, the doctor responded fairly quickly, but by this time the fire had been raging for around an hour. On being apprised of the situation, the doctor wasted no time making the necessary call and the two lads set off back to The Hall.

When they arrived they found the whole of the back of the old, timbered building well alight. With the audacity of youth, Frank Franklin climbed a drain pipe and looked into Mrs Bazley-White's bedroom but it appeared to be empty. Scrambling back to earth, he ran to the part of the building in which the servants' quarters were located and found this, too, was burning fiercely. Using a tyre lever from his taxi, he forced the front door and found that the main staircase was intact. He could hear sounds that he later described as being 'like the groans of an old lady' and so he made his way up the stairs. On the first floor he thought he heard shots but this was put down to the cracking of the burning timbers. The flames were blazing in the corridor and there was no way he could go any further so he went back downstairs.

Although on this occasion there was a telephone in the house, it was located in the study where the fire appeared to have started and where the flames were fiercest and there was no question of anyone being able to use it to call for help. Consequently, given the obstructiveness of the railway signalman, it was over an hour before the Maidstone Fire Brigade arrived at 1.17 am, by which time the whole house was well alight. The fire chief, William Wainscot, claimed that he was told that there was no one in the house, whereas in fact, the Captain and the rest of his family – wife, infant son and nurse – were trapped on the upper floor.

The fire brigade toiled until around 5 am before the fire was brought under control, but by this time the house had been totally destroyed. The firemen searched the smouldering debris and discovered the body of Mrs Bazley-White on the drawing-room floor. Shortly afterwards, the body of her husband was found under the ashes. Finally, the bodies of the nurse, Miss Weekes, and the infant son were revealed. The baby appeared to be lying on the remains of a bed, with the body of his nurse bent over him.

Just what caused the fire and where it had started has never been fully established and there were two distinct theories. The fire officer held that the fire had started on the first floor, probably in the Captain's bedroom, and had burned downwards whereas the Coroner believed that it had started in the ground-floor study and burned upwards. The jury at the inquest inclined to the latter theory.

It was generally assumed that, as she appeared to have been the first to detect the fire, Mrs Bazley-White effectively sacrificed herself in order to save her son and husband. There is no doubt she could have escaped the same way as the parlour maid before the flames really took hold, but even if she later found her way barred by the flames, it is strange that none of the family tried to escape via the large windows that were only some 10ft from the ground. This is what the other two servants had done, although Olive Selves, the housemaid, had clung to the sill for some time before she found the courage to let go and drop the remaining 4 or 5ft to the ground.

Another mystery seems to have been largely played down; in the remains of The Hall the firemen found two hand guns, a Webley revolver and an automatic. The revolver had not been used for some time but the automatic was loaded with six rounds, three of which had exploded in the heat. It could well have been this that Frank Franklin had heard as he mounted the stairs in his unsuccessful rescue attempt.

The verdict of the inquest was that the gallant Captain and his family and the nurse had all perished from smoke inhalation. They had apparently made no attempt to jump to safety before being overcome.

Fatal Fete Fire

On Thursday 11 July 1929 a grand, two-day fete was held in Gillingham Park in aid of St Bartholemew's Hospital, the climax of which was to be the customary firefighting and rescue demonstration put on by the Gillingham Fire Brigade.

The scenario was a mock marriage reception to be held in a specially constructed house with the parts of the bride, groom and best man being grotesquely played by firemen and with a dozen sea scouts and naval cadets acting as the guests. These were accompanied by Petty Officer John Nutton, performing his traditional role as 'Auntie' in the manner of a pantomime dame. Having wandered through the crowd to draw attention to the display, at the appointed time the whole 'wedding party' made its way to the 'house' for the festivities, watched by a very large crowd of spectators. The 'house' itself was constructed, as was the custom, of old doors, timber, matchboarding and hessian, all designed to burn freely and spectacularly.

The plan was for fire to be simulated by burning red flares behind the windows, upon which the 'wedding guests' would lean out of the windows, calling for help. Once they had been ostentatiously rescued and were safe, the structure would be set on fire in earnest and extinguished with great aplomb by the fire brigade. The whole display had been thoroughly rehearsed without incident. But this time, something went terribly wrong.

As darkness fell, it soon became apparent that the flames were not being simulated and that the mock-up building was really on fire. Starting on the ground floor, the flames rapidly spread to the upper storey, blocking all means of escape. It only took seconds for the wood and canvas structure to become engulfed in flames.

The spectators, little realising the drama that was unfolding before their eyes, cheered this realistic display and clapped the figures they could see running across the roof and calling for help. Only when these were seen to fall or leap into the inferno below did many of the spectators appreciate the full horror of the incident.

Chief Officer Frederick White of the Gillingham Fire Brigade ordered the two stand-by water pumps into action and attempts were made to get ladders up to the trapped and terrified lads. Policemen, firemen and St John's Ambulance crews tried to enter the building but the heat forced them back and several of them suffered burns as a result. The fire ladders themselves caught fire, the charred rungs crumbling under the feet of the firemen and a builder's ladder had to be pressed into service.

A searchlight that was on the scene was played onto the inferno and the horrified spectators, many of whom were related to the 'actors', saw two boys, who had made their way to the top of the structure, jump off to avoid being burnt to death, only to be killed by the fall. The burned body of another boy could clearly be seen, hanging half over the edge of the roof.

The incident was reported in the *Chatham, Rochester & Gillingham News* in the following emotional terms:

> A great burst of fire leapt from the bottom of the flimsy building and shot up to the top, piercing the whole structure at one terrible sweep and wrapping it in suffocating flames. The occupant . . . shouted in mad panic, 'Bring the Brigade, for God's sake.' Many women in the crowd fainted and had to be carried out of the Park, and several men were in tears. The firemen frenziedly dragged two escape ladders to the house . . . Two boys leaped the forty feet for their lives, the poor little fellows crashing into the blazing wreckage below.

Frantic efforts to save the people in the building were to no avail. Although the fire was quickly extinguished, not one of the fifteen people in the building survived, many being burnt beyond recognition. They included nine boys, aged from 10 to 14 years, and six men.

Many of the bodies were identified only through their belongings or scraps of clothing. The body of Fireman Albert Nicholls (56), the Fire Brigade Secretary, was only identified by his dentures which were examined by the mayor, Councillor Treacher, who was the deceased's dentist. Councillor Treacher later made a statement to the press and public, saying:

> We can only guess at the possible cause. One suggestion is that someone in a fit of aberration fired half-a-dozen tar barrels which

were in the lower storey. This seems the only explanation of the blaze which, within two minutes, completely enwrapped the house. I don't think the victims could have suffered much; within a few minutes they were probably half-suffocated and must have become unconscious shortly afterwards. It was a terrible sight to see them hanging out of the windows, imploring help in earnest, but everyone thought it was make-believe.

Councillor Treacher added that the families of the three firemen would receive a pension of 10*s* (50p) a week.

The presence of any tar barrels in the 'house' was strongly denied by the Chief Fire Officer and Councillor Treacher subsequently retracted his comment that there were any such things there. It later transpired that there were a number of pans containing oily waste, which were used to light the flares, and also an old oil barrel containing wood shavings and it seems that it was these shavings that first caught fire and started the blaze.

The funeral of the unfortunate victims was attended by thousands of people who lined the streets as ten coffins were carried on fire appliances to the cemetery, with the other five borne on carriages, all covered in wreaths and flowers.

The Coroner at the subsequent inquest summed up by saying:

Lieutenant Bines has told how the combustibles were placed in the building, and how he gave detailed duties to various firemen – all of whom, unfortunately, have since died – and, finally, how he detailed Fireman Cockayne to light flares on the first, second and top floors, and then report to him at the front door when the building was clear – that is, when those who had been taking part in the mock rescue should have got quite away from the building. Then and not till then, were the shavings to be set alight, and the whole building demolished. Well, that is what should have happened. If that had happened we should not be here today. I am perfectly sure that those orders were not carried out and the question is: why were they miscarried?

The jury returned a verdict of 'Death from misadventure, due to shock from burns received while taking part in a fire brigade life-saving demonstration, due to a fire being prematurely started by a person or persons unknown.' There was an inference that, for some unknown reason, Fireman Cockayne, who was responsible for lighting the flares to simulate a fire, had set fire to the shavings (provided to start the real fire) before lighting the flares, possibly under the erroneous impression that the shavings would only smoulder for some time. However, there was no proof of this. What was not in dispute was that Fireman Cockayne was very much involved in attempting to help others to evacuate the burning building and lost his life while bravely doing so. Whether this was the true cause of the disaster we shall never know and the culprit – if indeed any one person was culpable – perished in the flames with all the others.

The editorial of the *Chatham, Rochester & Gillingham News* on 19 July 1929 summed up the disaster and called for the cancellation of any similar events in the future:

> The terrible fire at Gillingham which has been so much in our thoughts . . . represents far more than a serious local accident, it must be regarded rather as a disaster of national importance. . . .We have no desire, we have no authority to apportion blame . . . but to see that such safeguards shall be taken in the future as will render a disaster of this nature impossible . . . One may go on placing one's head in a lion's mouth for years with inferred impunity, but the element of danger does not cease to exist just because no accident occurs. The knowledge that such an act is popular . . . does not render it less probable that someday the lion may bite.

This popular view prevailed and the 'Fireman's Wedding' display was never again staged.

Cathedral in Peril

For over two centuries, the great City Flour Mills building in Canterbury had stood as a proud testament to the strategic and industrial importance of that great cathedral city – the birthplace of Christianity in England. Built in 1792 as the city granary to ensure the storage of grain in the event of an invasion by the French, it was a great, six-storey timber building standing at the corner of St Radigund's Street and Mill Lane, on the banks of the River Stour.

In 1794 the building changed hands and was converted to a water mill and was worked by a series of tenant millers. One-hundred years later, in 1896, it came into the possession of the Denne family, which was still milling flour for the city and its surroundings in 1933.

It was around 8.30 on the morning of 17 October 1933 that a young employee of the mill, Bob Carroll, gave the alarm that the hayloft was on fire. Most of the workers were eating their breakfasts away from the mill but the few that remained set about extinguishing the fire with buckets of water. But their efforts were in vain and it soon became evident that professional help was needed. Indeed, the fire was spreading with such rapidity that by the time the Canterbury City Fire Brigade arrived on the scene, less than 5 minutes after receiving the call, the upper part of the building was burning fiercely. Given the wooden construction, it was soon apparent that the mill was doomed, despite the additional attendance of fire brigades from Sturry and Bridge.

The *Kentish Gazette*'s reporter described the incident very graphically:

The scene from the river side of the mill beggars description. The circular top of the mill was etched with fire and flames were belching from every window. The roof fell in, piece by piece, and masses of orange flame leapt skywards with a roar. Blazing beams and flaming masses of wood fell onto the adjoining houses. A big baulk fell right across the *Miller's Arms Inn* and set the roof alight, but the danger of this building becoming another casualty was averted by the swift work of the firemen, although the chimney stack became dangerous and had to be demolished, injuring one of the firemen.

The most spectacular sight was when the greater part of the river side of the mill fell with a reverberating crash into the river. The terrific blast of heat which swept across the river drove people back some twenty yards, with their hands shielding their faces.

The gaping side of the building revealed the sight of a raging inferno of flame on every storey. It was a scene of devastation which will not soon be forgotten. A remarkable incident occurred when a great sheet of white flame swept across the river as though some gaseous vapour had become ignited.

Crash after crash came from the doomed building – the flames leaped higher and higher. The powerful jets of water seemed innocuous against the all-consuming mass of incandescent material. At times it seemed as if the water from the jets was dissolving into steam in the intense heat before they touched the building.

Beams and joists, great sheets of woodwork, fell blazing all around, exposing more and more of the interior. Gradually the upper structure fell in, sending up showers of sparks and burning embers.The whole city reeked with the smell of burning material.

Two firemen, courageously standing between the burning mill and a similarly burning hoarding, directing their hose on the flames, had a lucky escape when a huge baulk of timber fell towards them. Fortunately the base of this beam was caught in the mesh of burning timbers in the mill and it remained suspended horizontally, like a pointing finger, over the heads of the two lucky firemen.

The danger to houses and other properties – like the Miller's Arms Inn – in Mill Lane and Abbott's Place was very real. Even the great cathedral, only a couple of hundred yards away across the rooftops, was in great peril. The City Police set about evacuating everyone in the immediate vicinity of the mill and forlorn groups of householders and workers were to be seen, wending their way through the streets, now swimming with water from the hoses, carrying their precious belongings and pets out of the threatened danger. The cottage occupied by Alf Wallis, the mill foreman, was in great danger and friends and neighbours rallied round to help him and his family move their belongings. Mr Wallis had rescued the mill's books and cash and taken them to his home for safe keeping; he had to rescue them again when his house in turn caught fire.

In a house next door but one to the mill, Mrs F Best was in bed, recovering from a serious illness and was unaware of the blaze. 'I heard a loud banging on the door and, running down, I was warned by the police to get out at once. I just threw on my coat and ran out with my six-months-old baby.'

The evacuation was well merited; the clouds of burning embers and sparks were raining down, starting numerous small fires in the area around the mill which were quickly extinguished by firemen and residents. One errand boy was galvanised into action when he noticed that his basket was alight. The area around the yard belonging to the firm G R Jackson Ltd was particularly affected and around thirty employees and a number of women from nearby houses were kept very busy beating out small fires. The great fear was that the wooden sheds, which housed a large quantity of flammable materials, could catch light but the efforts of the firefighters were successful.

The chimneys of two properties in Knott's Lane were set alight by falling embers and a neighbour warned Mr A A Sell, of the Little Rose Inn in King Street, that his attic was alight, the embers having set fire to the curtains at the open window and then spread to the bedding and furniture.

One of the mill workers, Mr B Halliday of 33 Mill Lane, was in bed after completing a late shift when he heard the commotion in the street outside. He quickly dressed and went out to see what the fuss was all about:

When I got into the street, I could see the top of the mill in flames. People were panic stricken by the terrible danger in which they found themselves. I myself realized the danger and advised householders to be prepared to clear out. Several women fainted. It was remarkable how people first thought of their pets and livestock. The pigs were removed from the nearby slaughterhouse and dogs, cats and fowls were removed to safety. Like many others, all day long I did what I could to help and then I helped the firemen during the night.

Fred Water, a millwright who had worked in the mill, commented: 'When in the mill one was very conscious of the large amount of dry timber everywhere. There were the bins, hoppers, partitions, worm conveyors, elevators, the floors and all the weatherboarding with many coats of paint on it – one often thought what a blaze there would be if it ever caught fire.'

Molten lead rained down from the roof before it collapsed and every few minutes, showers of sparks and burning material was flung into the air as machines and heavy beams lost their support and came crashing down through the lower floors. After only two hours all that remained of that lovely old mill was concentrated within the four brick walls of the ground floor.

The mill owner, Mr Garnet Denne, said the cause of the fire was not known but it had resulted in some £14,000 worth of damage. 'I was coming down the road when I was stopped and told the mill was on fire. I didn't believe it. When I got round the corner and saw the blaze it fairly took the wind out of my sails.'

Fortunately, the mill owners had other premises and mills so that not only was there only a small hiatus in flour production, but all the staff were absorbed into other parts of the firm, a very important factor considering the country was only just getting used to terms like 'depression' and there were many men on the dole.

Some months after the blaze, the remains of the mill were demolished and only a few heavy items survived, such as the waterwheel shaft, an iron pit-wheel boss and two cast-iron stanchions, which remained on the site for many years, a sad memorial to a once-great building. Fortunately, however, despite the great damage and destruction, there were no serious injuries or loss of life.

A contemporary writer, Dorothy Gardiner, in her book *Companion into Kent*, wrote of citizens flocking excitedly to see the greatest holocaust most of them would ever see. She, of course, had no way of knowing that, in less than a decade, in just one bombing raid, Canterbury would experience destruction and burning on a scale she could never imagine.

Blaze at the Crystal Palace

The star attraction at the Great Exhibition in Hyde Park in 1851 was the revolutionary building made of glass and pre-fabricated cast-iron sections which had been designed by the great Sir Joseph Paxton. It was classed as one of the wonders of the world by many of the thousands of visitors to the exhibition from all parts of the globe.

Once the exhibition closed there arose the problem of what to do with this great structure which had to be removed from Hyde Park. To destroy it seemed like sacrilege to many and there was great relief when a new site was found for it in Sydenham.

A little over a century and a half ago, Sydenham was just a sleepy hamlet in the Kent countryside but the coming of the railway and, now, the relocation of the great Crystal Palace, saw the area take on a new importance. The idea was to encourage Londoners to use the new railway system to have a day out in the Kent countryside where they could visit the enlarged exhibition hall and stroll in the magnificent gardens, complete with pools, fountains and even a dinosaur theme park.

The cost of relocating the building was considerably more than the cost of the original structure but, by 1854, everything was set up and the new Crystal Palace, with its gardens and its exhibition of treasures from all over the world, was open to the public.

Such was the success of the project that the population of Sydenham grew from just 2,800 in 1841 to around 40,000 by 1900. Although the town was absorbed into the new London County in 1889, it was still regarded by many as being part of Kent and the postal address remained a Kent one until comparatively recently, much like the neighbouring towns of Bromley, Beckenham and Orpington. The area became known as Crystal Palace, as did the local football team, and for four score years the great glass edifice towered over the site. But the end was nigh.

During the evening of 29 November 1936, Sir Henry Buckland, a trustee of the Crystal Palace, was walking his dog through the extensive grounds when he saw flames in the main transept. He rushed to the building, with his dog at his heels, and found two night watchmen struggling to contain what was then a small fire but which was rapidly getting out of control. Fanned by strong winds, it swept down the nave and into the south-west wing with great speed and there seemed to be no stopping the inferno. The players in an orchestra rehearsing in the concert hall were warned to leave and began packing up their instruments. 'Leave them. Run for your lives,' cried the messenger as the fire spread beneath their feet.

Sir Henry called the local fire brigade in Penge and appliances arrived just after 8.00 pm but the firefighters quickly realised that this fire was beyond their capabilities. Requests for assistance were swiftly met and there were soon nearly 500 firemen at the scene with more than 80 appliances from various Kent and London brigades. But there was little they could do other than try to contain the fire and prevent it spreading to nearby buildings. Gallons of water were played onto the crashing glass and the contorting, white-hot steel framework; but it was impossible to check the inexorable progress of the conflagration and the flames continued to leap hundreds of feet into the sky, fuelled by great explosions.

People came from miles around to witness the incredible scene; was it possible that glass and steel could burn and with such ferocity? But burn it did. There were soon sightseers from all over Kent and from all parts of London; special trains brought the curious from as far away as Margate and Hythe and the roads were gridlocked by the cars and vans of would-be spectators, hindering the approach of additional fire engines. Within 90 minutes of the discovery of the fire, a huge throng of sightseers had heedlessly trampled down fences and the contents of private gardens and mounted police had to be called to control them. There were even private aeroplanes cruising overhead.

One eyewitness described the scene:

> Great crashes and explosions could be heard, and billowing mountains of spark-filled clouds, about twice the height of the 350 foot towers, rolled away over South Kent, flaming with the glow of the fire. When we got to the Crystal Palace Parade at the top of the hill, we found a seething mass of people, cars, bicycles and pedestrians, and still more thousands streaming up from every hill and road. Fire engines trying to run out their hoses; cars and bicycles and humans rushing over the hoses and over and above all the blinding blaze of the Crystal Palace alight almost from end to end.

When the great transept finally collapsed, the noise was heard 5 miles away and the firemen continued to concentrate their efforts on the twin towers because if were these to succumb, the surrounding houses would be destroyed. In fact, their labours were crowned with success and the towers were saved (only to be destroyed deliberately during the Second World War to prevent them being used as a navigation aid by enemy aircraft).

Finally, all that remained of this great edifice, which had covered an area four times the size of St Peter's in Rome, was a heap of smouldering ashes and a pile of contorted metal. The great organ, alone insured for £10,000, was no more.

The cause of the fire was never officially determined. The widest held view was that an electrical fault was to blame but there were several other hypotheses bandied about, including the possibility that a forgotten cigarette in the ladies' cloakroom had ignited the wooden flooring, a bomb placed by extremists or sabotage by a disgruntled worker. One intriguing suggestion was that Paxton had unwittingly incorporated the demise of the structure in his design. Being aware that some housemaids had the habit of sweeping dust under the carpets in the larger houses he was acquainted with, he deliberately left quarter-inch gaps between the floor boards to ease the cleaning problems, allowing the dust and dirt to be swept into the space under the floor. Over the years this had accumulated into a foot-thick, dry and felt-like substance which reposed under the equally flammable wooden flooring. Once the fire started, it was bound to spread like wildfire.

But how had the fire actually started? One very plausible suggestion involves John Logie Baird, the 'father of television' who had his workshop and large storage facility in the undercroft. On the day in question, his workers knocked off at 5.30 pm and made their way home. An expected delivery of gas cylinders had failed to arrive, the British Oxygen Company's delivery truck turning up 15 minutes after all the workers had gone. With the aid of the night watchman, the driver unloaded the heavy gas cylinders and placed them for the time being in the watchman's hut in the basement.

With the departure of the delivery lorry, the watchman followed the usual British workers' tradition of first putting a kettle on the gas ring, then setting off on his rounds and finally returning to his hut to enjoy a cup of tea. Unfortunately, he never got round to the final part of the procedure as one of the cylinders had a small leak which, in the absence of the watchman, built up in the confined space of the hut until it had reached such a concentration that the low light on the gas ring ignited it. With the wooden hut alight, the flames rose and reached the thick layer of dust between the ceiling of the undercroft and the wooden flooring above it. The heat caused the other cylinders to explode, which would have accounted for the belief that a bomb was involved, and the burning gas spread sideways under the whole of the Palace.

Whatever the true cause, the Crystal Palace was gone and, according to the *Bromley Times*, even those who mocked its appearance and described it as an architectural monstrosity maintained a friendly affection for it. It was the centre for concerts, art shows, firework displays, cat and dog shows and many other activities. It was '. . . a meeting ground of a thousand interests and hobbies'. And it had all gone in one dreadful but thrilling night, happily without loss of life.

The Oakwood Park Tragedy

Towards the end of the eighteenth century there was felt to be a need for a central mental asylum to cater for the whole county, including those parts that now form part of Greater London. Between 1829 and 1833, a brand-new building was constructed on the Heath at Barming, a village on the outskirts of Maidstone which today forms part of the Maidstone conurbation. (It is widely believed that the derogatory term 'barmy' is derived from the name of this village.)

In 1833 the first pitiful patients were admitted to this new institution. Originally designed to accommodate 168 patients, such was the demand that the asylum was soon overcrowded and so it was progressively enlarged and extended until, by 1948, it held more than 2,000 mental patients.

Such was the situation in 1957 when, in the early hours of Friday, 29 November 1957, a fire broke out in what was now described as a hospital rather than an asylum, although its function was unchanged. The night nursing superintendent, who discovered the fire, called the fire brigade, which attended within 4 minutes of the call being received at 6.40 am. Part of the first floor, adjacent to the wards that contained 350 mentally ill patients, was found to be well alight and the fire officer in charge quickly sent a 'make pumps six' call back to his headquarters, indicating that this was a potentially very serious incident and that at least four appliances in addition to the two already on site were needed.

Having started in the first-floor tailor's shop, the fire had rapidly spread throughout the workshop wing, engulfing the print shop, the library and staff rest rooms and was rising to the roof. The additional appliances were quickly put to work and, with six hoses in simultaneous use, the fire was brought under control by 7.30 am when a 'stop' message was sent to brigade headquarters. An hour later it had been completely extinguished without any casualties and the fire crews set about damping down and clearing up the debris. Although the interior of the block had been gutted and the roof destroyed, the adjacent 120ft ventilation tower appeared to have escaped intact. As a senior fire officer later told the press, 'The fire itself was not serious and when it was put out about 8 am, it was thought that the tower was as safe as the Rock of Gibraltar.'

During the course of the clearing up process, a load 'crack' was heard but this was put down to the natural cooling of the masonry. However, at 10.00 am, there was an ominous rumbling and the tower suddenly collapsed onto the workshops, burying a number of firemen and workers as well as hospital staff. Others were trapped on all levels of the building, from the basement to the first floor, some being in considerable danger.

Retained fireman George Burden from Loose had been on the roof of the gutted building helping to pump contaminated water out of a water tank when, 'Suddenly I heard someone shout, "Look out, the tower's coming down!" I looked up and that was all I knew about it.'

George Burden lay face down under a pile of rubble for what seemed to him to be ages, but eventually rescuers reached him and he was pulled out of the wreckage and placed in an ambulance. At the hospital, where he was to spend eleven weeks, Fireman Burden was found to have a broken leg, a smashed pelvis and a broken ankle. He was off work for a further eleven months but eventually returned to his normal trade as a builder, although he was invalided out of the fire service.

George Partis, the hospital's chief administrative officer, had been walking towards the scene of the fire when he was horrified to see the tower collapse: 'I couldn't believe my eyes! All of a sudden I saw this huge tower collapse. It didn't topple to either side. It was just like a lift coming down. It was the blackest day of my long stay in Maidstone.'

The hospital's superintendent engineer, Alex Robinson, together with plumber Bernard Wilcox and hospital engineer Bob Smith were in the roof space, assessing the fire damage, when Bernard Wilcox looked up through the charred roofing timbers and shouted, 'It's coming!'

Bob Smith takes up the story:

> There was no warning at all, just a rumbling noise. We could feel the whole building shaking and we ran. A cloud of dust followed us along the roof and I can remember us hurdling over metal tie bars designed to support the walls. When Alex and I reached the end of the roof, we realized that Bernard was missing.

Bernard Wilcox had tried to follow his comrades but his foot got caught between some pipes and he was engulfed in piles of masonry. To their surprise and delight, when the other two retraced their steps to find him, they discovered him unhurt apart from a bruised heel.

The three descended to the ground, trying to close their ears to the cries and screams of the trapped and injured, and set about assisting others in the task of extracting them, a job that was greatly hampered by the lack of electricity. It was not until around 7 pm that Bob Smith finally got home and the enormity of the disaster hit him: 'When I got home the shock really set in. I had a tightness in my chest and a job to breathe. There were some very lucky escapes; if the tower had not come straight down more people would have been killed.'

The rest of the firemen, hospital staff and other helpers, who had been enjoying a well-earned cup of tea, also rushed to the rescue, subsequently aided by Civil Defence units from six towns. Working in extremely dangerous conditions, reminiscent of the Blitz, tunnelling under piles of bricks and rubble and wet, fire-blackened timbers, the rescuers struggled to find and extricate those who had been trapped.

One of the hospital's tradesmen, painter Graham Walkling, was quickly on the scene and used his bare hands to claw away the rubble to get to those who were trapped:

> We managed to crawl into the basement through a small gap in the rubble. We had to scratch around and move the masonry with our bare hands but we managed to get three people out before the Civil Defence people arrived and took over. It was a terrible scene; a lot of people were very badly injured. We knew a lot of the people we got out. It's something I shan't forget.

Sadly, of the first six men to be carried out of the debris, two were found to be dead. Station Officer S E Pearce, one of the 'retained' part-time firemen who had been called to the scene, discovered the partially buried body of a fireman which, to his horror, was that of his own brother, Assistant Divisional Officer Leslie Pearce. Not surprisingly, he collapsed and was himself taken to hospital by ambulance. Two other firefighters, Firemen Albert Farrow and John Hawkes, lost their lives in this incident, as did three civilians, the hospital's printer, Theodore Sheppard, staff nurse Clarence Hayes and a Polish patient, Karol Siwirski. It was nearly 24 hours before the last body was removed from the rubble. A number of firemen and others were injured but fortunately escaped with their lives.

It was later ascertained that the cause of the fire was a clothes iron which had been left switched on overnight in the tailor's shop. The likely reason for the tower collapsing was held to be the unequal cooling and contracting of the brickwork after the blaze.

Destruction of the Seaside Piers

For some inexplicable reason, despite being surrounded by sea, seaside piers seem to suffer greatly from fire. This has occured not only in Kent but also in places such as Brighton and Weston-super-Mare.

So far as Kent is concerned, one of the earliest (at least within living memory) occurred at Folkestone. The Victorian pier off the beach, below the famous Leas Promenade, was a great attraction in the early part of the twentieth century. Built in 1887/8, it was 700ft long and 30ft wide and the pavilion at the end seated a thousand people.

However, with the outbreak of the Second World War in 1939, it was decided that the pier would be useful to any enemy landing parties and so a section of the structure between the shore and the pavilion at the end of the pier was destroyed. In 1943 an easily removable temporary footway was constructed to join the pier head to the shore and so provide limited access to the end of the pier. The whole of the seafront was a restricted area under the Defence Regulations and so, even with this limited access, only military personnel could get to the pavilion end of the pier. Theoretically, it was therefore impossible for unauthorised persons to reach the end of the pier from the beach or vice versa.

The military authorities relinquished their control over the pier after the D-Day landings in June 1944, by which time the pier had become very run down and was described in that year as 'a derelict eyesore'. This afforded an opportunity for a few young lads and daredevils to clamber precariously along the rickety and rotting temporary footway and gain access to the dilapidated and ghostly pavilion.

On Whit Sunday, 20 May 1945, the war-weary and beleaguered inhabitants of Folkestone were celebrating the bank holiday in full peace-time style, the war in Europe having finished less than a fortnight before. A number of these merrymakers, their courage bolstered by alcohol, scrambled onto the pier during the day and, as the evening approached, a few small wisps of smoke were seen rising from the pavilion and, surprisingly quickly, it was well alight. The now-alarmed holidaymakers cavorting on the pier began to panic and struggled to reach the shore and safety.

The local fire brigade was called and attended but the narrow and dangerous footway, together with the explosion of a number of oil drums that had been stored in the pavilion, made it impossible to deal with the flames in any meaningful manner and it was decided that the pier should be left to burn itself out.

Fanned by strong winds, the ferocity of the flames caused the sea beneath the pier to steam and the ornate Victorian ironwork became white-hot and buckled into incredible shapes.

How the fire was started will never be known, although there were several theories, ranging from a carelessly dropped cigarette, sunlight through glass, gases given off by the items stored in the pavilion and, by far the most popular idea, arson by some over-intoxicated reveller.

Having survived sea mines being washed up against it and a Spitfire crashing close by, the old pier finally succumbed to this ignominious end. It was subsequently decided that renovation of the pier was not viable and it was finally completely demolished in 1954.

Margate's was the next Kentish pier to yield to the ravages of fire. At around 9.15 pm on 7 November 1964, Eric Berry was working in the ships' pilot radio office at the end of the pier when he heard the fire siren sound the alarm. Looking out of the office window, he could see flames in the pavilion and so, picking up the only fire extinguisher he could find, he began to tackle the blaze.

'I had the flames out, but it was still smouldering,' he told the *Isle of Thanet Gazette*. 'By the time the firemen had arrived the flames had burst out again and got a good hold.'

The fire rapidly spread from the pavilion to the pier bars and kiosks, fanned by a gale-force wind. The flames could be seen by the crews of ships 15 miles out to sea and they bombarded the coastguards with radio messages, believing it to be a ship on fire. The lifeboat was lying in the water nearby and the crew had to remove rockets and flares to avoid these adding to the confusion.

'From the police station we could just see a small flicker of light,' said a police sergeant. 'This seemed to go out and, a second or so later, the building went up like a bomb, with flames coming out of the roof of the big building.'

The fire brigade quickly attended but was frustrated to find that bollards had been installed on the approach road, preventing the appliance from getting nearer than a ¼ of a mile from the pier. They then discovered that the water main that supplied the hydrants on the pier had been drained as a frost precaution measure, without the brigade being informed. In the end, hoses had to be coupled together and stretched the whole length of the pier. More than thirty firefighters attended the scene from all over Thanet and eventually got the blaze under control. But it was too late to save the pavilion and the other buildings on the end of the pier, all of which had closed down for the winter and were being used to store deck chairs and other flammable holiday equipment.

'The fire had a firm hold,' said a fire officer, 'because the wind was passing above and below the affected building and we had to make sure that the flames did not spread along the under part of the decking.'

Fortunately, the firemen had managed to save most of the decking and the supporting piles, which remained intact.

The police and firemen highly praised the actions of a party of about thirty Royal Engineers Junior Leaders who were on a coach trip to the town from their training barracks in Dover. These young lads carried hoses for the firemen and assisted the police with crowd control and clearly demonstrated the value of their training as future Army NCOs.

'They very promptly buckled to and helped us keep back the crowds as well as helping the firemen run out their hoses,' said the police inspector in charge at the scene.

As the fire was extinguished before the pier had been completely burnt out, it was possible in due course to restore it. However, it was to succumb to a violent storm in 1978 when it was totally destroyed.

Six years later it was the turn of Herne Bay. Built in 1899, at 1,147m long the pier was the second longest in Britain (after Southend), the extreme length being necessary to reach water deep enough for the visiting pleasure steamers to berth at the pier head.

The pier complex suffered its first fire in 1928 when the shore-side theatre, built in 1910, was destroyed. The pier itself was badly damaged in the great storm in 1953 and was finally closed in 1968 when it was found to be in a dangerous condition. The Grand Pavilion, constructed at the entrance to the pier, continued in operation for a couple of years, but while the skating rink and concert hall were undergoing renovation and repairs on 12 June 1970, it caught alight. A total of eight pumps and other emergency vehicles attended and, although it proved impossible to save the Grand Pavilion, the fire was extinguished before the pier itself was destroyed, but not before it suffered severe damage. A new sports and leisure centre was built on the site of the burnt-out buildings and was opened by Sir Edward Heath in 1976.

Catastrophe at the Crypt

In 1836, some major building works were being carried out in Bench Street, Dover, which included the destruction of an old tower that for centuries had stood beside the already old Shakespeare Hotel – one of Dover's major watering holes and a prestigious family concern. When the tower was finally pulled down, a hitherto unknown vault was discovered beneath it and, although the origins of the structure are obscure, it is believed to have been used as a place of refuge for Huguenots who were fleeing persecution in France in the sixteenth century. This hypothesis is supported by the discovery of numerous Flemish tiles there.

For some time the vault was used as an underground wine store for the hotel but, in 1921, the hotel was renovated and converted to a bar with a number of flats above, the vault being brought into use as the Crypt restaurant. This large, four-storey building occupied the whole of the space between York Street and Bench Street – one of the main shopping and business areas of the town. The ground floor and first floor of the building fronting onto Bench Street contained bars and the restaurant, as did the semi-basement and ground floors of the York Street side. The two further floors were used as living accommodation.

In the early 1970s the Crypt was a very popular eating place; the restaurant and bar had an enviable reputation for good food combined with a pleasant ambiance and attentive staff and, on the evening of Saturday, 26 March 1977, the restaurant was full and the kitchen was working flat out. By the time the restaurant closed late that evening, the staff were only too pleased to seek their beds and perhaps look forward to a lie-in on the following morning. Meanwhile, the occupants of the living accommodation in the three storeys above the restaurant were snug in their beds.

It was just before 3 in the morning that a man walking his dog in Bench Street noticed smoke coming from the building and called the fire brigade. At the Ladywell Fire Station, White Watch was on duty and most of the members were resting when the station alarm went off. Simultaneously Station Officer Peters was alerted at his home, as were a number of retained firemen scattered around the town. The six members of the watch leaped onto the water tender and, with commendable promptness, arrived on the scene 6 minutes after the emergency call was received at the Brigade's central control room.

The leading fireman in charge was informed that there were people cut off on the upper floors of the building and he quickly called for assistance and the provision of two turntable ladders to reach the trapped persons. In all, fifteen appliances of all sorts ultimately attended to scene.

The rescue operation commenced immediately and, by the time an hour had passed, the firemen had carried nine persons out of the now blazing building. Sadly, two of these proved to be already dead.

It was soon ascertained that the fire had started on the ground-floor level and had quickly spread to the upper floors through a number of voids before advancing horizontally through the living accommodation, which was described as 'a mass of rooms and passages which could be compared to a rabbit warren'.

Before long firemen had penetrated all parts of the building in pursuance of their dual task of dousing the fire and rescuing any other persons trapped by the flames and smoke and, while so doing, the central part of the premises suddenly collapsed, without warning, burying three of the firefighters, all from the Folkestone station. Fireman John Davison, also from Folkestone, told the *Daily Mail*, 'There were six of us working at the seat of the flames. We were just about to be relieved when the girder collapsed. The other five were completely buried in hot rubble and debris. I was the lucky one – I was only half-buried.'

Their colleagues hastened to their aid but their efforts were hampered by the still-spreading fire on the upper floor above the would-be rescuers and on two sides of them. The work was both difficult and extremely dangerous. Mechanical cutting gear, lighting and an airline were brought in and, after about 20 minutes, two of the trapped firemen were extricated and the third, Leading Fireman Sharp, was also pulled out of the debris. In total, six other firemen had been injured in the incident and they were all taken to hospital but Leading Fireman Sharp (31) was certified dead on arrival.

Chief Officer Reg Doyle, the newly appointed head of the Kent Fire Brigade, attended the scene in person and instructed that further searches of the building should be made but these, together with the continuing firefighting measures, had to be abandoned because of the increasing precariousness of the building.

Throughout the firefighting and rescue operations there were confusing and contradictory reports as to the number of persons trapped and how many people in total needed to be accounted for. Once the fire was under control and the smoke had cleared somewhat, it was possible to confirm that three women and three children, all of whom resided in the accommodation over the restaurant, had died from acute carbon-monoxide poisoning and asphyxia. Among these victims were the wife and two children of the manager of the restaurant, Colin Clay, aged 35. He told the *Dover Express* that his attractive wife, Marion, a former beauty queen, would have lived if she had not gone back into the blaze to try to rescue her children. He explained that he had been woken by his 11-year-old son, Lionel, who rushed into his bedroom to tell him there was a fire. Telling his wife and children to stay by the window of the flat, he went to investigate but was overcome by the smoke and fell down a flight of stairs. He went on:

> My brother-in-law, Ronnie, was just coming home as the fire was discovered. He pulled me out through the Duck Bar door and dragged me out into the street.

Ronnie went up the Duck Bar steps and got hold of my wife's arm but she pulled herself away so she could go back to the flat to save our child, Shane, Mrs Conlon and our great friend, Anita Lee.

If she had not gone back up the stairs to go to the flat she would be alive now.

Mr Clay pleaded with the firefighters to let him have a breathing apparatus so that he could go into the blazing building to rescue his wife but they understandably refused. His little daughter, Antoinette, was rescued by firemen, as was Lionel and another of his children, but 6-year-old Shane and his baby daughter, Charlotte, both died in the inferno with their mother. The barmaid, Anita Lee, was also a victim, as was the Clay children's friend, 5-year-old Janus Ashton. Her grandmother, Phyllis Conlon, who was also staying with the Clay family, was rescued but later died in hospital. With the demise of Leading Fireman Sharp, the final death toll was therefore seven.

It was discovered that the cause of the fire was an electrical fault and the Coroner subsequently praised the courageous and determined efforts made by the firefighters, both to control the fire and to rescue those trapped. While regretting the deaths of the six occupants of the living accommodation, it was pointed out that many others had been saved, a number of whom were suffering from smoke inhalation and minor burns and who owed their lives to the actions of the firemen and other rescuers.

The funeral of Leading Fireman Sharp in Canterbury was attended by over 600 firefighters from all parts of the United Kingdom and even a contingent from France. The coffin, draped in the Union Flag, was carried on a turntable ladder.

The owners of the premises were subsequently refused planning permission to reinstate the damage but were authorised to demolish the remains. Demolition was carried out in April 1985 and, over two decades later, the site is still vacant, the space being occupied by scaffolding to support the buildings on either side.

Chapter 2

In Peril from the Sea

The actual words of the hymn are, of course, 'For those in Peril **on** the Sea' but, as we shall see, the sea can also be perilous for those on dry land.

If fire is both a boon and a bane, its counterpart, water, is no less so. Without water to drink man could not survive and without water to wash in we would be living in a very unpleasant world. Fire often requires water to extinguish it; the fish we eat need to live in fresh or salt water – the list of situations that necessitate the presence of water is endless.

But, like fire, water, in its various forms, also represents a great danger to mankind. Essentially, the ultimate danger is that of drowning which can occur both at sea and in rivers, lakes and other inland waterways. Less perilous, perhaps, water can also cause immense damage to property and this chapter looks at some of the disasters that have afflicted the county of Kent and in which water, in some form or another, was a major factor.

Ever since man first constructed a craft in which he could take to sea, there have been natural disasters and accidents arising from this element, usually aggravated by storm, fog, collision or negligence. The Goodwin Sands, off Kent's eastern seaboard, have alone accounted for hundreds of shipwrecks and loss of life and it is difficult to know where to start.

Women and Children First!

In comparatively recent times, a number of incidents have occurred and lives lost through vessels colliding with each other. For example, in January 1873, the *Northfleet*, a fully rigged sailing ship of 876 tons and named after the Kent town where she was built in 1853, was sunk with the loss of 243 lives – Kent's worst sea disaster to date.

The *Northfleet* had been captained by Captain Thomas Oates for a number of years but, at the last minute, he had been ordered off to attend the famous Tichbourne Trial, being probably the last man to see the real Sir Thomas Tichbourne in Rio de Janiero. Consequently, when the

Northfleet was towed out of Gravesend early on the morning of Friday, 17 January 1853 by the London steam tug *Middlesex*, she was under the command of her former chief officer, Edward Knowles.

This was a great moment for Gravesend-born Edward Knowles; not only was he taking up his first real command but, having recently married, he had been granted permission for his wife Frederica to accompany him on the voyage to Tasmania. He had a crew of 34 experienced seamen under his command and the vessel was carrying 343 passengers, many of whom had been contracted to work on the new railway being laid in Australia. The *Northfleet*'s hold contained over 400 tons of cargo, mostly rails and other railway paraphernalia.

Off Dungeness, the tug cast off and departed back to London, leaving the *Northfleet* to continue its voyage under sail with a Channel pilot on board. A storm had been raging in the North Sea and English Channel for some days and, after battling unsuccessfully against strong headwinds for some hours, Edward Knowles and the pilot, George Brack, agreed that there was no alternative but to turn back and seek shelter further up the coast until the storm abated. At around 3 pm on Sunday, 19 January, the *Northfleet* dropped anchor in the Margate Roads and rode out the worst of the storm there.

This was not a pleasant time for the passengers, many of whom were violently seasick. This, coupled with a number of births that took place on board during these few days, kept the ship's surgeon's hands very full.

As the weather began to improve, Captain Knowles decided to try once more to battle his way down the Channel but, while he was off Folkestone, the wind changed direction and increased in force. There was only one course of action open to him: to make for the shelter of Dungeness and ride out the storm there. Eventually, on Wednesday, 22 January, the *Northfleet* dropped anchor 2 or 3 miles off Dungeness in 11 fathoms of water, almost opposite the coastguard station.

Many of the passengers were still suffering from seasickness and, by 10 pm that night, when the ship was secured and showing all the necessary lights, most of them had sought the comfort of their cramped sleeping quarters. It was about half an hour later when the crew members on watch, two seamen and a petty officer, were startled to see an outbound steamer heading for them at full speed. They called out to the rapidly approaching ship, asking who she was and where she was bound, but their voices were lost in the howling of the wind and the unidentified vessel continued to bear down on them without altering her course in the slightest.

The lookouts' voices woke Captain Knowles and the pilot, both of whom hurried on deck, just in time to see the steamer ram their ship broadside amidships. The impact holed the wooden *Northfleet* below the waterline, crushing the great oak timbers traversing the main deck as if they were made from balsa wood. Immediately after the collision, the steamer cleared the ship and, before more than a very few of the terrified passengers below could get up on deck, she pulled away. With the *Northfleet* obviously in serious danger of foundering, the crew and passengers called out to the steamer for assistance but she seemed anxious to get well away from the holed sailing ship.

By the time most of the passengers had made their way up on deck, the steamer was heading away in the distance, having ignored the *Northfleet*'s distress and was soon out of sight. The badly holed ship was taking on water very fast and clearly sinking despite the valiant efforts of the crew; the first mate, Mr Gloack, and the second mate, Mr Blyth, were manning the pumps, while the ship's carpenter vainly tried to stem the inrush of water with mattresses and blankets. Attempts to fire off distress rockets failed as the gun malfunctioned but flares were lit and two lifeboats were lowered with Bo'sun John Easter in charge of one of them. The remaining four lifeboats were entangled in the collapsed rigging and could not be lowered.

By this time panic was raging among the passengers and, in an instant, both the boats were surrounded by more than a hundred frantic men. Having put his wife into one of the lifeboats (despite her protests), Captain Knowles gave the usual and recognised order: 'Women and children first' but some of the male passengers seemed intent on getting on the lifeboats regardless. Pulling out a revolver, Captain Knowles repeated his order, adding: 'I shall shoot anyone who disregards my orders.' Nevertheless, at least one of the 'navvies' cried out, 'I'd as soon be shot as drown!' and rushed for a boat. Knowles fired a shot over their heads and, when that seemed to have little effect, shot one of the men in the leg. Yet still a dozen or so made a rush and jumped into the second boat as it was being lowered, stoving it in. As it filled with water and turned turtle, the occupants frantically held on to the keel and most were eventually picked up.

Because of the appalling weather, nearly a hundred other vessels were anchored and riding out the storm nearby so Captain Knowles called out to his wife in the half-filled lifeboat, 'Goodbye and God bless you!' and ordered the bo'sun to pull for the nearest ship. Incredibly, none of the nearby ships appear to have realised what had happened; some later said they thought the signals were to call for a pilot and it was up to half an hour before a serious rescue operation began. This delay was to have catastrophic implications.

With the vessel rapidly going down, some men took to the rigging, hoping that the masts might remain above the water once she settled but when the *Northfleet* foundered many of these were thrown into the sea. The pilot, George Brack, managed to cling on to the top of the mast from where he was eventually rescued.

By the time the seaworthy lifeboat had pulled clear, the *Northfleet* was sinking fast. The sea was pouring through the breach and her bow had begun to slide beneath the waves. The stern, where most of the passengers and crew had gathered, was lifted high into the air before it, too, followed the bow to the bottom, leaving them struggling in the icy water. In less than half an hour, the *Northfleet* had sunk, leaving just the tops of her masts above the water. The cries of those who still survived could be heard several miles away on shore and by those on the other vessels in the area but gradually the cold and fatigue silenced them as they followed their ship under the waves.

The first rescue ship on the scene was the merchant steam tug *City of London*. Although its skipper, Samuel Kingston, had also misread the distress signals, he eventually decided to investigate and, in doing so, came across the lifeboat which handed over its precious human cargo and, despite the damage it had suffered, set off back to search for any more survivors. It found four in the water and took these back to the tug, which continued to search and eventually saved thirty-three people.

The lugger *Mary*, out of Kingsdown, also saved 32, while the *Princess*, out of Dover, picked up 21, including 10 from the *Northfleet*'s rigging, among whom was the pilot, George Brack. When the final tally was made, only 86 of those on board had been saved, including the captain's wife Frederica Knowles. The remaining 243, including Captain Knowles and 23 of his crew of 34, lost their lives in the icy waters of the Channel. Among those passengers who perished were 43 children and 41 women (only 1 of each survived).

One of the fortunate survivors was George Mason, who described his experience in graphic terms:

> At this time last night all of us was as jolly as waggoners. Some of us was playing dominoes and cards and some a-singing songs, and my mate, he'd got his fife. He could play a bit on the fife you know, my

mate could. And, bye and bye, us all turns in for the night – all but the watch on deck – and I was soon asleep, thinking o' course, we was safe enough 'cause we are at anchor. Well, the fust thing I knows is that I was woke up and I sits up in my bunk and sings out and says I, 'What's up mate?' 'Dunno,' says he. 'I thinks it was a gun fire.' Well, I look around and I sees the bunks on the starboard side all drove in, and I hears a chap a-groanin'. My mate goes and puts his head on deck and he come back and he says, 'For God's sake turn out; the vessel's half in two.' I turns out pretty sharp and drags on some of my things and goes on deck and I sees the side of the ship was drove in . . . The decks was shoved up and the water was pourin' in upon us. Some on us tried to shove the decks down and some was a-trying to caulk the leaks but it was no good and we then hung on to the pumps . . . I stuck to the pumps till there was only six of us left and then I went below and fetched a jacket . . .

Well, down she plunges head fust and up springs the pilot into the rigging and up I springs after him but the vessel went down and carried me under water . . . However, I keeps going up the ratlines and I gets above the water for the main topsail was just clear. There was twenty-one of us in the rigging of the three masts – three of the ship's crew, seventeen passengers and the pilot. We held on as well we could in the wind and rain till the pilot cutter came and took us off.

Seafarers and the public alike were outraged that the steamer that had rammed the *Northfleet* had failed to stop and render assistance and the Board of Trade offered a £100 reward for information. Exhaustive enquiries revealed that the most likely suspect was the Spanish steamer the *Murillo*, which had sailed from Antwerp to Lisbon. When the ship was arrested off Dover some eight months after the collision, the owners and crew stoutly denied being involved and swore that the evident light damage to her bow had been caused two years previously. But two Englishmen aboard, a passenger and the second engineer, both said they had heard noises and felt a jolt around the relevant time. They also said they heard cries and tried to get the Spanish crew to stop and make a search but they were ignored. A Court of Admiralty ordered the *Murillo* to be sold and severely censured her officers.

Curiously enough, the *Murillo* was a replacement for a ship of the same name that had been lost when it was rammed by another, unknown vessel in 1864, at almost precisely the spot where the *Northfleet* went down.

Death of a Battleship

On Friday, 31 May 1878, three German warships, having left their base at Wilhelmshaven bound for Gibraltar via Plymouth to join the German Mediterranean Fleet, were steaming majestically down the English Channel, just off Folkestone. It was a lovely, early summer's day and a large crowd had formed on the Leas, Folkestone's renowned cliff-top promenade, to watch the progress of these great ironclads. The spectators were thoroughly enjoying the spectacle of these warships sailing past when, to their horror, it suddenly became apparent that two of them were on a collision course.

The Folkestone fishing lugger the *Emily*, commanded by Richard May, had a grandstand view of the disaster as it unfolded, being only a matter of yards from the German squadron:

> Just before ten o' clock, we were about two and a half miles off shore, preparing to make for Folkestone harbour, when we saw the three large ironclads bearing down on us so we naturally slowed down to watch their proceedings. The *König Wilhelm* and the *Größer Kurfürst* were nearly abreast, the former leading by about a length. A barque was retching off, and the *Größer Kurfürst* altered her course slightly to allow her to go clear. Just at that instant the *König Wilhelm* put her helm hard a-port and, swinging round with great rapidity and going ahead, she struck her consort just before the mizzen mast, making a terrific hole in her side. Almost immediately she turned over and, within about five minutes she went down, turning keel uppermost.

Richard May wasted no time in heading the *Emily* for the spot as soon as it was safe to do so. 'The cries and shrieks of the hundreds of the human beings thus, at a moment's notice, cast into the sea was appalling. About a hundred of the poor creatures, who were clinging together in one vast heap, sank en masse.'

May bravely took his little vessel into the midst of the struggling men and managed to save twenty-seven of them. Other luggers came up, including the *Susannah* and the *Five Brothers*, and they succeeded in saving more than thirty other survivors. The *Prüssen* lowered its boats and rescued 167 more but some 300, including the captain of the *Größer Kurfürst*, perished.

It was clear that when the *König Wilhelm* collided with the port side of the *Größer Kurfürst* between the main and mizzen masts, it tore a great hole in the armour plate well below the waterline. The sea had rushed in, quickly drowning most of the unfortunate seamen below decks, and the great ship began to slide gracefully beneath the waves. In just 8 minutes it was all over and she had sunk to the bottom, leaving some 600 seamen bobbing about in the water. The horrified spectators on the Leas could hear the cries of these shipwrecked mariners as they called for help – and help was not long coming. The South Eastern Railway's cross-Channel packet, the *Lord Warden*, steamed out of Folkestone harbour, accompanied by a small armada of local fishing smacks, five of which picked up seventy-seven survivors between them.

The *König Wilhelm* and the third German warship, the *Prüssen*, between them rescued another 218 wet and cold mariners but, by the time other vessels, including another cross-Channel ferry, the coastguard boats from Folkestone, Sandgate and Dungeness, and the Sandgate lifeboat, had reached the scene it was too late to save any lives. The *König Wilhelm* was also severely damaged and appeared to be in a sinking state, with a large sail fastened around her bows in an attempt to keep the water out but refused any offers of assistance, later continuing on its way with the *Prüssen*.

Nearly 300 members of the crew of the *Größer Kurfürst* had joined or followed their ship on its way to the bottom, the speed of her sinking leaving very little time for some to get out of this 6,663-ton, 370ft-long warship before she did so.

The bodies of most of the victims were washed up along the coast between Dungeness and the South Foreland, so many arriving on the beach at Sandgate that they were referred to as 'Sandgate Soles'. More than one-hundred were buried in Folkestone's Cheriton Road Cemetery, where a large monument was erected by the townsfolk a couple of years later. It is to be hoped that some of those who grew comparatively rich on the £1 reward given to the finder of each body contributed generously to the fund set up to pay for the monument.

Some thirty-five years later, during the First World War, the worthy burgers of Folkestone trusted that the welcome they had extended to the survivors of the disaster and the respectful manner in which the dead had been buried would ensure that they would be spared any direct attack by the country's enemies, but this was not to be. On 25 May 1917, the town was raided by a number of Gotha bombers, leaving seventy-two people dead.

Perhaps sentiment has no place in war.

Disaster on Gallions Reach

If the open sea can be perilous, so too can navigable rivers, such as the Thames and the Medway. One early disaster took place on 3 September 1878 in the River Thames, off what is now the town of Thamesmead, just a few miles upstream from the present Dartford river crossing.

The 250-ton London Steamboat Company paddle-steamer the *Princess Alice* was one of a number of large steamers that ran daily trips from London to Sheerness. On this occasion, the vessel had left Swan Pier near London Bridge around 10 that morning with some 700 daytrippers, dropping many of them at Northfleet to enable them to visit the Rosherville Gardens near Gravesend. This 20-acre pleasure garden boasted a zoo, an aviary, botanical gardens, a maze, two theatres, sideshows and stalls and many other attractions, including the popular tearooms. A band played for the entertainment of the visitors, many of them young children who came down from the capital for an exciting day out. The remainder of the ship's passengers stayed on board for the cruise to Sheerness. It had been a very poor summer but, at long last, the sun had come out and everyone was out to enjoy themselves. The men were formally dressed in serge suits, many sporting a flower in their buttonhole, while the ladies wore their Sunday best.

At about 4.15 pm, the *Princess Alice* began her return journey, picking up the passengers at Northfleet on her way. Equipped and licensed to take 936 passengers, she now had about 800 passengers and crew on board and was heavily laden as she paddled her way up the River Thames under the command of her captain, William Robert Hattridge Grinstead, with helmsman John Eyres at the wheel. On board a band played the popular tunes of the day, including *Nancy Lee* and *We Don't Want to Fight, But By Jingo If We Do*, and there was an atmosphere of good-natured high spirits. The passengers were a mixed bunch and first and second-class ticket-holders mixed together, united by the holiday atmosphere. The children ran up and down the deck, while the adults stood in little groups, chatting amiably, breaking off occasionally to rebuke their children when they became too boisterous or ventured too close to the ship's rail. Some of the passengers frequented the bar where a beer cost between 1½*d* and 3*d* a pint and gin was 4*d* a double. The river was very busy, as indeed it usually was in those days, but it was a fairly clear evening with only a light breeze and just beginning to get dark.

To quote from a contemporary poem:

As they're wafted to shore on the evening breeze
How happy those voices sound!
There is nothing the listening ear can please
Like a pleasure-boat homeward bound.
There is laughter on deck – there is love below –
Ah! Little their danger the doomed ones know!

William Digby Seymour, 1878

By 7.40 pm that evening the *Princess Alice* had reached the area of the River Thames known as Gallions Reach and the band ceased playing and put away their instruments, ready to go ashore. The stewards busied themselves tidying the deck chairs and clearing the rubbish created by hundreds of holidaymakers.

Opposite Beckton Gasworks, off Tripcock Point, the river took a sudden, sharp bend to the left, obscuring the view into Gallions Reach. Vessels on opposing courses approached each other blindly at this point, although their pilots had some view across the flat marshy spit between the two reaches in daylight. At night or, as now, at dusk, the red and green navigational lights and the white masthead lights of ships could also be seen if the angle of approach was right. In fact, it was a well-known danger point where more than one collision had taken place in the past. Captain Grinstead on the *Princess Alice* was well aware of the dangers and ordered the two sons of the steamship company's superintendent to leave the bridge and rejoin their mother, so as not to distract him. He then ordered the engines to run at half speed.

It was now that the prudent and conscientious 46-year-old Captain Grinstead appears to have made a curious decision. One of the passengers, the brother-in-law of one of the crew, was an experienced seaman – although totally unacquainted with this stretch of the River Thames – and it was to him that Grinstead handed over the helm of the paddle-steamer. As it rounded the bend in the river the vessel moved slightly over to the right, no doubt to gain a better view.

Among the other vessels using the river was the 800-ton, screw-driven collier the *Bywell Castle*, which was sailing in the opposite direction to the *Princess Alice* on its way downstream, bound for Newcastle. This vessel, under its master, Captain Harrison, was travelling in the centre of the river but gave the crew of the paddle-steamer no cause for concern until it was quite close. After all, the river at this point was 600yd wide and it was a fine

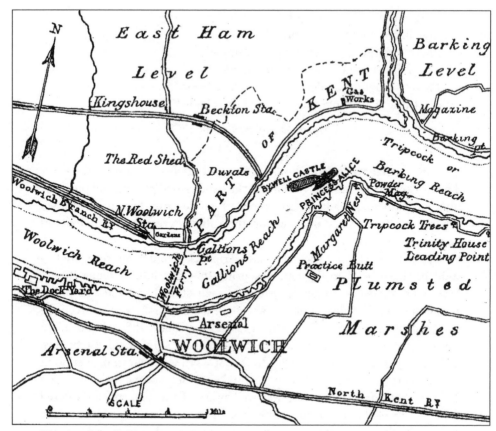

The site of the Gallions Reach disaster. (Greenwich Heritage Centre)

evening with fair visibility. Captain Harrison, however, was beginning to wonder what the *Princess Alice* was up to and expected her to turn to port, towards the south bank.

Captain Harrison later stated: 'I observed the Alice turn towards the north shore, appearing to cross in front of my bow. To avoid a collision, I told my pilot [Christopher Dix, a qualified Thames river pilot] to angle towards the south shore. My aim was to pass safely past the stern of the Alice.'

The log of the *Bywell Castle*, as quoted in the *New York Times* of 6 September 1878, recorded:

The master and the pilot were on the upper bridge, and the lookout on the top-gallant forecastle; light airs prevailed; the weather was a little hazy; at 7.45 o'clock pm, proceeded at half speed down

Galleon's [*sic*] Reach; when about the centre of the reach observed an excursion steamer coming up Barking Reach, showing her red (port) and masthead lights, when we ported our helm to keep out toward Tripcock point; as the vessels neared, observed that the other steamer had ported the helm. Immediately afterward saw that she had starboarded her helm and was trying to cross our bows, showing her green (starboard) light close under our port bow. Seeing that a collision was inevitable, we stopped our engines and reversed them at full speed. The two vessels came in collision, the bow of the Bywell Castle cutting into the other steamer with a dreadful crash. We took immediate measures for saving life by hauling up over our bows several passengers, throwing overboard ropes' ends, lifebuoys, a hold-ladder, and several planks, and getting out three boats, at the same time keeping the whistle blowing loudly for assistance, which was rendered by several boats from shore, and a boat from another steamer. The excursion steamer, which turned out to be the Princess Alice, turned over and sank under our bows. We succeeded in rescuing a great many passengers, and anchored for the night.

Unfortunately, it seems that, at the crucial moment, Captain Grinstead on the *Princess Alice* mistook the intentions of the captain of the other ship and had also turned his vessel to the south. On realising the danger, the helmsman on the *Princess Alice* attempted to take avoiding action but it was too late; the *Bywell Castle* rammed the *Princess Alice* just aft of her starboard paddle wheel and she broke into three parts and quickly began to sink. Being screw-driven, the *Bywell Castle* had no way of stopping quickly and, being carried on the ebb tide, Captain Harrison and the pilot had to run her engines at half speed in order to maintain way and enable the vessel to be steered as it drifted down the river.

Another curious fact was disclosed at the later inquiry. It seems that some of the *Bywell Castle*'s crew were so-called 'runners' – mostly experienced seamen who, having married, preferred to engage on short coastal voyages, rather than deep sea. One of these 'runners', John Hardy, was employed as lookout on the top-gallant forecastle and another, William Haynes, had the ship's wheel. Neither of these men was known to the captain, although the pilot was acquainted with Haynes.

And so, the captains of both ships, which were rapidly approaching each other, had placed complete strangers at the helm – men who had no idea of the quirks and idiosyncrasies to which the vessels might be prone.

Seymour's poem continues:

They are midway now, on the Thames' broad stream,
And above them a clear, calm sky;
Hark! Heard you not then a dismal scream
And the shouts – as of agony?
The river runs – but the music's gone –
Two ships have met – and there floats just one!

As water poured into the crowded saloons below decks aboard the stricken paddle-steamer, there was no question of giving precedence to the women and children. The weakest were trampled underfoot in the stampede for the exits and many were found jammed in the doorways when the ship was raised later. There was pandemonium with some of the passengers jumping overboard, while others tried to climb up the smoke stack, burning themselves in the process. They, too, fell back into the water. One of the paddle-steamer's stewards, William Law, realising that there had been a serious collision, took the hand of a young lady of his acquaintance and dragged her onto the deck. Pushing through the confused crowd to the ship's rail, he hoisted her onto his shoulders and jumped overboard but lost her in the water. A powerful swimmer, he managed to support a man who was struggling in the water until such time as they were both picked up by a rescue board but was unable to help any of the other distressed victims in the river around him. Some had attempted to climb up the collier's anchor chain, only to be dragged under the water when it dropped its anchor. Two clergymen were heard singing hymns as the ship went down.

At the time of the collision, the *Bywell Castle* was sailing unladen and was consequently floating very high in the water. This meant that, even when the collier was stationary and trying to rescue the passengers and crew of the foundering paddle-steamer, few were able to reach the decks of the *Bywell Castle* high above them. Only those on the forward deck had a slim chance of boarding the other ship and it appears that one fortunate passenger was standing right on the bow of the *Princess Alice* when she was struck and, as the bow section of the severed ship rose in the air before sinking, he simply stepped across onto the deck of the collier. But most of the hundreds of passengers fell into the river and had to cling to the pieces of flotsam resulting from the collision and wait and pray for rescue. In less than 5 minutes the *Princess Alice* had sunk beneath the waters of the Thames and the river was full of bobbing heads and the air full of the screams and cries of the drowning passengers. 'The whole river seemed alive with heads – they looked like coconuts,' said one horrified watcher. 'I shall never forget the screams and the demented faces,' said another.

'They were like bees swarming around us,' said the captain of the *Bywell Castle*. Life-belts thrown to those struggling in the water proved useless; so many hands grabbed at them they simply sank like stones. Small craft put out from the banks of the river in a gallant rescue attempt and managed to save almost 200 survivors but the rest, mainly women and children, went down with the *Princess Alice* as she sank in just 18ft of water. Few of the passengers knew how to swim and the voluminous costumes worn by the women in any case made swimming very difficult. Most of the children, some in the little sailors' outfits so fashionable at that time, perished in the murky waters of the river.

One survivor told the *Illustrated London News* of his experience and described the approach of the other vessel:

My wife expressed a fear that the great vessel towering so much above us would come into collision. She was some lengths off, but coming nearer in a direct line . . . As the large vessel came nearer to us, while I believe we were standing still, I distinctly heard the captain shouting to her, 'Where are you coming to?' . . . The collision must have occurred at that moment for, although there was no crash, we felt the *Princess Alice* tremble under us – a kind of strong, shivering motion . . . Screaming had then begun and I saw a lot of people . . . rush, as I believe, across the gangway . . . We found ourselves, my wife and I still holding together, in the water . . . I could not swim and could scarcely hold my wife up . . . My wife and I also shouted and ropes, I believe several, were thrown over us by the men [on the *Bywell Castle*]. I grasped one of the ropes, my wife still holding on to me. The vessel moved on and, holding the ropes, we floated down the river along with her . . . A small boat hailed us and took us on board . . . and rowed us to Greenwich . . . The men in the boat told us we were picked up two miles from the scene of the collision.

Another surviving Londoner, George Haynes, told his story to the same periodical: 'After quitting Gravesend . . . our vessel nearly collided with a large brig and a serious accident was only averted by our captain reversing the wheels full on. This incident caused no small amount of consternation among the passengers.'

Mr Haynes then described the collision with the *Bywell Castle*:

I cannot describe the scene of confusion and maddening perplexity which seized upon everybody . . . One of the crew rushed up to the stern and tried to loosen the ropes connecting one of the davits on the port bow in order to utilise the boat but he could not get the ropes unfastened and said, 'Who's got a knife? Have you one, Sir?' I replied that I had and handed it to him when he cut the rope and . . . let the boat down into the water without a single person in it, although by proper management people could have been got in. I might have seated myself in it easily enough, but I thought it was intended for the ladies and children. After being let down it must have drifted away with the tide. I relied upon my good nerves and swimming powers to save myself . . . Events went speedily on, and at last the portion of the vessel on which I stood slipped away from my feet and I found myself struggling in the water. I seized hold of a lady next to me who was drowning and supported her in the tide. . . . I went under several times for there was a great surge on then, caused in great part by the screw of the big ship near us . . . After a while a little boat hove in sight commanded by Mr Trewby, the manager of Beckton Gas Works . . . Mr Trewby put out an oar which I seized. Mr Trewby took the lady in first and I followed.

Among those who hurried to the river side on hearing of the disaster was a journalist, W T Vincent, who wrote:

Soon policemen and watermen were seen by the feeble light bearing ghastly objects into the offices of the Steampacket Company, for a boat had just arrived with the first consignment of the dead, mostly little children whose light bodies and ample drapery had kept them afloat, even while they were smothered in the festering Thames. I followed into the steamboat office, marvelling at the fate which had brought the earliest harvest of victims to the headquarters of the doomed ship, and, entering the board-room, the first of the martyrs was pointed out to me as one of the company's own servants, a man employed on the Princess Alice and brought here thus soon to attest by his silent presence the ship's identity. The lifeless frames of men and women lay about, and out on the balcony, from which the directors had so often looked upon their fleet through the fragrant smoke of the evening cigar, there was a sight to wring out tears of blood from the eyes of any beholder. A row of little innocents, plump and pretty, well-dressed children, all dead and cold, some with life's ruddy tinge still in their cheeks and lips, the lips from which the merry prattle had gone for ever. Callous as one may grow from frequent contact with terrors and afflictions, one could never be inured to this. It was a spectacle to move the most hardened official and dwell for ever in his dreams. Then to think what was beyond, out there in the river. It was madness!

One of the 'company's servants' referred to in the above report was William Towse, the general manager of the London Steamship company, who died along with his parents, his wife and his sons – three whole generations of one family destroyed in a single incident.

With just one lifeboat, one longboat and only a dozen or so life-belts there was a distinct lack of life-saving equipment, although the arrangements were considered satisfactory by the Board of Trade. In all, some 600 passengers lost their lives that day, all within a hundred yards or so of the banks of the river. It was the worst disaster the river has ever known – indeed, it resulted in the greatest number of fatalities in any peacetime incident to date, especially as many of the original survivors later died from ingesting the polluted waters of the Thames. Since the Becton North Outfall Sewer, which pumped thousands of gallons of raw sewage into the river, lay just to the north of the site, and the nearby industrial plants of Silvertown and North Greenwich similarly allowed their waste to flow into the river, this was one of the most polluted stretches of river in England.

By the time around a hundred survivors had been rescued, it became apparent that this was now more a question of recovering the dead rather than rescuing the living. The steamboat office, which was taken into use as a temporary mortuary, soon proved far too small for the task and bodies were taken to the town hall and, later, to a huge shed at the Woolwich dockyard. For weeks afterwards, the Thames watermen were involved in what the *Illustrated London News* described as 'the doleful and shocking task of groping in the bed of the river by means of poles and grapnels' and continued pulling an average of one-hundred bodies out of the river each day, for which they were paid 5s per body. But it is evident that not all the victims were found; no one knows for sure what the final death toll was but it is generally believed to have been between 550 and 650. Some bodies were obviously washed out to sea and never recovered; even those bodies that were brought ashore were not all identified and around 120 remained unclaimed. A large number were found still trapped inside the steamer when the two halves were later brought to the surface.

The normal putrefaction of the corpses was hastened by the horribly disfiguring pollution, making the task a most disagreeable and sickening one for the recovering parties, and rendering many bodies unrecognisable. Around 115 unidentified bodies were buried in Woolwich cemetery and elsewhere. Among the living survivors was a small boy who gave his name as Edward Newman who was taken to hospital but was never claimed, his parents presumably having perished in the disaster.

Comments made by witnesses who appeared before Mr Charles Carttar, the West Kent Coroner, at the subsequent inquests are pathetically revealing:

'There were fifty of us, all middle-aged women from a Bible class – I am the only survivor.'

'We were returning from honeymoon. We jumped overboard but she was swept away.'

'Two of my children and my brother . . .'.

'My daughter and five grandchildren were on the boat. All were lost.'

William Towse, the steamboat company's superintendent, counted himself lucky to have lost only four of his eight children – including the two lads who had earlier been on the ship's bridge. Edmund Wool, the licensee of the Granby Arms in Hampstead, had that morning seen his family off from the Swan Pier, the party of eight comprising his wife, their five daughters, aged between 16 months and 14 years, the pub's barmaid and the children's nursemaid. Not one of these was to survive.

The captain of the *Princess Alice* went down with his ship, together with his chief steward, and the skipper of the *Bywell Castle* was so shocked by what had happened that he never put to sea again, even though the subsequent inquest returned a verdict of 'death by misadventure', the jury accepting that the collision was an accident. The foreman of the jury added a rider, however:

The *Bywell Castle* did not take the necessary precaution of easing, stopping and reversing her engines in time. The *Princess Alice* contributed to the collision by not stopping or going astern. We think the number of passengers on the *Princess Alice* was more than prudent. We think the means of saving life on the *Princess Alice* was insufficient for a vessel of her class.

The Board of Trade inquiry concluded that 'If two vessels under steam are meeting head on the helms of both should be put to starboard so they pass each other on the port side.'

The disaster spelt the end of the London Steamboat Company, which went into liquidation six years later. Coincidentally, the *Bywell Castle* itself disappeared without trace in the Bay of Biscay just four years after the collision, while returning from a voyage to the Mediterranean.

A memorial was erected in Woolwich cemetery, the cost being raised by a public sixpenny subscription to which more than 23,000 persons contributed. The town of Woolwich (then part of Kent county) spent £1,380 on the recovery and burial of the victims and an appeal to the county justices (the predecessors of the County Council) was rejected. The Treasury donated £100 and the unfortunate Woolwich ratepayers had to provide the rest.

These days, politicians and others are quick to say that 'lessons have been learned' but, in this case, there were some very real improvements as a direct result of the disaster. For example, the 'keep right' rule was introduced for river traffic – the same as had already been adopted for sea-going vessels – and the Thames Division of the Metropolitan Police was issued with steam launches to replace the rowing boats used hitherto.

Rescuers Lost at Sea

Over the years, many types of boat have been used to assist vessels in distress and to take off the passengers and crew of the stricken vessel. Since 1824, the Royal National Lifeboat Institution have provided lifeboats at key points along the coast for this express purpose, while local seamen and fishermen often kept a surfboat for the same purpose. These surfboats were strongly built sail boats, specially constructed to be launched from the beach and used in heavy surf and rough weather but they were not self-righting.

At Margate, towards the end of the nineteenth century, there was an RNLI lifeboat, the *Quiver*, and two surfboats, one of which was owned by a co-operative of around fifty boatmen, none of whom seemed to be prepared to spend much time or money on maintaining it. It is therefore not surprising that the boat was later described as 'a boat totally unfit for the dangerous service', although its volunteer crew was described as 'deserving of the highest praise'. The other Margate surfboat, the *Friend to All Nations*, was bought by the boatmen as a replacement in 1878.

The week covering the end of November and the beginning of December 1897 was a terrible one for Margate and nearby towns. For days they had been battered by hurricane-force winds and raging seas including a tidal surge. The stone pier, jetty and headquarters of the Pier and Harbour Company in Margate were all destroyed, while sea walls, buildings, roads and coastal defences were all washed away. The Westgate Promenade and the Ramsgate colonnade were destroyed and Broadstairs Pier was breached.

At around 7.30 on Monday morning, 29 November 1898, the *Friend to All Nations* was called upon to assist a ketch, seen to be riding heavily in the trough of the sea off Birchington. The weather conditions were such that it was impossible to launch the surfboat from Margate and so it was taken by horse-drawn transport to Birchington where it was possible for the launch to take place. It is a tribute to the skill and determination of the crew that, in atrocious weather, the surfboat reached the ketch, which was found to be the *William and Elizabeth Little*, owned by a Mr Keep. Bound for Broadstairs with a cargo of coal from Greenwich, she had parted from one anchor and was dragging heavily on the other cable and noticeably drawing nearer and nearer to the shore. The main sail had been carried away by the hurricane-force winds, the ship's boat had been smashed during the night and the cabin was full of water.

Exhausted from manning the pumps all night, the three-man crew, drenched to the skin by rain and waves, were delighted to see the little surfboat draw near, the crew hauling manfully on the oars. But, even in the delirium of rescue, the crew did not fail to remember the fourth member of the crew: their little dog which had shared the danger with them. 'Can you take off our dog?' called out the skipper of the ketch, Captain William Dolden. 'Aye, aye,' came the reply, 'We've come for all of you and want everything living.'

And so, with the crew of the ketch and their faithful dog safely on board, the surfboat headed for the shelter of Margate Pier where they arrived at around 11 am. 'We not able to save anything and were glad enough to get off with our lives,' said Captain Dolden.

The surfboat and the Margate lifeboat were in great demand in the next couple of days. On the morning of Thursday, 2 December 1897, rockets and distress flares were seen coming from the *Persian Empire*. She had been in collision with another vessel on the far side of Margate Sands and the *Friend to All Nations*, together with the RNLI lifeboat *Quiver*, put to sea at about 5.30 am to go to the aid of this vessel. A gale was raging from the NNW and even the experienced crew of thirteen had difficulty in handling the *Friend to All Nations*.

As the surfboat left the harbour mouth and drew near to the inshore low-water obstruction known as Nayland Rocks, the decision was made to lower the sail. As the seamen were doing so, they were hit by a sudden squall and the boat and the partially lowered sail rapidly filled with water. Before the boat had time to recover, another wave ran up the mast, swamping the sail, and she turned turtle. At this time four of the crew were still with the boat – one inside and three somehow clinging to the hull.

The capsized surfboat drifted on the wind and finally beached on the shore near the Rocks. A passing lamplighter, busy extinguishing the lamps along the promenade, heard voices from the beach near the Nayland Rocks and saw the survivors clinging to the hull of their upturned boat. Some of these now struggled to the beach which, with the ebbing tide, was close to the rocks and were aided by the lamplighter and people from nearby houses. The respected local doctor Charles Troughton, a powerful swimmer, had attempted to swim ashore but was found to be dead from exhaustion and shock on the beach. Not until around twenty men had arrived on the scene to assist could the stricken surfboat be righted and the man inside, whom they thought to be dead, extracted alive – albeit only just. This man, Joseph Epps, had survived a previous capsize in 1866 but appeared to be indomitable for he went on to live to the ripe old age of 93.

The other nine crew members, none of whom inexplicably was wearing a life-jacket, were lost, their bodies eventually being washed ashore, battered by the seas and the rocks and scarcely recognisable. The lives of nine more brave men had been taken by the implacable sea.

In recognition of the bravery and sacrifice of these men, a fund was set up and sponsored nationally by the *Daily Telegraph* to provide aid to their families. Including donations from Queen Victoria and the RNLI, this raised the very large sum of around £10,000 which should have ensured that the dependants of the victims were suitably cared for. However, the management of the fund was entrusted to an Executive Committee of local politicians and other dignitaries who decided to spend a large proportion of it on lavish funerals and a sizeable and ornate memorial in Italian marble. Apart from the very high cost of this monument and its delivery to Margate, roads had to be strengthened and a special carriage constructed to carry the monument to the cemetery where it was to be erected. All these costs were met out of the fund, Margate Corporation contributing nothing towards them. Thus most of the money intended to give succour to the bereaved was misappropriated to an unnecessarily grandiose scheme and little of it reached the intended beneficiaries, some of whom ultimately had to apply to local charities to help them meet their simple living costs.

Around the turn of the century another monument was erected on the Margate seafront, consisting of a life-size bronze figure of a seaman in oilskins and a sou'wester hat, wearing an old-style cork life-jacket, shading his eyes and looking out across the sea towards the Nayland Rocks. A fitting, permanent memorial to those brave men who lost their lives trying to save others.

The *Friend to All Nations* was replaced by another surfboat of the same name in 1901, this time a self-righting one which gave sterling service until 1940, when it was the Duty Lifeboat during the Dunkirk evacuation. It was decommissioned later that year and was sold off.

HMS *Bulwark* and the *Princess Irene*

On a dull, wintry afternoon in November 1914, Winston Churchill, the First Lord of the Admiralty, rose from his seat in the House of Commons and, in his inimitable growling voice, made the following statement:

> I regret to say I have some bad news for the House. The Bulwark battleship, which was lying in Sheerness this morning, blew up at 7.35 o'clock. The Vice and Rear Admiral, who were present, have reported their conviction that it was an internal magazine explosion which rent the ship asunder. There was apparently no upheaval in the water, and the ship had entirely disappeared when the smoke had cleared away. An inquiry will be held tomorrow which may possibly throw more light on the occurrence. The loss of the ship does not sensibly affect the military position, but I regret to say the loss of life is very severe. Only twelve men are saved. All the officers and the rest of the crew who, I suppose, amounted to between seven hundred and eight hundred, have perished. I think the House would wish me to express on their behalf the deep sorrow with which the House heard the news, and their sympathy with those who have lost their relatives and friends.

The 15,000-ton 'London' class battleship, HMS *Bulwark*, which had been launched in 1899 at a cost of more than £1 million, was a modern and important member of the great British Fleet in the early part of the twentieth century. She boasted four 12in guns and twelve 6in guns as well as an assortment of other artillery pieces and torpedoes. In November 1914, she was lying at anchor, with other vessels of the Fifth Battle Squadron, in Kent Hole in Saltpan Reach, just off Sheerness. The Squadron was busily engaged in taking on coal and victuals before setting forth to engage the next maritime target to which it was directed but, at present, its main task was to foil any attempt to invade England.

By this time, the First World War had been in progress for some three months. There had been heavy fighting in France and Belgium, including the bloody battles of Mons, Ypres and the Marne, and the troops were now beginning to dig in and settle down for what was to become a long period of trench warfare.

At sea, there had been significant British losses with three cruisers sunk by a U-boat in September 1914, followed shortly after by the loss of another three cruisers, sunk by the German cruisers *Scharnhorst* and *Gneiseau*. These worrying losses were somewhat compensated for by the destruction of a German squadron off the Falkland Islands.

But, nearer home, many of the members of HMS *Bulwark*'s crew had been granted shore leave on Wednesday, 25 November 1914 and had been relaxing, as only sailors can, in pubs, theatres and dance halls in Sheerness and Chatham. In accordance with their orders, all were back on board by 7.00 am the following morning and were going about their normal business. Some were eating breakfast on the mess deck or in the wardroom, others were performing their allotted duties on deck, on the bridge, on the guns or in the galley. The ship's band was busy rehearsing their repertoire for a concert later.

This busy but peaceful scene was brutally interrupted at 7.35 am when a roaring and rumbling sound was heard and a great sheet of flame and debris was projected into the sky. The ship rose bodily out of the water before falling back and disappearing under the waves in a great fog of thick, grey smoke, accompanied by the sound of further explosions. When the fresh breeze blew away the smoke this great vessel was found to have sunk virtually without trace.

Such was the noise of the explosion that it was heard 20 miles away in Whitstable and Southend's pier was shaken but not damaged. The nearest towns to the incident, Sheerness and Rainham, suffered structural damage with hundreds of windows broken by the blast.

A great rescue operation was launched, both from the shore and from other ships. Progress was hampered by the debris that littered the scene, including hammocks, life-belts, furniture, cases, not to mention the great number of bodies. It quickly became apparent that the task was not really one of rescue but of recovery of the mutilated bodies, which numbered hundreds.

A witness on one of the nearby ships told a local newspaper that he went on deck when he heard the explosion, thinking it might be the firing of a salute by one of the Dreadnoughts but soon saw that something terrible had occurred:

> We were at once ordered to the scene of the disaster to render what assistance we could. At first we could see nothing but when the smoke cleared a bit we were horrified to find the battleship Bulwark had gone. She seemed to have entirely vanished from sight, but a little later we detected a portion of the huge vessel showing about four feet above the water. We kept a vigilant look-out for the unfortunate crew but only saw two men.

In fact, of a complement of around 750 men of all ranks, only 14 initially survived the disaster, although 2 of these later died from their injuries. None of the officers survived.

Although officially a Portsmouth ship, with most of her crew being 'Pompey' ratings, the *Bulwark* had undergone a refit at Chatham two years previously and had been stationed with the Nore Division at Sheerness before the war. As a result, many of the locals and dockyard 'maties' regarded her as one of theirs and were horrified at the disaster and the great loss of life. Many theories were postulated concerning the cause of the explosion. An attack by Zeppelins was quickly ruled out, as was the possibility of a marauding U-boat. Had the explosives in the magazine become unstable and spontaneously ignited? Had a sailor dropped one of the great shells? Was it the result of a skiving crewman having a crafty smoke somewhere where he shouldn't have been? The true cause will never be known as anyone who might have thrown some light on the subject would have perished.

At the subsequent inquest, Lieutenant Benjamin Carroll, the assistant coaling officer at Sheerness, said he was passing down the River Medway and saw the *Bulwark*. He was looking at her signal flags to see what her coaling requirements were when he saw a spurt of flame abaft the after barbette turret which seemed to rush towards the after funnel before the whole interior of the ship blew into the air and everything seemed to be on fire. He added that the sea remained quite calm and there was no tide or disturbances on the water. He was convinced that what he had seen was an internal explosion and so turned his boat about and picked up one or two men from the water.

The battleship had eleven magazines, all of which appeared to have exploded in a chain reaction. Asked if he thought a carelessly discarded cigarette might have caused the explosion, Lieutenant Carroll replied that, as the 12in charges were in brass cases, he thought this most unlikely.

Sergeant John Budd, Royal Marines Light Infantry, gave evidence to the inquest by way of deposition as he was still in hospital suffering from burns and a broken leg. In this, he said that he was serving on HMS *Bulwark* at the time and was finishing his breakfast on the port side second mess deck when he saw a sudden flash aft. The deck then seemed to open up under him and he fell down into the water. He remembered resurfacing and seeing that the ship had disappeared. He did not hear any explosion.

Another witness was Charles Drage, a young midshipman on board HMS *London*, who wrote in his diary:

> When the catastrophe occurred I was reading a signal exercise on the port boat deck and had my back turned to the *Bulwark* who was our next astern. I experienced a slight shock, coupled with a blast of hot air and, on turning, saw a vast flame as high as the main truck, around which thick smoke was already beginning to form. Such debris as was in the air consisted of small objects and appeared to be largely composed of wood stored in the booms. There were two distinct explosions and then debris began to fall on our port quarter, a strong wind blowing it away from us. The place where the *Bulwark* had laid was entirely covered in smoke and it was impossible to ascertain the nature, extent or cause of the damage.

An Admiralty Court of Inquiry was held, presided over by Rear Admiral Gaunt, to which Midshipman Drage was called to give evidence: 'I . . . went in wearing my dirk and what I imagined as a composed expression.' His evidence did not add much to the findings, merely confirming that the explosion had been internal.

Rear Admiral Gaunt told the Coroner's inquest that exhaustive inquiries and scientific investigations had been made but these failed to find any evidence of the explosion being caused by external means. Everything pointed to the explosion being caused internally and, in this respect, he told the inquest: 'There was no evidence of treachery and no evidence either of loose cordite and, although there may have been loose cartridges in the ammunition passages, I do not think they had any bearing on the explosion.'

In response to a question posed by the Coroner, he added: 'All the evidence we had was that the explosion had occurred. After that, there was no proof of the actual cause. There were many possible causes, but no direct evidence and there have been many theories which are untrue.'

Although the Coroner was clearly not completely satisfied with the evidence, he told the jury that it was impossible to determine exactly how the explosion was caused and it duly returned a verdict of accidental death.

If the loss of this great battleship and the deaths of so many sailors was not enough, only a couple of months later another great explosion at sea was to replicate somewhat the *Bulwark* story and further foster the sabotage theory.

This time the unfortunate vessel was the *Princess Irene*, a former Canadian Pacific passenger liner which had been converted in Sheerness dockyard to act as a mine-layer. In May 1915 she was anchored in Saltpan Reach, just off Port Victoria Pier, only a mile or so from the wreck of the *Bulwark* when, once again, an unexplained explosion literally blew the vessel out of the water. The spectacle was likened to an eruption of Vesuvius and, as the flames died out, the scene was cloaked in a great pall of white smoke. When this cleared, few remnants of the ship were to be seen. The force of the explosion had hurled great pieces of the ship in all directions: part of the boiler landed on a passing collier and other parts damaged the Admiralty oil tanks on the Isle of Grain, where a piece of metal weighing 10 tons also landed.

Loaded with mines, the explosion was even greater than that of the *Bulwark*, although, fortunately, with a much smaller complement, the loss of life was less. Even so, the explosion took the lives of 273 men, including almost all the officers and ratings, as well as 76 dockyard workers who were carrying out repairs on board at the time. Only one sailor from all those actually on board at the time survived. Stoker David Willis was blown overboard but despite suffering severe burns he, alone, lived to tell the tale.

A further casualty was 9-year-old Hilda Johnson (referred to in some documents as Ida Barden) who was killed by a piece of metal as she was playing in the garden at her home on the Isle of Grain. Elsewhere on the island, a 47-year-old farm labourer died of shock while working in the fields and another man, working on a ship more than ½ mile away from the scene, died from injuries received when a piece of debris hit him on his head. Many other civilians were also injured by the wreckage.

An eyewitness, W G Moore, writing in *Early Bird*, described the scene:

> The whole thing was too awe-inspiring for me to appreciate the horror of it immediately. It started with stabs of flame spurting up

from her deck from stem to stern, then a colossal roar, and everything was hurled into the air – a column of smoke then went up, up, up, spreading out to a mushroom head at about 1,200 feet. . . . I was blown onto my back but not stunned. The aeroplane hangar doors on the aerodrome behind me were all blown in and pieces of plate from the ship's side were found half a mile away in the marshes beyond the aerodrome. . . . The Air Station launch, with its crew on board, was lying off our slipway so I hailed it and went with the Station Engineer Officer straight out to the scene of the disaster to see if we could pick up any survivors. We were the first launch there, but there was absolutely nothing to be found. There might never have been a ship there at all, save for the flotsam and oil. She had just disintegrated and sunk.

Part of the ship and its crew were found miles away from the scene, a case of butter landing 6 miles from the scene in Rainham. Books, papers, furniture, uniforms and, more horrifically, parts of bodies were found scattered over a very wide area. Human heads were found at Hartlip and Grain, and sundry other gruesome discoveries were made. Most parents in the Medway towns and surrounding area forbade their children to play outside until the area had been checked for body parts or any dangerous pieces of equipment or munitions.

Wartime censorship shrouded the incident in secrecy but there seems to have been no evidence of enemy action or sabotage. The most likely explanation for the disaster was an improperly fuzed mine, as the *Princess Irene* was carrying around 500 of these highly explosive and volatile weapons at the time.

The loss of two more warships – the cruiser *Natal* in December 1915 while at anchor in the Cromarty Firth and the battleship *Vanguard* at Scapa Flow in July 1917 – raised once more the possibility of sabotage. One suspect was an ordnance fitter at Chatham Dockyard, a certain John Harston. It was known that he had worked on both the *Natal* and the *Vanguard* at the time of their loss and, as a Chatham Dockyard worker, it was very possible that he would have had access to the *Bulwark* and the *Princess Irene*.

Harston was a witness at the inquiry into the loss of the *Natal* where his testimony raised certain suspicions, in particular his claimed lack of knowledge about the magazines on the ship – this despite the type of work in which he was engaged. He was thoroughly investigated by Special Branch officers but was cleared of any blame.

Although the possibility of sabotage by a person or persons unknown remained a remote possibility, it seems that the age and design of the vessels was more likely to be to blame. In the case of the *Bulwark*, a veritable powder trail existed with each of the magazines being connected by passages running the entire length of the ship. An explosion in one magazine would flash across to all the others in an instant. Boilers, which created 'hot spots', were situated dangerously close to the magazines and would cause the cordite to deteriorate rapidly and become unstable.

With the passage of nearly a century, it is unlikely that the true cause of the explosions on the *Bulwark* and the *Princess Irene* will ever be discovered – not that this would be any comfort to the hundreds of seamen and dockyard workers who lost their lives in these tragic incidents.

A Stricken Submarine

Some thirty-five years passed between the loss of the *Princess Irene* and the next naval disaster in the River Medway. The Royal Navy submarine, HMS *Truculent* (P315), after a distinguished record in both home and far-eastern waters, had been undergoing a refit in the Royal Dockyard in Chatham.

On 12 January 1950, she set off for sea trials with a full crew, together with a number of civilian marine engineers, on board. The submarine completed its surface trials and was in the Thames Estuary near the Shivering Sands fort, returning to Sheerness in the dark at 7 pm when the lookout saw lights ahead in the Channel. In addition to the usual red and green navigation lights, there was an extra, all-round red light on the masthead which baffled the crew of the submarine.

Lieutenant Charles Bowers, in command of the submarine, decided that the other ship was only showing part of a two-red light signal, which would indicate that she was not under command and was at anchor. This proved to be a fatal error as the other vessel was in fact a small Swedish oil tanker, the *Divina*, bound for Ipswich from Purfleet, and was actually on the move. The additional red light, which had so confused the submarine's crew, was a Port of London requirement to indicate that the vessel was carrying explosive materials. The men on the *Truculent* were apparently unaware of this regulation (which, indeed, did not apply in the Thames Estuary) and, by the time the captain realised his mistake, the two vessels were on a collision course.

The presence of shoaling waters prevented the submarine from passing the approaching ship to starboard, in accordance with the 'Rule of the Road' and the captain ordered the helmsman to steer to port. The other vessel was much closer than first appeared, however, and the *Truculent*'s bow had only just started to swing onto its new course when the two ships collided. Lieutenant Bowers ordered 'Full astern – hard to port'.

On board the *Divina*, the Thames pilot had not even seen the *Truculent*'s lights, which were set very low down near the water line, and it was not until the last minute that the master of the tanker saw the submarine. Even as he took avoiding action the bow of his ship carved its way into the *Truculent*'s hull.

Although only a small ship of 643 tons, the *Divina* had a specially strengthened bow to enable it to break through the Scandinavian ice and the bigger, but thinner skinned, *Truculent* did not stand a chance. At first the master of the *Divina* thought he had run down a Thames lighter that had ignored the Rule of the Road and crossed his bows in the dark. He ordered 'Full astern' and lowered a boat to pick up anyone in the water but the submarine sank by the bows after just a few seconds.

The Bridge Party of four officers and a seaman, who were in the submarine's conning tower at the time of the collision, were thrown into the sea by the impact and were rescued by a passing vessel. Inside the stricken submarine, the crew responded promptly to the order to go to collision stations. Ventilators and valves were shut and the conning tower hatch and voice pipes were closed off. The order was given for all watertight doors to be closed but this apparently was not done. The ballast tanks were filled with compressed air and the crew crowded into the aft compartments. The lights went out and carbon dioxide was rapidly building up and the First Lieutenant decided that an immediate escape was called for. Although the required SUBSUNK distress call had not been made, he reasoned that there would be plenty of other ships in the area to rescue the crew from the water. An indicator buoy was released to mark the position of the sunken ship. The well-trained seamen, up to their armpits in water and covered in oil, quietly followed the escape procedure and the dockyard workers followed suit. The Davis Escape System and the well-rehearsed Submarine Training Progamme enabled the trapped crew to reach the surface, one by one. As there were not sufficient escape appliances for every man, it was agreed that those issued with the kit would help those without and the system worked perfectly. By this means sixty-seven men came to the surface, and this number did not include those who had been thrown from the conning tower. As they bobbed on the water, they looked around for the rescue vessels but the estuary was dark and empty.

This perhaps premature escape attempt led to most of the submarine's crew being carried away towards the North Sea by the strong ebb tide. The *Divina* and a Dutch ship, the *Almdijk*, picked up the Bridge Party and another twelve men from the sea, including two dockyard workers and the captain, but the rescue vessels were unable to find the remaining sixty-odd seamen and dockyard engineers, nearly all of whom perished from cold in the icy waters, or on the equally cold mudflats in the Thames Estuary. Few of those who had escaped from below decks stood any chance of survival in the wintry conditions. In all, forty-eight seamen and fifteen dockyard technicians lost their lives in the worst submarine disaster since the sinking of HMS *Thetis* in 1939.

A whole fleet of rescue vessels, including Admiralty ships and the lifeboats from Margate and Southend, rushed to the aid of the doomed vessel and the Commander-in-Chief of the Nore, Admiral Sir Henry Rethven Moore, instructed all shipping in the area to 'Keep silence for distress calls on all ship-to-shore wavelengths.' But it was all too late.

The Admiralty Board of Inquiry decided that the *Truculent* was 'most seriously at fault'. The president of the inquiry, Rear Admiral Hughes-Hallett, said: 'The central fact remains that Lieutenant Bowers turned to port on sighting the lights when sound seamanship and the rule of the road dictate that he should have held his course, turned to starboard or stopped. It was from this initial error that the train of events which led to the collision followed almost inevitably.'

The Admiralty Board considered that if the watertight doors on the *Truculent* had been closed, she would have settled bow down, with her stern above the water, thus considerably improving the crew's chance of survival.

This incident led to a special light, known as the 'Truculent Light', being shown on the bows of British submarines to make sure they could be easily seen by other ships, and improved escape training was given and better survival suits issued.

Coincidentally, a film, *Morning Departure*, had been completed immediately prior to the sinking of the *Truculent* that mirrored almost exactly the circumstances of this incident. In view of this tragic, real-life situation, the film's release was delayed and the film was almost withdrawn. However, it was eventually decided to go ahead with the release, with the addition of a special tribute to the officers and men of the Royal Navy.

The Zeebrugge Disaster

In the late 1970s, the Townsend Thoresen car ferry company (then known

The Kent Fire Office provided two engines in Maidstone in 1804. This manual pump belonging to the insurance company's brigade is seen outside their offices in the High Street, *c.* 1883 (the year painted on the side of the engine). (Kent Fire & Rescue Service's Museum)

Bromley Council bought this Shand Mason steam pump in 1897 at a cost of £430. It still exists and reposes in the Kent Fire & Rescue Service's museum in a restored condition. (Kent Fire & Rescue Service's Museum)

The City Flour Mills in Canterbury well alight in 1933. (Kent Fire & Rescue Service's Museum)

The end of the Crystal Palace.

Oakwood Hospital, after the fire but before the tower collapsed, killing six people. (Kent Fire & Rescue Service's Museum)

Folkestone Pier in its heyday, before fire destroyed it. (Kent Fire & Rescue Service's Museum)

The burning pier at Margate lights up the whole area. (Kent Fire & Rescue Service's Museum)

Thick smoke pours out of the Grand
Pavilion on Herne Bay Pier.
(Kent Fire & Rescue Service's Museum)

The scene of the disastrous fire
at the Crypt restaurant in
Dover.
(Kent Fire & Rescue Service's Museum)

A fireman descends the ladder
with a pathetic little bundle in his
arms at the Crypt fire in Dover.
(Kent Fire & Rescue Service's Museum)

The SS *Northfleet*.

Captain Knowles
preventing men from
storming the lifeboat.

A contemporary drawing of the
German battleship, the *Großer
Kurfürst*.

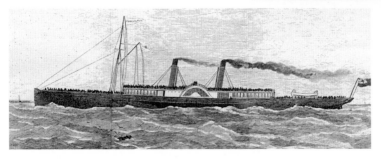

The saloon paddle-
steamer, *Princess
Alice*.
(Greenwich Heritage
Centre)

The struggle
for life as the
Princess Alice
sinks.
(Greenwich
Heritage Centre)

The collier
SS *Bywell Castle*.
(Greenwich Heritage
Centre)

The *Bywell
Castle* ploughs
into the *Princess
Alice*.
(Greenwich Heritage
Centre)

The search for bodies in
the Thames.
(Greenwich Heritage Centre)

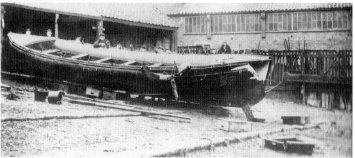

The surfboat *Friend
to All Nations* before
the disaster.
(Margate Museum)

The inscription on the plinth of the Margate memorial. (Author)

The 'London class' battleship HMS *Bulwark*, the victim of a mysterious explosion in November 1914.

HMS *Princess Irene*, another explosion victim.

The Royal Navy Submarine HMS *Truculent*, lost in the Medway.

The Dover cross-Channel ferry MV *Herald of Free Enterprise*, which sank off Zeebrugge with the loss of 187 lives in March 1987. (Greenwich Heritage Centre)

The inhabitants of Whitstable take to rowing boats in the flooded streets of the town in February 1953.

The cross-Channel ferry *Hengist*, high and dry near Folkestone during the 'Great Storm' of 1987.

as Townsend Car Ferries) ordered the construction of three identical car ferries from the Schichau Unterweser ship builders of Bremerhaven. This was a time when the cross-Channel traffic was growing enormously with the introduction of roll-on/roll-off (Ro-Ro) ferries which made the turn-round time so quick.

The three ships, named the *Spirit of Free Enterprise*, the *Pride of Free Enterprise* and the *Herald of Free Enterprise*, came into service in 1980 when they were hailed as the most advanced and prestigious of the cross-Channel ferries. They began service on the Dover–Calais route in May 1980 and obviously greatly impressed John Hendy, writing in *Sea Breezes* (Vol. 54, No. 417):

> As Dover rushed on towards its frantic summer, the two German-built Townsend-Thoresen sisters continued to plough their way across the Channel and the Herald of Free Enterprise crossed to Calais in a force eight gale in 54 minutes 53 seconds (pier to pier), thus breaking her sister's previous best by nearly a minute. The twins really are an impressive sight in the Strait. With their rounded, blunt bows, they seem to bulldoze their way across and 'appear to swallow their loads with the greatest of ease.'

In September 1983 the *Herald of Free Enterprise* was switched to the Zeebrugge–Dover route, for which she was not entirely suited, as the linkspan at the Belgian port had not yet been adapted for the *Herald*. Consequently, it was not possible for both the main and the upper vehicle decks to be loaded at the same time and so loading was slower than at Calais. In addition, in the spring, with the ferries being berthed bow first, it was also impossible for the ramp to be raised high enough to reach the level of the upper vehicle deck due to the high tides experienced at that time of the year. This problem was well known to the ferry captains who commonly resolved the problem by filling their forward ballast tanks to lower the bow and so raise the stern.

As John Hendy wrote in a subsequent issue of *Sea Breezes* (Vol. 58, No. 457):

> It was an unusual and interesting experience, crossing to Zeebrugge in the Herald and, although perhaps her accommodation is not really suited to the longer run to the Belgian port, at this time of year passenger loadings are usually light and the extra space availability for the passengers was a pleasant bonus. In spite of the few passengers and the longer crossing, the stewards busied themselves

with cleaning and polishing and were justifiably proud of their ship. Down in the engine room, the engineers had closed the starboard engine to renew the fuel injectors but, even running on two engines, we managed the crossing in a very creditable four hours and eight minutes. . . .

The enthusiasm and pride of the captain were plainly evident – he expects high standards from those around him and they really respond by giving it. . . . Even some ten months after her last refit [the *Herald*] was in remarkably fine condition both inside and out. She was a delight to sail in.

But despite these enthusiastic comments, disaster was to strike.

At 6.05 pm (British time) on 6 March 1987, the *Herald of Free Enterprise*, under the command of Captain David Lewry, sailed from No. 12 berth in the inner harbour at Zeebrugge, bound for Dover, with a crew of 80 hands, laden with 81 cars, 47 lorries and 3 coaches. The 459 passengers were in high spirits, anticipating a smooth crossing in the prevailing good weather – there was a light easterly breeze and very little sea or swell.

The *Herald of Free Enterprise* took 19 minutes to proceed from her berth to the outer mole where she entered the North Sea proper. In another 4 minutes or so she had capsized. During her final moments the ferry turned rapidly onto her side and was prevented from sinking totally only because her port side had grounded in the shallow water, less than 7 cables (1,400yd) from the harbour entrance. This great vessel was now lying on her side like a beached whale, only 100yd from the shore.

How could such a thing have happened? Before casting off, the normal practice was for the First Officer to remain on the car deck to ensure that the assistant bosun closed the doors to the vehicle decks. The Channel crossings were highly competitive and the various ferry companies were anxious that their vessels were punctual and made the turn-rounds and crossings without undue delay. It was for this reason that, for once, the First Officer left the car deck to return to the bridge before the moorings had been dropped, leaving the assistant bosun, Mr Stanley, to close the doors unsupervised. Although contrary to official procedures, this was not an unusual or serious matter as the assistant bosun was a very experienced hand and perfectly capable of ensuring the doors were secured for sea. However, once he had ensured that the car decks had been cleaned following the ferry's arrival at Zeebrugge, Mr Stanley was released by the bosun, Terry Ayling, and had returned to his cabin for a rest before the return journey. He was still asleep when the ship cast off and set sail and failed to hear the call to 'harbour stations'. The captain on the bridge had no means of knowing that the doors had not been closed. It is unclear why no other member of crew on the car deck realised that the doors had been left open and that the vessel had set sail in this condition and in a bow-down trim. Mr Ayling, the bosun, had other duties and was not responsible for overseeing the closing of the doors and others simply thought the assistant bosun was there as usual.

The ferry accelerated quickly to keep to schedule and, less than 2 minutes after leaving the harbour, when she had reached nearly 19 knots (around 20mph), she began to ship water through the still-open car doors at the rate of 200 tons a minute. The huge car decks had no partitions, bulkheads or other form of sub-dividing baffle to prevent movement, and the weight of this unhindered water sloshing about the car deck quickly upset the stability of the vessel. It only needed the slightest roll to the left and all this water rushed to the port side of the deck causing the ferry to roll over onto her side and sink in comparatively shallow water close to the shore, leaving about a third of her hull and superstructure above the water.

So sudden and so unexpected was this incident – the whole event took less than a minute – that there was no time to send any distress calls before the sea water destroyed the main and emergency electrical power systems. There had been no chance to launch any of the ship's lifeboats. A large number of passengers and crew were now trapped in those parts of the ship which were now under water or found themselves unable to get out because their escape route was blocked by water-filled compartments.

Dutch and Belgian rescue ships were quickly on the scene, while helicopters fluttered over the scene and divers were summoned to assist. The rescue craft were confronted by the sight of dozens of panicking passengers trying to escape through the windows onto the starboard side which was still above water. Maureen Bennett, who had been on a day trip with her husband, Frank, to celebrate their wedding anniversary, later described her ordeal: 'It was so cold – all we wanted to do was just get out. It was so frightening, it really was.'

Another survivor told how her husband had made himself into a human bridge so that she and her daughter could climb across to safety but when she called him to follow them, he said there were others who needed help. He was not seen again.

A dozen members of the ship's crew were eating their evening meal in the crew's mess when disaster struck. Moyna Thompson, the senior perfume-shop stewardess was just finishing her meal when she was flung across to the port side of the ship with water up to her waist. Like her colleague, steward Graham Merricks, she thought she was going to drown as the water quickly rose up to their necks. 'The lights went out, throwing the ship momentarily in complete darkness,' said Steward Merricks. 'People were screaming; it was horrific.' He was saved by a rope thrown down to him by crew members and Mrs Thompson was helped out of the water by other crew members who pulled her across with a fire hose. Then, after a further agonising wait while others were hauled up a corridor by a rope, it was her turn and she was dragged through a door, which had been smashed in, before clambering over the rail onto the side of the hull which was now horizontal. Eventually she slid on her bottom alongside a rope into a waiting tug.

'We were trapped, initially,' said senior barman John Hudson, 'but we knew we wouldn't be evacuated immediately because others would be worse off and so we got ourselves organized. We were in the water for about an hour and freezing. We did our best for each other and the passengers.'

One of the seamen, Bill Walker, had just finished his dinner in the mess room – fortunately on the starboard side of the vessel:

> We were half-a-mile to a mile out to sea when the ship went hard to starboard, as though it was avoiding another ship. Things were falling off tables and then it went too far and people started falling. We realised something was very wrong and people started trying to get out of the mess room door. Within thirty or forty seconds, water started rushing up in a big wave . . . I was standing waist-deep in water just outside the mess when I felt something bump against my legs.

Looking down, Bill saw it was an unconscious female passenger. He pulled her head out of the water and gave her mouth-to-mouth resuscitation and was delighted when she began breathing. He and another crew member took turns in supporting her and eventually they managed to haul her out through a door before returning to help others.

The last to leave his part of the ship, Bill Walker remained outside on the side of the ship to help other crew members rescue those still inside. They laboured on for hours until the bosun, who was leading the rescue operations, realised that they were so exhausted that it was taking six or seven of them to lift one person and so he ordered them onto the waiting tug for a hot drink and a rest.

Assistant steward 18-year-old Martin Barnes was clearing tables in the crowded passengers' cafeteria when the ship suddenly listed, throwing him about 6ft into glass windows before about a dozen passengers fell on top of him. Held face down under the water by the weight of the people lying on top of him, Martin truly believed his last moments had come but he managed to struggle to the surface and take a few deep and satisfying gasps of air. 'Once I was under the water I didn't think I was going to get out alive but I managed to push my way to the top of the water. Then the lights went out and it was pitch dark. People were shouting to keep in contact – it was just complete chaos.'

Using the now vertical tables (which were fixed to the floor) as a ladder Martin was able to break through a window and eventually make his way, with half-a-dozen others, onto the side of the ship where they were ultimately rescued.

Within hours, scores of divers, both civilian and Royal Navy, were on the scene and quickly set about trying to locate those passengers who were cut off in the part of the ship that was underwater, some of whom were in pockets of air but were unable to get out of area in which they were trapped because the adjacent compartments were flooded. Mostly, however, the divers found only the bodies of those who had perished in the cabins or on the bridge. Couples and whole families died together in the freezing cold (3°C) water, many of whom came from Dover or other parts of Kent, as did virtually all the crew.

Coupled with the tragic stories of those who died in the disaster there were many tales of heroism and brave deeds. Assistant purser Stephen Homewood, from Folkestone, worked unceasingly for several hours in the gloom and coldness of this huge 'tomb', paying little regard to his own safety. 'The first thing on everybody's mind as soon as they got out was helping others to escape. Time didn't mean a thing.' Mr Homewood was subsequently awarded the Queen's Gallantry Medal for his courageous efforts.

The bosun, Terry Ayling from Cheriton, was one of the first to escape but he quickly went back with three colleagues and succeeded in extricating the Captain, David Lewry, who was badly injured, together with the Chief Officer. He later informed the press: 'She went over to about 45 degrees. It reminded me of a horror film. The port side was like a forty-foot well and when we broke one of the portholes, all we could hear was pushing, screaming and crying. One baby was still strapped in his pushchair when we pulled him out.'

Jenny Leslie from Folkestone was a stewardess selling perfumes in the duty free shop when the ferry started to list. The woman she was serving disappeared leaving the baby she had been carrying behind. Mrs Leslie knotted the baby in her skirt, so as to leave her hands free to climb, swim or otherwise make her escape as the water was coming in quickly. Both she and the baby survived the disaster.

Graham Drury was on a day trip to Zeebrugge with his wife and three children:

> One minute we were all watching a video when it all happened. There was no warning – nothing. People were hurled through plate glass windows, partitions buckled. My baby son, Michael, was thrown to the other end of the room. I saw my daughter Julie being lifted out of the water into a different tug to ours but I don't know which hospital she has ended up in.

The ship's restaurant was full of diners just starting their meal when the ferry started to founder. With the sound of glass breaking and crockery smashing on the deck, the head waiter, Mick Skippen, did his best to calm the situation but panic was spreading as the windows collapsed and the sea poured in. One of the stewards was swept into the galley where he managed to smash a window and gain access to the television lounge. Clambering over cupboards and scaling up shelves in total darkness he eventually managed to extricate himself, later to find that he was one of the very few survivors from the restaurant. Among these was Mick Skippen, who was subsequently decorated for his endeavours.

Truck driver Larry O'Brian from Ireland told the *Daily Mail*:

> I was in the restaurant when it happened. Suddenly plates started to leave the table and in forty-five seconds the boat was on its side half filled with water. While I was sitting in the restaurant, trying to hold on to the table, water burst through the portholes and people were sucked out like you see in films about air disasters. The people who went that way had no chance.

Rosina Summerfield from London said:

> I was in the cafeteria. Water came in and flooded it all out from the side. The ship just fell on its side. The water came up higher and we climbed higher to get out of the water. We were trapped inside – it was terrifying. It was fifteen to twenty minutes before help came but it was a long time. We were in the dark. The lights went out. They [rescuers] smashed the windows and put ladders down. People were panicking, screaming and shouting.

An armada of tugs, lifeboats, fishing smacks and other small craft ferried the survivors to a rescue centre in scenes reminiscent of the Dunkirk evacuation nearly half a century before. One survivor, Miss Susan Hames from Coventry, stayed up in a Bruges hotel, hoping that her boyfriend would appear. He never did. Dressed in borrowed clothes, she recalled, 'We were in the restaurant and I remembered thinking, "Oh, my God, we're sinking!" I tried to get to my boyfriend but he was washed away and I never saw him again.'

How could such a disaster occur to a ship that was only seven years old and the pride of Townsend Thoresen's fleet? The answer may be put down to over-familiarity leading to a negligence of prescribed procedures. It may seem obvious that the ferry's bow doors, through which the roll-on/roll-off vehicles entered the car decks, should be closed and secured before putting to sea. But this fundamental safety precaution was ignored, allowing the sea to enter the hull before the doors were fully closed. The subsequent inquest returned a verdict of unlawful killing on the 187 victims, and the official inquiry that followed accused the company of 'sloppiness from top to bottom'. The inquiry castigated the company's management, saying:

> . . . a full investigation . . . leads inexorably to the conclusion that the underlying or cardinal faults lay higher up in the company. The Board of Directors did not appreciate their responsibility for the safe management of their ships. They did not apply their minds to the question, 'What orders should be given for the safety of our ships?'
> . . . from top to bottom the body corporate was infected with the disease of sloppiness . . . It was the failure to give clear instructions about the duties of the Officers . . . which contributed so greatly to the cause of this disaster.

Manslaughter charges were levelled against the company and seven members of crew, including the Captain, the case being heard at the Old Bailey some three-and-a-half years later. Expected to last twelve months, the case was dismissed after only five weeks but established an important point of law regarding corporate responsibility.

Storm, Flood and Tempest

While most of the disasters occurring at sea involved ships and seamen, the sea can be a cruel friend even to those on shore. And not just the sea: rivers swollen by heavy rain, gale-force winds and snow blizzards can all bring misery and disaster to landlubbers and sailors alike.

The year 1927 ended with the worst weather ever known in Kent as heavy rain fell throughout Christmas Day, to be quickly followed by driving snow on Boxing Day. Houses were buried up to their roofs and those areas that escaped the worst of the snow were subjected to continuing heavy rain, causing serious flooding in various parts of the county. Along the length of the Thames, from Woolwich to beyond Gravesend, rushing flood water flowed through the towns and villages of northern Kent, causing chaos to road and rail traffic and seriously disrupting the telephone system. Further upstream, fourteen people lost their lives, overwhelmed by the waters. The River Medway burst its banks in several places such as Tonbridge and Maidstone where the water reached nearly to the top of the lampposts sited along the embankment. Canterbury was described as experiencing the 'greatest natural disaster ever known' and all the urgently needed boats, which used to take tourists along the River Stour, had sunk. In many places, the only way of reaching people marooned in the upper floors of their houses was by boat, the water in the streets being too deep even for horses and carts.

Twenty years later, a somewhat similar situation arose as a result of the harsh winter of 1946/47. By the end of January 1947, an easterly wind had caused the already low temperature to drop significantly and the Rivers Thames and Medway were freezing over. Even the sea began to freeze into great ice floes at Whitstable. This exceptionally cold weather was to last for several weeks more, bringing considerable hardship for the people of Kent who were still suffering from rationing, shortages and general austerity as a result of the war that had not long ended. To add to the food problems, the Kentish fishing fleets were unable to put to sea for several weeks and on occasions the cross-Channel packet services were suspended. Power cuts, which had started even before the worst of the weather, continued to plague people in their homes and places of work. Oil lamps had to be used to light a production of the well-chosen *The Winter's Tale* by the girls of Tonbridge Grammar School, but this, according to the local press, merely added to the atmosphere.

Whole villages were cut off by walls of hard snow 5ft deep and the Isle of Sheppey lost all contact with the mainland. In Folkestone, huge icicles formed on the façade of the town hall, weighing several pounds and the area had to be cordoned off for safety's sake. Temperatures of -19 °C were recorded in Tunbridge Wells in February.

Not until the middle of March did the temperature rise and herald the approach of spring, but even this simply added to the problems by melting the great banks of snow and so causing the added misery of flooding.

This time the freak weather was directly or indirectly responsible for the deaths of several inhabitants of the county but, despite the great privations and hardships experienced everywhere, the death toll was not as great as that six years later when the North Sea inundated the northern coast of Kent, as well as the east coast of Britain.

This time it was not snow, or even heavy rain, that was the problem but the great power of the sea, an exceptionally high tide being whipped up into a frenzy by hurricane-force north-easterly winds. The raging sea struck the north Kent coast in the early hours of 1 February 1953 and destroyed whole beaches and eroded mighty cliffs, breaching the sea defences in 400 places. Not a single community along the coast from Woolwich to Margate was spared, the water being 9ft deep in some places. The sea wall on the Isle of Grain collapsed, flooding the newly built oil refinery and the water simply came over the top of the new sea defences at Whitstable.

A submarine in dry dock at Sheerness was picked up by the force of the water and flung bodily over the gates and deposited on the other side, while a frigate was turned on its side in the dry dock. At Margate, the sea wall held but the lighthouse at the harbour entrance was undermined and collapsed. The police station in Margate was evacuated, an 'overlooked' drunk in one of the cells being discovered by a photographer.

Animals suffered too; many cows, horses and sheep – even dogs and cats – lost their lives in the flood waters, although others miraculously survived. A horse that had spent two day in freezing water up to its neck at Sheerness was finally rescued, as were many other animals that had managed to find a small area of dry land or a piece that was only covered in a few inches of water. There were 600 acres of fruit trees destroyed and numerous glasshouses wrecked.

In all, the sea claimed 307 lives, although Kent was largely spared this toll and only 1 person in the county, a sluice-gate keeper, lost his life in the storm. It was this great flood disaster that proved to be the spur for the building of the Thames flood barrier a few years later, as well as the strengthening of the many sea defences along the coast.

The year 1987 was notable for the number and variety of weather conditions: heavy rain, floods, blizzards and snow drifts. But the greatest natural disaster that hit the county in the October of that year was not caused by the sea, rain or floods, but by exceptionally high winds (although the generally wet conditions in the preceding months undoubtedly played a part).

Although gales had been forecast, no one had anticipated the 100mph gusts, which caused havoc and uprooted hundreds of trees. Their roots loosened by the saturated soil, the still leaf-bearing trees took the full force of the wind and fell singly or in serried ranks like dominoes. Whole forests, woods and orchards were decimated. Of the traditional seven oaks in the town of Sevenoaks, six were uprooted and other great trees, which had stood for hundreds of years in places like Knole Park and Chilham Castle, were similarly blown down, often taking others with them. Over 5,000 acres of mature trees were destroyed in the Bedgebury Forest alone. Roofs were blown off houses and caravans, cars and lorries were overturned and aircraft blown onto their backs.

In Folkestone, the cross-Channel ferry the *Hengist* was securely tied up to the harbour pier, fully prepared to ride out the expected storm with a skeleton crew of twenty-four on board but the seas, whipped up by the increasing violence of the wind, began to rip the vessel from her moorings. As these were re-secured by the vigilant crew, so they were torn away again and eventually the captain, Sid Bridgewater from Dover, decided to put to sea. It was too dangerous to remain in harbour. But the sea was not to be denied its pleasure and the ship pitched and rolled to such an extent that the engines were tripped and the vessel had no power. Rolling helplessly the great ship was thrown onto the concrete apron at the Warren, between Folkestone and Dover, where she finally beached at about 5 am in the morning.

There is no doubt that the all too-recent *Herald of Free Enterprise* disaster was very much in the minds of the beleaguered crew as the beached craft continued to be battered by the wind and waves. Ropes were run from one side of the ship to the other so that, should she capsize, the crew would have something to hold onto. 'We all thought we were dead when she was rolling,' said the chief engineer, Peter Philpott, later. 'We thought it was another *Herald of Free Enterprise*.'

Fortunately, the worst fears were not realised and rescuers were soon on the scene and the crew were taken off by breeches buoy. As for the ship, this was eventually refloated and repaired.

Further along the coast in Dover, although the port was kept open for any vessels that sought to enter the haven, the waves were such that it was extremely perilous for any ship of any size to attempt to get through the comparatively narrow gap between the harbour piers. A small coaster, the *Sumnia*, had been sheltering in the lee of Dungeness like so many other ships before her, but she dragged her anchor and was in distress. The skipper decided to make a run for Dover but, as he tried to turn into the harbour entrance, the coaster was blown onto Admiralty Pier and the breakwater by winds now gusting to 100mph and rolled over. A Dover Harbour Board tug was dispatched to see if it could pull the stricken vessel off the breakwater but its offer of a tow was refused, no doubt with an eye to the salvage costs this would involve. The Dover lifeboat also hurried to the rescue, aided by the tug, and between them they took three of the six-man crew off the foundering ship before a huge wave, estimated by one of the lifeboat crew to be some 70ft high, finally destroyed the *Sumnia*.

Abandoning hope of rescuing any more of the crew, the lifeboat headed for the eastern harbour entrance rather than risk the western one which had proved so disastrous to the *Sumnia*. This proved to be a very fortunate decision for 21-year-old Mike Traynor, a deck hand from the sunken vessel. A sharp-eyed lifeboatman espied him clinging to a life-belt and about to be swept out to sea and rescued him from the sea in the nick of time.

The next day the body of the *Sumnia*'s first mate, Ron Horlock, was recovered from on the breakwater but the master of the vessel, David Birch, was lost at sea and his body was never recovered.

Having sailed from Calais at 3.30 am, the cross-Channel night ferry *St Christopher* was unable to enter Dover harbour, partly because of the weather but also because of the operations in progress to rescue the crew of the *Sumnia*, and spent the whole night lying off Dover waiting for the winds to abate, much to the consternation of the passengers, many of whom were feeling decidedly unwell. The 40ft waves battered the stationary ship, buckling the steel doors on the upper car deck and three lorries fell onto their sides and began to slide across the deck, causing considerable damage to the cars parked nearby. The ship did not dock until early the following afternoon, some 10 hours after she had left Calais on a 90-minute crossing.

With a good number of electricity distribution poles and power cables blown down, many areas were without the comfort of electricity for some days after the event despite the valiant efforts of the electricity supplier's workers. Small wonder that the 'Great Storm' or 'Hurricane' of 1987 has passed into local folklore as the weather event of the century.

Chapter 3

Going off the Rails

The arrival of the railways in the middle of the nineteenth century was seen by most, but not all, as a great blessing. No longer was it necessary to travel uncomfortably from place to place on horseback or by carriage or cart along the rutted and often muddy roads. This new, fast and comparatively clean and safe means of transport was a great improvement.

That is not to say that the railways were universally accepted; some towns, such as Maidstone, resisted the arrival of the train until a comparatively late date, by which time other towns had been better served.

For many years, the Kent countryside was scarred by the excavations, tunnelling and cuttings made by the navigators, or 'navvies', who were preparing for the laying of the tracks. Not only the countryside but the towns and villages on the route of these railroads were beset by hordes of these itinerant workers, many of whom came from Ireland to avoid the famines and shortages that afflicted their home country. These labourers were hard workers and hard drinkers and were always ready for a fight or a bit of petty larceny. As such, they were a constant headache for the parish constables and infant police forces and a source of great annoyance to the bucolic residents of the county.

But by 1853 the East Kent Railway had been created, incorporating a number of small railway companies that had been formed earlier, and had access to the new Victoria station. The existing network was extended to Dover and Ramsgate in 1859 and the name was changed to the London, Chatham & Dover Railway Company. Meanwhile, a rival company, the South Eastern Railway, had also more or less completed its own network through mid-Kent but its access to London was inferior to that of the London, Chatham & Dover Railway Company and so a direct line through Sevenoaks to Tonbridge was constructed between 1865 and 1868, which involved huge earthworks. Once these lines had been laid and a regular service was being provided by the two companies, the railway quickly became the accepted means of transport between the main Kentish centres of population, and between these and London.

For some years Ashford, Chatham, Dover, Gravesend, Margate, Ramsgate, Rochester, Sevenoaks, Bromley, Canterbury, Maidstone and Whitstable were all served by both companies, each using its own lines and stations but the London, Chatham & Dover Railway Company was constantly in financial difficulties and so both companies merged in 1899 to become the South Eastern and Chatham Railway. The second station in each town was closed apart from those in Bromley, Canterbury and Maidstone, which have two separate stations to this day. The South Eastern & Chatham Railway became the Southern Railway in 1923.

Despite the awesome appearance of the steaming and snorting locomotives, the railways proved to be a very safe, reliable and reasonably comfortable means of transport but, even so, from time to time accidents did occur.

A Dickens of a Crash

One of the earliest railway accidents involving a significant loss of life occurred on 9 June 1865. In total ten passengers lost their lives and around fifty were injured when the boat train from Paris to London via Folkestone went off the rails where the track crossed the narrow River Beult near Staplehurst. The Beult at this point scarcely justified the nomenclature of 'river' at this time of the year, being but a few feet wide and with a depth of some 2ft of water over perhaps 6ft of mud. But the area was prone to flooding and, following heavy rains, the river was a more substantial obstacle.

The viaduct over the river, or Hockenbury bridge as it is known locally, was about 70yd long, constructed of cast-iron girders supported on brick buttresses and spanned by 25ft-long timber beams to which the rails were affixed. The bridge was surrounded by open fields with just a few cottages in the vicinity and was a scene of rural tranquillity.

On this particular day, the track over the bridge was in the process of being repaired by railway workers who had to remove a pair of rails to replace one of the wooden beams beneath them. Harry Benge, the foreman, watched the 2.50 pm train steam past and then, consulting the South Eastern Railway's time book, estimated that he had plenty of time to effect the repairs before the arrival of the boat train, scheduled for 4.15 pm. Without wasting any time he sent his flag man, John Wiles, the usual ten telegraph poles (550yd) up the line to act as lookout and instructed the rest of his team to lift the two 21ft lengths of rail and install the new supporting beam.

Benge was happy to be engaged on this job as he lived a fairly easy walk away in Headcorn with his wife and three young children. Aged 33, he had been employed on the railway for ten years, during which time he had built up a reputation for conscientiousness and reliability, a reputation that was earning him 3*s* a week more than the rest of the gang's wage of 18*s*. Despite being only semi-literate, Benge could read a timetable but, what the young foreman had failed to realise, was that he had followed the wrong line in the closely printed schedule and had been looking at the times for the next day, Saturday.

The timing of the boat train was subject to fairly wide variations, it being governed by the time of high tide at the port. On this day, it left Folkestone at 2.20 pm, an hour or more earlier than the Saturday time that Benge had read by mistake. When the lookout, John Wiles, first noticed the express, it was just approaching Headcorn station, some 2 or 3 miles away, travelling at around 50mph. At this speed the train would reach the bridge in less than 5 minutes. Wiles shouted a warning to his colleagues but he was too far away for them to hear him over the noise of the work they were carrying out. Running as fast as he could back towards the bridge, Wiles kept calling and eventually he was seen by one of the labourers but, by this time, the train was only a mile or a little over a minute away. Henry Benge went white with horror: 'God! It's the boat train. What shall we do?'

But there was nothing they could do but save themselves and get clear of the track before the train reached them. The horrified platelayers could only watch as the express hurtled towards the bridge where the two rails had not yet been replaced.

Driver Crombie on the boat train saw the lookout waving his flag frantically as a warning and, realising something was seriously amiss, shut down the steam and applied the brakes, meanwhile sounding two short blasts on the train's whistle – the recognised danger signal. But the bridge was much too close for the fast-approaching express to stop in time.

The boat train comprised fourteen carriages, half of which were first class, hauled by one of the latest and most powerful locomotives owned by the South Eastern Railway Company. It was carrying some 110 passengers, described in a later newspaper report as 'chiefly moving in the higher circles of life', most of whom were making the 8-hour journey from Paris to London.

Despite fierce braking, the train ran onto the bridge at a speed later estimated at 30mph and the locomotive, together with its tender, the brake van and the two leading first-class carriages, managed to reach the further side of the 43ft gap in the rails by running on the timber ties before the cast-iron girders cracked and the bridge collapsed, sending most of the carriages into the river. There were no guard rails or any other kind of protection to prevent the carriages from tumbling into the water and this contributed significantly to the scale of the disaster. The *Illustrated London News* reported the catastrophe: 'Then ensued such a scene of agony and bewilderment as, happily, is but rarely witnessed. . . . In more than one carriage a wife lay dead, or on the point of death, beside her unconscious or helpless husband.'

The horrendous wail of the steam whistle, the screech of the brakes, the sound of the crashing rolling stock and the collapsing bridge, together with the screams of the terrified passengers were heard for miles around and people began running to the scene from far and near. The noise then ceased and soon, apart from the cries of the injured and the hiss of escaping steam, there was a moment's quiet from the shattered train. The uninjured passengers began extricating themselves from the wreckage and from the few undamaged carriages, assisting those among them who were only slightly injured. Some of these passengers alighted into the shallow river, only to become mired in the deep, glutinous mud beneath.

Although some way from any paved road, help began to arrive by every conceivable means: on foot, on horseback, by cart, by pony and trap and, especially, by rail. Special trains ran from London, Ashford, Tonbridge and elsewhere, bringing railway officials, engineers and medical aid. Soon there were twenty doctors at the scene. The Staplehurst surgeon, Dr Frederick Wilkin, later told the inquest:

A railway porter came up to my house and told me that an accident had occurred and had a trap ready to bring me down immediately. I came forthwith. I was at the scene of the accident, I should think, about half-past three. Some of the bodies had been taken out before I was there and others were taken out while I was there. I examined some of the bodies . . . I can say they all died from injuries they received by the accident, or by drowning.

Dr Wilkin's home was converted into a hospital, as were some other houses in the village, while local ladies volunteered their services as nurses.

When the smoke and dust had subsided it was found that ten persons had lost their lives in this, one of the earliest recorded rail accidents, and fifty more had suffered injuries.

Among those passengers who '. . . moved in the higher circles of life' was one Charles Dickens. The by now famous author was seated in the foremost first-class carriage with his companion and mistress, Ellen Ternan, and her mother. This trio, like so many of the other passengers, was returning from Paris and looking forward to arriving in London in an hour or so. Fortunately, the carriage in which Mr Dickens and his party were ensconced was one of the two that leapt the gap and did not fall into the river, although it was leaning at a perilous angle. Once the carriage had settled and stopped swaying, he reassured his companions and told them not to move while he climbed through the window and made his way to the guard's van where he obtained a key. Returning to the carriage, he opened the door and helped his lady companions to descend. Once assured that they had come to no serious harm and were now safe, Dickens produced a bottle of cognac that he was bringing back from Paris and then went to lend a hand to those passengers less fortunate than himself, one of whom, a Mr Dickenson, claimed he owed his life to the writer's actions.

Climbing down the brick buttress into the water, Dickens distributed sips of brandy to all who would accept them and, using his cap as a basin, he gathered water from the river and bathed wounds. Sadly, several of those to whom he offered succour were too far gone and expired before more-expert medical attention arrived. He recorded the situation he encountered:

> I came upon a staggering man, covered with blood . . . with such a frightful cut across the skull that I couldn't bear to look at him. I poured some water over his face and gave him some to drink, then gave him some brandy, and laid him down on the grass, and he said, 'I am gone!' and died soon afterwards.

Dickens's efforts did not go unnoticed and he later received a letter of appreciation and a gift from the management of the railway.

When things had quietened down a little, Dickens suddenly remembered that he had left the manuscript of his latest book, *Our Mutual Friend*, in the carriage and he clambered back inside to retrieve it, together with his luggage. He later caught a special train to London where he admitted that he had suffered from an 'attack of the shakes'. He added, 'I had to cling tightly to the seat to prevent myself falling off. I felt pale and sweaty and was unable to look at anyone directly. The doctor tells me I may be suffering from nystagmus [a disorder of the eyes].'

The day following the accident, Charles Dickens wrote the following letter to his doctor, Francis Carr Beard:

My Dear Frank Beard,

I was in the terrible accident yesterday and worked some hours among the dying and the dead. I was in the carriage which did not go down, but hung in the air over the side of the broken bridge. I was not touched – scarcely shaken. But the terrific nature of the scene makes me think that I should be the better for a gentle composing draught or two.

I must away to Gad's directly to quiet their minds. John would get made and would bring down any prescription you might let him have here. Don't come to me at Gad's yourself, unless you can stay all night and be comfortable. In that case, do.

Ever yours,

CD (I can't sign my flourish today!)

There is no doubt that, although physically uninjured, Dickens suffered delayed shock and the incident had a profound and lasting effect on him. He avoided train travel whenever possible after this traumatic experience and it seems probable that the psychological after-effects of this incident were at least partially responsible for his early death just five years later at the age of 58, coincidentally on the anniversary of the train crash.

By 6 pm, all the survivors and all the bodies had been removed from the wreckage, the latter being placed in the charge of Superintendent David Ovenden, the policeman in control of the Cranbrook Division of the County Constabulary, and were stored in a shed at Staplehurst, belonging the the railway authority.

At the inquest that was opened on the afternoon of the following day, the Coroner referred to the incident as 'the most lamentable event that has happened on the main line of the South Eastern Railway' and it is true that, since it was opened in 1842, there had been no serious incidents on the line.

The inquest was informed that the Company's rules provided that, in cases where rails were removed, detonators should be placed on the line at 250yd intervals for 1,000yd, so as to give train drivers adequate warning of the danger. This had not been done. In addition, the flag man should have been 1,000yd from the bridge, not 550yd. It was considered that, had the proper warnings been given, there would have been time for the driver to have brought the train to a halt before it reached the bridge.

Henry Benge admitted that he now realised that he had read the wrong entry in the timetable and both he and his superior, Joseph Gallimore, the district inspector, were charged with manslaughter. Both the flag man and the train driver were exonerated from any blame.

Both defendants were indicted to appear at the Kent Summer Assizes where they both pleaded not guilty to manslaughter. Benge admitted he had been given a copy of the company's rule book but said he had never been asked if he could read it. Gallimore told the Court that he was responsible for a number of gangs and could not be with all of them all of the time to ensure the rules were being followed. It was argued on his behalf that, if he were held liable, then so should others higher up the management chain. However, this argument had been dismissed by a Board of Trade inquiry held prior to the trial, stating that Gallimore must have been aware that the rules were being broken and, if he did not, he should have done.

Having heard the evidence, the jury retired briefly before returning a verdict of guilty against Henry Benge and he was sentenced to nine months' hard labour, described by the judge, Baron Pigott, as 'a comparatively mild sentence'. The case against Gallimore was dismissed on the judge's direction, although the official Board of Trade inquiry placed some of the blame on him. An article in the *Illustrated London News* was scathing about both men but was particularly critical of Gallimore, expressing the view that the post of District Inspector should be filled by a 'Gentleman', preferably a military man.

A 'Battlefield' in Kent

Sixty years were to pass before the next serious rail accident was to occur within the county when the London–Folkestone express was derailed at Riverhead, on 24 August 1927. The scene was at the point where the railway passes under the bridge carrying Shoreham Lane (a minor road linking the main A25 road with the A224) about ½ mile north of Sevenoaks station.

Leaving Cannon Street at 5 pm, the journey passed unremarkably until the catch points near the site of the accident were passed. On crossing these points, the train began to rock slightly from side to side, this rocking motion increasing as the train came round a left-hand bend until one of the wheels derailed. The train was completely derailed about 30m after crossing the next set of points, tearing up the permanent way for some 150m. The engine and the front few carriages struck the abutment of a bridge over the line causing serious damage and injuries to the passengers.

A *Sevenoaks Chronicle* special correspondent described the scene on the railway as 'like a corner of a battlefield'. He continued,

> As I made my way to the scene of the accident there was a steady stream of injured making their way towards Sevenoaks, reminiscent of the flow of wounded along the duck-boards of Flanders, and when I approached the bridge, the feeling of being on a battlefield was intensified. Half-buried in the bank on the downside was the engine *River Cray*, steam rising from it in clouds. Piled up behind it was all that remained of a coach in which a railway worker had travelled. It looked just as though someone had taken a giant razor and razed off everything from the floor upwards. The passenger had the most miraculous escape of all, I learned afterwards, being flung right through the windows on to the line and yet escaping injury.

Although unhurt, it was some time before this fortunate but greatly shocked man was able to speak.

Much of the remainder of the train had suffered similarly; behind the coach described above was another, the side of which had been ripped away, probably by the central pier of the bridge as it passed under it. Parts of the roof of the third coach appeared to be hanging by a thread, while the remainder of the coach was strewn all over the lines and it was here that the first of the fatally injured casualties was found. The *Sevenoaks Chronicle* special correspondent continued: 'It was that of a man of possibly thirty years with dark hair and, from the position of the body, it looked as though one leg had been jerked right out of its socket and twisted at right angles to the body.'

Railway cushions, newspapers and magazines that the passengers had been reading and huge pieces of woodwork – later taken into use as stretchers – were scattered across the line. A large consignment of evening papers was lying close to the train, and these were later used to cover the dead as they were placed in a long row nearby.

Under the bridge itself, about 30m from the third coach described above, another coach had piled itself up, completely filling the archway with wreckage. It was here that the body of a woman could be seen, but it was many hours later before the body could be recovered.

On the London side of the bridge an easily identified Pullman coach was stretched across the two lines with its end on the bank, high enough for rescuers later to be able to pass underneath. The remaining coaches were in a better condition than the front three or four, one still upright, while the others were leaning at a 45 degree angle.

Being close to the town centre and easily accessible from the road, rescuers were soon on the scene and heroic efforts were made by police, passengers, railway employees, ambulance men, doctors and nurses, hundreds of whom rushed to the site. While some reverently covered the bodies of the obviously dead until the living could be attended to, others searched the debris for possible injured and/or trapped survivors. Even the train driver, although wounded, helped in the rescue work.

A dozen or so members of the Sevenoaks division of the County Constabulary had just returned from a cricket match when a telephone call was received from the landlord of the White Hart Hotel in Riverhead alerting them to the incident. The officer in charge, Superintendent Edwin Fowle – a distinguished member of a contemporary police family and previously the county's first official detective sergeant – jumped in his car, which happened to be waiting outside the police station, and was immediately driven to the scene. The cricketers followed close behind, at least two of them without their tunics.

By 7 pm there was an audience of several hundred people on the bridge, displaying the usual macabre curiosity that such incidents engender. By the time the breakdown and heavy rescue gang had arrived about an hour later, the number had risen to thousands. Courageous women busied themselves bringing tea and refreshments to the workers, steeling themselves to ignore the more gory and gruesome aspects of the incident.

Mr Goddard, the licensee of the White Hart Hotel, having notified the police, grabbed a bottle of brandy and, like a St Bernard dog, set out to provide some sustenance to the shocked and injured survivors. He crawled beneath the archway and found the arch of the bridge packed with wreckage, some of which partially covered three dead bodies:

> Two of them were men and both were terribly smashed about. I stepped over them and as I went on down the line I saw a woman seated opposite the track just as if she were asleep. She was dead. One little girl was terribly injured and her poor little mangled body had to be taken away in a sack.

A witness remarked that, despite the terrible injuries that some had suffered, there was very little screaming or other noise. This view was borne out by Mr W H Pelling from Riverhead: 'All who could get out of the coaches were standing or sitting about quietly. One middle-aged passenger was awfully worried about a parcel he had had with him in the compartment. To satisfy him I had to search among the wreckage until I found it and gave it to him.'

Another *Chronicle* reporter described his horrific experience.

I went down onto the line and ran to the Pullman car where frantic efforts were being made to extricate the body of a woman believed to be buried in the debris. It was not until torches were brought, however, that I could see her but even then only a glimpse of her back. One of the wheels was right across her body. She must have died a terrible death. It was not until the early hours of the next morning that, with the aid of heavy-lifting jacks, her terribly mangled body could be recovered.

A Mr Spalding from Kingsdown, near Sevenoaks, told a graphic story:

The train suddenly rocked and jolted violently and I and other passengers in my compartment were all thrown together in a heap. As soon as we sorted ourselves out, so to speak, I shouted to the others to keep still. The roof of the carriage had been sliced off and the sides ripped open, whilst the carriage next to ours was practically untouched. The Pullman car was at right angles to the bridge but leaning over dangerously. I saw four people dead in the third coach. In my compartment, opposite me, sat a sergeant of the Royal Marines with his four-year-old son sitting on his knee. The child escaped but the sergeant had his left arm badly cut and torn from the wrist downwards. I helped him get out and then placed the child beside his father.

I then rushed along the carriage to assist and do what I could to assist with the dead and dying who were lying all around. It was a heart-rending job but we who were fortunate enough to escape untouched thought it our job to assist in the work of rescue. In one carriage I saw two little kiddies who appeared to be either dead or dying and, only a few yards away, there lay a woman whom I took to be their mother. She was very badly injured and unconscious.

What struck me most was that the disaster happened all in a second, there being no warning whatever. In fact, at the time it occurred, I was sitting comfortably reading my magazine.

All night long the work of rescue and the recovery of bodies continued, with some passengers being notified as 'missing' until their remains were eventually found. In all, a total of thirteen passengers lost their lives in this terrible accident with more than twice that number seriously injured.

The usual inquiry and inquest were held which found that the rocking motion had been caused by a combination of hard suspension on the locomotive and the poor state of the track bed at the point where the rocking started. Heavy rains in the preceding weeks had seriously undermined the track bed, washing much of the gravel away. So far as the engine was concerned, this accident led directly to a new, improved type being introduced.

Fatalities in Fog

Although in point of fact the area concerned ceased to be within the administrative county of Kent in 1889, Lewisham still had close ties with Kent in the middle of the twentieth century and many of the older inhabitants preferred to regard themselves as residents of rural Kent, rather than part of the urban conglomeration that was the County of London.

In the 1950s the London area was still subject to the choking and blinding 'smog' – a mixture of natural fog and the sulphurous results of the burning of fossil fuels such as coal and coke – that had the effect of reducing visibility to virtually zero. It was on such an evening, on 4 December 1957, in the early winter gloom that these conditions caused the delay or cancellation of all trains coming into and out of the London termini. The 4.56 pm Cannon Street–Ramsgate express, hauled by the Southern Rail's 'Battle of Britain' class steam locomotive *Spitfire* and packed with home-going commuters, was therefore late leaving the station and was near St John's station on the Lewisham by-pass line when it collided with the equally delayed ten-coach electric 5.18 pm Charing Cross–Hayes train. The impact shunted the express into an over-bridge which collapsed onto the packed carriages, adding to the casualty list.

The subsequent inquiry revealed that the electric train was stationary at a red light at the Parks Bridge junction when the steam train ran into its rear. The steam train had apparently passed a red light in the fog and was travelling at around 30mph at the time of the collision. As the stationary train was on a rising gradient, the brakes were fully applied which made it an unyielding, virtually immovable object incapable of absorbing any of the impact. The ninth coach of the electric train was forced over and through the one in front which was completely destroyed.

In the Ramsgate train, the front of the leading coach was crushed against the rear of the engine tender and the two units were thrown to the left. They crashed against the middle steel column which supported two of the four heavy steel girders of the bridge that carried the Nunhead–Lewisham line over the four-track main line on which the collision had occurred. The two girders immediately subsided onto the steam train below, completing the destruction of the leading coach and crushing the second coach and the front part of the third.

Fortunately, about 2 minutes after the collision, the alert driver of a train slowly approaching a red light on the overhead line saw the girders of the bridge over which he was about to pass were at an unusual angle and brought his train to an emergency halt just before the bridge. Had he not done so his train would have fallen onto the two trains, creating an even more serious incident.

Both the trains on the main line were packed to capacity because of the disruption of rail services through the fog. The electric train had 958 seats but was carrying nearly 1,500 passengers, while the steam train had 480 seats and was estimated to be carrying 700 passengers. As a result of this overcrowding, the casualty list was much higher than it might otherwise have been and a total of ninety persons lost their lives, including the guard of the electric train whose van took the full brunt of the impact. There were over a hundred casualties with serious injuries, including the fireman of the steam train and two other locomotive drivers who were travelling in that train on duty.

Fortunately there was good road access to the scene of the accident and the emergency services were quickly in attendance. Thanks to the prompt action of the uninjured railwaymen who threw out the steam engine's fire and smothered its remains with ballast to prevent overheating, there was no fire and so the fire brigade was able to apply all its resources and expertise to the extrication of victims from the wreckage. Doctors and nurses from local hospitals attended, as did the St John's Ambulance Brigade, the WVS (as it then was) and the Salvation Army, all of whom did sterling work in succouring both the victims and the rescuers. Many local residents threw open their houses and placed their belongings at the disposal of the rescuers and medical teams.

Despite being on the footplate of the engine that ran into the other train, the driver of the steam train, W J Trew, was not physically injured but suffered severe shock. He was later tried for manslaughter but the jury failed to agree and he was acquitted at a second trial. Whereas signals were normally sited on the left side of the line, those on this particular stretch were on the right and it was accepted that, with the driver sitting on the left side of the footplate with only a narrow spectacle glass through which he could look, signal lights on the right side of the track were difficult for him to see, especially in conditions of poor visibility such as fog. In addition, the boiler of a 'Battle of Britain' class locomotive was particularly wide, further restricting the driver's forward vision.

This problem was mentioned by the drivers of other trains that were running in the area around the same time. The driver of a Cannon Street–Hastings steam train told the inquiry that, although it was running very late, having left Cannon Street 38 minutes later than scheduled, he was losing more and more time because of the conditions and these signalling arrangements. 'I was sitting on the left-hand side and my view of the signals on the right hand side was partially obscured. As we proceeded slowly on towards Hither Green, I asked my fireman to stand on the right-hand side of the engine to look out for the signals through the fog.'

The fireman confirmed this and said that some of the signals could not be seen when they were only 20yd away. The driver of the diesel–electric train in front of the steam train did not have the same problems as the drivers of steam trains, as his driving position was right up at the front of the train with nothing to obscure his view – apart from the fog. The driver had noted a sequence of yellow cautionary lights and was driving very slowly when he came to a red light and stopped his train at the Parks Bridge junction. It was still stationary when the following steam train ploughed into its rear.

The railway network was disorganised for some time after the accident, although a diversion enabled some services to by-pass the scene by the next morning. The girders and steelwork that had fallen on the front of the steam train were estimated to weigh 350 tons and had to be cut into sections to enable their removal. A 'temporary' bridge was erected to carry the Nunhead–Lewisham line to serve until a permanent bridge could be erected. This 'temporary' bridge is still in use fifty years later.

Guy Fawkes Night Disaster

Ten years were to pass before the next serious rail accident in the Kent area, once again occurring on the busy London part of the Southern Railway's network. Like Lewisham, a short distance to the north-west, Hither Green had become part of the capital and now fell within the London Borough of Bromley but still retained close historic and sentimental ties with Kent, of which it had been a part for so many centuries.

At 9.16 pm on Sunday, 5 November 1967, any Guy Fawkes celebrations in Hither Green were brought to an abrupt end when the Hastings–Cannon Street express train went off the rails at 70mph, just before it crossed the bridge over the busy A205 road. Most of the twelve coaches overturned, the sides of two of them being completely ripped off.

What could have caused this disastrous derailment? No other train was involved, the signals were in its favour and the speed, while fast, was not excessive and in keeping with the customary rate of progress on this so-called 'Up Fast line' on which the maximum permitted speeds were up to 90mph, depending on the type of train. The scene was closely examined by railway experts who soon detected the cause: a small, wedge-shaped piece of steel, about 5in across the top, had broken away from the end of one of the rails, causing the third coach to derail when its wheels hit it. The train continued to run with this carriage off the rails for about a ¼ of a mile until the derailed wheels struck a crossover when the second coach and all the other coaches behind the originally derailed coach also came off the rails. The second to the fifth coaches tipped over onto their sides before the train finally came to a halt some 200m further on. All these coaches were severely damaged and the fifth to ninth coaches jackknifed. The last three coaches were derailed but remained upright.

Being a Sunday, the train was well filled with a number of passengers standing in the corridors of the coaches and forty-nine persons lost their lives, while a further twenty-seven were seriously injured. Few passengers escaped without some injury or other.

The emergency services responded very promptly, the police arriving within 5 minutes and the first ambulance only a minute later. The fire brigade was on the scene only 2 minutes after the ambulance. In all thirty-three ambulances and twenty-eight fire-brigade vehicles attended the incident and, once again, the voluntary and welfare services soon arrived to support the workers and the casualties.

The derailed coaches caused short circuits of the power supply and the lines were closed to traffic for up to three days, causing widespread disruption of rail services.

At the inquiry held some six months later, the driver, D S Purves, said he had been driving diesels for nine years and took over the train when it reached Sevenoaks. He did not notice anything wrong with it and slowed down for the 60mph section at Chislehurst, after which he accelerated again to 70–75mph. As the line began to descend, he shut off the power and coasted towards Hither Green. He said it was his usual practice to apply the Westinghouse brake between Grove Park and Hither Green, in order to reduce speed from 70mph to 60mph in accordance with the Inner London speed restriction after Hither Green. On this occasion, he put the brake handle into the lap position, ready to apply it and:

I then felt a drag on the train. I thought I might have accidentally thrown the handle slightly into the Westinghouse position and made a small brake application so I waited for the thing to sort itself out before applying it again. I now think I didn't put the handle into the Westinghouse position and the drag I felt was the carriage coming off the rails.

Soon afterwards the drag became severe with a lot of snatching until:

. . . there was a severe snatch with a terrific bang. The brakes came hard on and the coach stopped a short way ahead. I realized that the train had become divided but it was not until I looked out after stopping that I realized that the division had occurred behind my motor coach. I then went forward and protected the Down lines and telephoned the signalman.

With the help of the guard, Driver Purves then started to detrain the passengers.

Goods Guard J Gray also gave evidence, confirming that the run had been uneventful and conducted at the normal speeds until they reached a point between Grove Park and Hither Green when:

I noticed a lot of debris flying past the nearside window of my brake compartment. When I opened it to look out my hat was knocked off my head. I realized something was seriously wrong and lay down on the floor and shouted to nine or ten passengers who were travelling in the passage adjacent to my compartment to lie down too. I did think about applying my brakes but things happened so quickly that I didn't have time to do it.

Once the train had stopped I got down and detrained the passengers from my coach. I went towards the back of the train and saw that it was not badly damaged . . . so I went forward to find the driver and helped him to detrain the passengers from the front coach.

It was Guard Gray who later, in company with two policemen, found the wedge-shaped piece of steel that had sheared from the end of the rail.

A company director, Mr G Dean, was a regular passenger on this train, travelling to Town from Battle. On the fateful day, he was seated in a first-class compartment with one other passenger, '. . . although I believe the second class carriages were well filled'. He continued,

Up until the train approached Hither Green it had been a normal run, although on that line the coaches always swayed a lot and I have always had an uneasy feeling that they were going too fast. When the train got near Hither Green, my coach started to sway more than usual and then there was a noise that sounded to me as if the train was running over splintered glass. The coach then started to rock very much more until suddenly there was a crash. The lights went out and the coach turned over on its right-hand or corridor side. Luckily, I was not hurt.

Mr Dean added that he thought the train was going too fast, but not faster than these trains usually travelled.

Another witness, Mr J Brennan, had the misfortune to be in the toilet when the train started to sway excessively and he had a job to open the sliding door to get back to his seat.

Mr Brennan and several other witnesses said they thought that trains habitually ran too fast over this particular stretch of line. However, it is clear that speed was not a primary cause of the accident, although it is possible that, had the train been moving more slowly, the extent of the damage and injuries would have been reduced. What does seem to be clear is that the line was in a poor condition. Just two weeks before the accident, no less than five separate cracks had been detected by ultra-sonic equipment a little further south. With the line in such a poor state, the speed limit was undoubtedly too fast and it was immediately reduced to 60mph.

Marden Mayhem

The evening of Saturday, 4 January 1969 was a dark and miserable one, with thick fog hanging over much of the South East. Nevertheless, the 8.00 pm passenger express train from Charing Cross to Ramsgate was speeding along through the mist and murk at anything between 70–90mph. Despite the conditions, with visibility down to 50yd in places, it had not been thought necessary to bring the fog safety system into operation.

Meanwhile, at 8.45 pm, just west of Marden station, near where the railway line crosses the little River Teise and close to Brook Farm, the 7.18 pm parcels train from London Bridge to Dover Priory had stopped for a red signal. The driver patiently waited until he got the signal to proceed and then, just as he was moving off, the express train, travelling on the same line and in the same direction, ploughed into the rear of the almost stationary goods train.

The express train had around 170 passengers on board, distributed between the 12 coaches and it was a miracle that this high-speed collision resulted in the deaths of just 4 people – the driver of the express and 3 of his passengers, although many more were injured, some seriously.

The site of the incident was in the middle of open country, the best part of a mile from any road, and then only minor country lanes. Hearing the sound of the crash, David Winch, who ran Brook Farm, set off with a handful of his workers towards the place where the sound seemed to have come from. Feeling their way across the lush but somewhat marshy meadows, criss-crossed by streams and dykes, the little band of volunteers, some on foot, some on tractors and other agricultural machinery, soon came across a scene of complete chaos.

Without waiting for the emergency and railway services to arrive, these workers set to, helping the shocked and injured passengers. Using their tractors, they ferried casualties across the fields to where the ambulances were soon waiting, on the road.

Stephen Nye, aged 16, spent the evening in the Chequers public house in Marden with a couple of friends, the landlord being tolerant of their young age provided they behaved themselves. Soon after 8.30 pm the trio of lads set off for their respective homes, their parents apparently imposing quite a strict curfew on them.

As they walked along the dark, cold country lanes, they heard a rumbling sound, rather like thunder but, given the weather, they knew this could not be the case. Stephen ventured that it was a train crash but his companions were scornful of this interpretation. Nevertheless, they decided to make their way to Marden railway station to see if there was any news there.

Full of excitement, the three youngsters burst into the station and asked the clerk if he knew what the noise was but he, cosily closeted in his office with the doors and windows tightly closed against the inclement weather and with his radio full on, denied hearing anything and obviously thought the whole thing was a practical joke.

Disappointed, the lads had no sooner left the station when they heard the siren being sounded, calling out the retained firemen in the village as the nearest full-time station was several miles away in Maidstone. Still anxious to know what was going on, one of the boys suddenly had a brain wave; his father being one of the firemen, he knew that a log was kept at the fire station and that they could get some information by consulting the log book.

They arrived just as the fire engine was leaving and, the station being unoccupied, there was no one to question their presence. A quick glance at the log made it all clear: 'Train Crash – Brook Farm', so back to the railway station they went where the clerk had just been notified of the incident. He was doubtful about accepting the lads' offer of help but, just then, he received a telephone message from Tonbridge signal-box that the power had been cut off and it was safe to venture onto the line. The clerk asked the signalman if it would be alright for the boys to go to the scene to assist and he agreed, provided they made themselves known to the police on arrival. Stephen Nye recalled his experience in an eyewitness account which he gave to the Marden Heritage Centre some years later.

> As we were talking, a man staggered into the station from the platform. His face was a complete mess of cuts and bruises and he could hardly walk. He had walked from the crash site to raise the alarm, not knowing that this had already been done . . . He could not have known where the crash was or how far he would have to walk. He must have staggered blindly through thick fog and total darkness to reach the station, about a mile away.

Stephen Nye and his colleagues found their enthusiasm waning as they groped their way along the railway track in pitch darkness and swirling fog but suddenly a huge diesel engine loomed out of the murk, the hot engine still ticking as it cooled down. This was the mail train with its wagons stretching out behind it into the darkness.

They could now hear sounds and the odd light and, as they approached the rear of the mail train they could see two fire engines in the field, their spotlights playing on the scene of total devastation. With some difficulty the newly arrived helpers could determine that another train had run into the rear of the parcels train. A policeman appeared and the young men reported to him that they had come to help, if they could. As they were among the first to arrive, he was grateful for the offer. Many of the emergency service vehicles were having difficulty in locating the site due to its remoteness. Stephen Nye's account continued:

> The policeman told us that we could help get the less hurt people across the field to the nearest place the tractors could stop. We were quite happy to do this, as it was better to leave the serious injuries to the experts who were arriving all the time. Apart from that we were by now all scared stiff! As we looked around there were groups of people dotted about, some dazed and disorientated. Others were crying and shaking with shock. Some were bleeding from head wounds and some had fallen into the mud as their legs were so shaky. We began to lead them carefully across to the waiting tractors. . . .
> The field was wet and soft and it was hard work.

When they looked at the wreckage they could see that the front carriage of the express train had totally disintegrated and the next had split in half lengthwise. It was obvious that most of the passengers had escaped death by the skin of their teeth.

In the aftermath of the accident, there was much criticism of the failure by the management to implement the fog safety system which would have caused train drivers to reduce speed and could therefore have either prevented the accident or at least reduced the number and seriousness of the injuries.

Collision at Cowden

Saturday, 15 October 1994 dawned dull, dreary and foggy and Steven Webb, the duty signalman in the Oxted junction signal-box, was quietly going about his business. Occasionally he would glance out of the windows but all he could see was the mist swirling about his box. It was a miserable morning and was due to become even more miserable and a date forever imprinted on his mind.

Suddenly, the quiet efficiency of the signal-box routine was disturbed by the sound of an alarm and a glance at his control panel told him that a London-bound train had gone through a red signal near the Kent/Sussex border. To his horror, he realised that another train, which had passed his box earlier, was already on the single-track line concerned, going in the opposite direction.

Despite the recommendation of the railway inspectors after the Clapham rail crash in London six years earlier, no two-way means of communication had been installed in the trains on this vulnerable line and so the signalman had no means of warning the drivers of the two trains that were now hurtling towards each other. 'When I realized they were heading on a collision course, I telephoned Railtrack control at Croydon and asked them to get the emergency services out because I believed there was going to be a collision. I had no means of contacting the trains myself.'

Steven Webb's forecast was to prove terribly accurate. At a point near Cowden, a very short distance into Kent over the border with Sussex, the inevitable happened with horrendous results; the two trains met head-on at speed, the driver of neither train being aware of the impending disaster. One can only imagine their horror as each saw the other's train bearing down on them. Both trains were around forty years old and were six-carriage diesels and they should have passed each other at the loop in the line near Ashurst. As it was, they ended up both on the single track, travelling at speed in opposing directions.

The frightful impact caused the leading coaches of the two trains to telescope into each other and the remains of a diesel–electric power unit was among the wreckage, which came to rest precariously against some flimsy trees and bushes on top of the extremely high embankment, making rescue attempts by the emergency services very difficult and perilous. Firefighters had to lay ladders and lines down the embankment to provide the rescue parties with some foothold in the undergrowth, which was very slippery with dew.

John Horscroft was one of the many firemen called out from Tunbridge Wells fire station:

> The silence at the scene was eerie. It seems hard to believe that such a collision left no echo. The wreckage was unrecognisable but was a hideous reminder of how much worse things could have been, how many lives could have been lost had it been a working day. No amount of training can fully prepare you for an incident of this scale.

The fireman's testimony was echoed by Barbara Lawton, one of the survivors from the crash, who also mentioned the 'eerie silence'. She was travelling on the London-bound train on the way to visit her mother when the collision occurred. She thought the trains were travelling at between 50–60mph. 'There wasn't a bang, it was more like a dull thud. One second the train was moving, the next it had stopped dead. I was catapulted into the air along with seats and other loose objects, onto the seat opposite. All went quiet; there was no screaming or shouting – just an eerie silence.'

Having descended from the train with nothing more serious than extensive and painful bruising, Miss Lawton found the front of the train 'a tangled mess'. All that could be heard was a gentle hissing noise from the remains of the engine, mingled with faint moaning sounds from some of the carriages. 'I knew the driver must be dead,' Miss Lawton told a reporter. 'There could be no doubt about it – it was a horrifying fact.'

Not without a great deal of difficulty, the fire and ambulance crews were able to extricate eleven survivors from the wreckage, the position of the train making the removing of casualties a slow and arduous process. Over a further period of time, first two bodies, then two more were discovered and removed. Finally, the body of the driver of the wrecked power unit in the wreckage was located but it was clear that it would not be possible to remove the body without putting the lives of the rescuers themselves in danger.

Discussions with the British Rail engineers confirmed that the only solution would be to lift the wreckage back up onto the lines at the top of the embankment – something that would have to be done in any case to clear the line. However, the only pieces of equipment capable of lifting the great weight of the power unit were the huge, 300-ton capacity cranes belonging to British Rail, but which were currently both in the north of England. These were sent for and soon began their long, slow haul down from the north.

In the meantime, steps were put in hand to construct a temporary road across the field beside the embankment to enable these great lifting machines get to the wreckage. In little more than a day, bulldozers had cleared a 300m path, laid some road stone and tarmacked it over, ready for the cranes. By the Sunday evening, the field adjacent to the railway line had been transformed from a peaceful pasture into something that seemed to resemble a scene from a science-fiction film. 'There were huge lamps on masts filling the crash site with a harsh light and two enormous cranes were over the trains like giant praying mantis,' said John Horscroft. 'Fortunately, this is the kind of thing most firefighters see only once in a career. None of us was sorry to leave.'

Not until early on the Monday, almost two days after the crash, was the last body released. This was that of Brian Barton, 31, who had been the driver of the 8 am service from Uckfield to Oxted, who went through a red light when he should have stopped and waited until the late-running 8.04 am train, which was on the return journey back to Uckfield, had gone through. The driver of the latter train, David Rees, 49, who had been employed by British Rail since he left school, was also killed.

An inquiry revealed that the guard of the northbound train, Jonathan Brett-Andrews, was, contrary to regulations, in the driver's cab when the train went through the red light. This 36-year-old railwayman had ambitions to be a driver and there was a possibility that Driver Barton had let him take the controls. The report on the accident concluded: 'The presence of the guard in the cab of the driver's train on the up–line seemed to be the only explanation for why the driver Barton had ignored the danger signal.'

Guard Brett-Andrews was never to be in a position to dispute the findings as he, too, lost his life. Dr Peter Jerreat, a consultant forensic pathologist, said that: 'From the injuries the two men [Barton and Brett-Andrews] sustained, it was impossible to tell who had been in the driving seat. There was nothing specific to tell me that either one of them was sitting down or standing up.'

Wayne Burton, another railway employee, reported seeing the guard in the cab of the train. 'He was in the cab when the train left East Croydon . . .

The scene of the fatal accident at Staplehurst, involving Charles Dickens, in 1865. (*London Illustrated News*)

The scene at Staplehurst today, showing the present railings along the sides of the bridge, the lack of which in 1865 increased the severity of the incident. (Author)

Heavy cranes removing the debris at Riverhead in 1927. (Courier Newspapers)

The scene at Lewisham before the accident in December 1957. (Ministry of Transport)

The scene of the Lewisham train disaster following the accident. (Ministry of Transport)

The broken rail, cause of the Hither Green rail accident in November 1967.
(British Rail)

Marden farmworkers, who toiled through the night to transport victims of the rail crash to the nearest point the ambulances could get to the scene of the accident.
(Marden Heritage Centre)

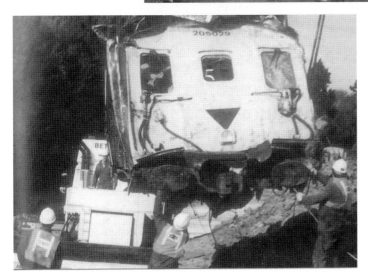

Removing the wreckage of one of the trains involved in the rail crash at Cowden in 1994.
(Courier Newspapers)

An old drawing of the Hartlake bridge before the accident in 1853.

The new Hartlake bridge. (Author)

Plaque under the new Hartlake bridge commemorating the accident. (Author)

Memorial in Hadlow churchyard to the thirty victims of the Hartlake bridge disaster. (Author)

The crashed Dover tram on Crabble Hill, 1917. (Dover Museum)

Dock Road, Chatham, the day following the deaths of the Royal Marine cadets, 1951. (Kent Police Museum)

Police line Dock Road, Chatham, awaiting the cortège conveying the victims of the road accident to the funeral. (Kent Police Museum)

The bus that killed the twenty-four cadets. Note the crumpled nearside wing and the broken headlamp. (Kent Police Museum)

Memorial plaque to the victims of the Dock Road disaster. (Author)

Scene of the multiple-vehicle accident on the M25.
(Kent Police Museum)

the guard got out of the cab door at Edenbridge to look along the train to see if anyone was getting on.' This allegation was supported by at least one of the passengers on the train.

Not only were the three railwaymen killed in the collision, but two of the passengers, Raymond Pointer, 61, and his wife, Moira, 56, from Crowborough, and another thirteen were injured.

Strong protests were levelled at Rail Track in the press and elsewhere about the use of a single-track line where there used to be two. Barbara Lawton was one of many who wrote to the Transport Secretary to complain about the single-track Uckfield line, vowing never to use it again until safety improvements were made. A retired teacher, Michael Steadman, added his voice to the clamour. 'I am sorry to have to say it in such grave times but it will happen again some day unless something is done to put it back to a double-track.'

Chris Jago, a director of Rail Track, disputed these allegations and said that the red warning lights on the track had 'a piercing aspect' and even if they were ignored, visual and audible indicators would have alerted the driver in his cab. 'There was nothing to suggest that this system wasn't safe. It was a tragic accident,' he said, stressing that, when single tracking was introduced in 1989, it was accompanied by 'state-of-the-art' signalling to upgrade and safeguard the line which had been threatened with closure. But not everyone was convinced.

Chapter 4

Risky Roads

For the generations of people who have always lived with the motor car and the internal combustion engine there is a tendency to assume that road and traffic accidents are, like these, a modern phenomenon. Not a bit of it. It is true that the weight, size, speed and ubiquitous nature of modern means of transport mean that modern accidents are more frequent, violent and destructive than those of yesteryear, but there have been road accidents ever since there have been roads on which they could occur. Perhaps the wheel coming off Julius Caesar's chariot as he drove it up Watling Street from Richborough didn't make the *Kentish Express* or the contemporary *acta diurna* – whatever that may have been – but it would have been a road accident. But the scale of accidents in Kent in ancient times, and the number of those killed or injured, would have been minimal – until perhaps we get to the case of the Hartlake Hoppers.

The Unhappy Hoppers

For hundreds of years, Kent was the centre for the cultivation of hops and each autumn tons of these pungent, aromatic vines would be plucked and sent off to the local breweries (of which there were hundreds) for the making of ale and other forms of beer. So concentrated was the harvest time and so labour intensive that it was not long before the local agricultural workers were insufficient in numbers to handle the enormous quantities required. Wandering labourers, gypsies and other travellers would make their way to the Kentish hop gardens for this annual ritual; hard work but very remunerative for those prepared to put in the effort. But even these were not enough and, by the beginning of the nineteenth century many families from the slums of the East End of London were making it their practice to go 'hopping down in Kent' each autumn as a means of earning some cash while benefiting from the wholesome country air. Mother, grandmother, sons, daughters – all came to stay in the tents and huts provided for them by the farmers, the menfolk arriving at the weekend or whenever they could be released from whatever job they normally did in the capital.

The arrival of the railways in the middle of the nineteenth century made the journey down to Kent much easier and special trains were laid on for the purpose, arriving at Paddock Wood or Tonbridge in the early morning where they would await the transport laid on by the farmers to take them to their place of work and their home for the next few weeks. The accommodation left a lot to be desired – leaky ex-Army tents, barns, cow sheds and a few specially built huts with timber walls and corrugated iron roofs. But it was often no worse than what the pickers were used to in the city slums and they usually came back year after year.

This, then, was the situation at Cox's Farm in Hadlow in October 1853. It had not been a good summer and the River Medway was swollen from the heavy rains, overflowing in places into the adjoining fields. Farmer Cox's pickers, largely made up of gypsies and other travellers, were lodged in sheds and farm buildings in Tudely, on one side of the river, and were carried to their place of work in the hop gardens on the other side by horse-drawn wagons because of the floods.

On Thursday, 25 October, the day's work finished, the waggoner, John Waghorn, began the task of conveying parties of hop-pickers to their homes and camp sites across the river, starting with the locals – the families of the regular farm hands and local villagers who came to make a little extra cash to tide them over the forthcoming winter. He returned at about 6 pm to collect the next and last batch of about forty 'strangers' – folks from London and itinerant field workers and take them to their encampment across the river. It had been a long day and they were all anxious to get back to the camp site for a meal, a rest and then perhaps a drink and some jollification, either at the camp or at the Bell Inn in Golden Green village.

With all this party on board, the wagon was full to the brim with people sitting on the tail board and sides as well as crushed together in the body of the wagon. The two sturdy cart horses, harnessed in tandem, needed all their mighty strength to haul the 2 tons of humanity along the rutted and bumpy track to the river, for the most part up to the axles in flood water. John Waghorn was walking beside the lead horse, while one young hopper, Benjamin Hearn, was proudly astride the other horse, much to the envy of those crammed into the cart. As they neared the bridge, Waghorn mounted the leading horse, to avoid having to wade through the water, which had overflowed and was covering the approaches on either side of the wooden bridge to a depth of up to 2ft.

The Hartlake bridge was a timber construction, resting on wooden piles and curving over the River Medway which, at this point, was normally about 20ft wide. There was a 3ft-high fence on either side of the bridge, made from close-boarded planks and the roadway over the bridge was set with metal rungs to give the hooves of horses something to grip as they made their way across the often slippery wooden decking.

With the waggoner astride, the leading horse was just over the apex of the bridge and descending the other side when the second horse stumbled. The waggoner tried to steady his mount, as did the lad behind on the second horse, but the wagon veered to one side and the wheels came close to the low hoarding which skirted the bridge. This hoarding, which had been installed twenty-seven years previously following an accident in which a farmer and his wife and their horse were drowned, appears to have been old and rotten, as were the ends of the timbers on which it rested, and the hoarding gave way and the wheels sank in the gravel or earth under the bridge. The driver tried to drive out of the sinking rut his wheels were making but more and more of the hoarding collapsed as if it were matchwood. In a moment, the wagon had gone over the side, taking both horses and their riders and nearly everyone on the wagon into the fast-flowing, cold and muddy waters of the river. In the evening darkness, only eleven passengers who had been sitting on the sides or tailboard were able to jump off onto the bridge before the wagon went over.

Few ordinary people knew how to swim in those days before the masses had begun to take holidays by the sea and everyone was swept away by the current towards the Stilstead sluice. Their pitiful cries for help were heard as far away as Golden Green. The contemporary *Kentish and South-Eastern Advertiser* described the scene in graphic terms:

> The screams and shouts of those who were not immediately taken below the surface – the fierce struggles of the horses – the momentary struggles and bubbling cries of the drowning – the efforts of those who were safe to rescue the others – and then, in a few seconds, when the eleven survivors stood again upon the bridge, their blank dismay at the utter disappearance beneath the surrounding waste of waters of so large a body of their friends, who a few moments before were as hale and lifelike as themselves.

After the initial shocked silence, a great wailing cry for help arose, so loud that it was heard at the Bell Inn, a good mile distant. The landlord and some of his customers set off to assist but were thwarted by the extent of the flood waters.

Almost all those who fell into the water were drowned, despite the attempts by locals and the survivors to pull them out using hop poles and ropes. At the final tally, only eleven persons had survived the incident, the remaining thirty-five having all drowned. Out of this latter number, no less than sixteen were members of the Leatherland family from the Rosemary Lane area of London, several of the others being Irish travellers. It took a number of days before all the bodies had been recovered, all being buried in one grave in Hadlow churchyard. The two horses appear to have escaped from their harness and managed to scramble up the bank to safety.

The fact that all the victims were of the same or similar background prompted a number of rumours and allegations. The Revd R Schindler, a great campaigner for better conditions for hop-pickers, commented:

> There is something mysterious about the incident, for those thirty persons were all gypsies or Irish and not only had a party of home-dwellers been conveyed across the bridge in safety a short time before, but certain trivial circumstances had prevented several residents uniting with the party that met with so melancholy an end. Some may say, 'This fact explains all; they were notorious sinners, I doubt not, and God has punished them for their sins with a dreadful sudden death.'

Despite this uncharitable castigation of the poor victims of the accident, the clergyman went on to suggest that the fated party was no better or no worse than some of the home-dwellers – a rather begrudging admission that only serves to underline the way these 'strangers' were regarded by the locals. To their credit, the villagers of Hadlow had an impressive memorial erected in a corner of the churchyard, bearing the names of all the victims and some details are displayed to this day in the porch of Hadlow church.

A reporter from the *Kentish and South-Eastern Advertiser* visited the scene two days later:

> We found groups of the bereaved friends and relatives standing about in mute despair – others with animated gesticulations were describing the terrible catastrophe – some with long poles were probing the eddies and backwaters of the river for those that

were lost. A little bare-headed, shoeless girl was pointed out to us as having lost father and mother and infant brother. One man had lost fourteen relatives – another whose face and mien were the personification of grief itself, threw a piece of wood to direct the men with poles to the spot where he had last caught a glimpse of his drowning wife. Only six of the bodies had been found and thirty more it was believed were then to be discovered. It is scarcely possible to perceive a more distressing sight. We were, however, astonished to find that, although two and forty hours had elapsed since the accident, no boat had been obtained, and no systematic plan of dragging had been adopted. The poor fellows with their poles, who ran hither and thither at the call of the relatives and friends of the deceased, were pictures of hopeless, aimless exertion.

It appears that the bridge had been in a very poor state for some years, although no one had thought to mention the fact to the owners, the Medway Navigation Company. Despite evidence from witnesses about the bridge's dangerously defective condition, the inquest jury returned a verdict of accidental death, which absolved the Medway Navigation Company from all liability. None of the victims' dependants received any form of compensation. The damaged and unsound wooden bridge was replaced in due course by a more substantial stone bridge which exists to this day.

Dover Tramcar Tragedy

In 1897, work started on the construction of the Dover electric tramway system, it being one of the earliest towns to apply for and be granted government permission to do so under the Tramways Orders Confirmation (No. 1) Act of 1896. Astonishingly, the track was laid and the system ready for the opening ceremony by the mayor on 6 September that same year. The mayor took great delight in driving the first tram (No. 3) from the town hall to Buckland, then to the Harbour station and back to the town hall.

For the rest of that day a single tram was available to the public, with two more added the next day. The lack of trained drivers meant that the trams only ran every 15 minutes.

The tramway ran between Clarence Place (near the entrance to Admiralty Pier) northwards via the Market Place, Biggin Street, the town hall to Buckland. A further line along the Folkestone Road to Maxton came into use later that year and the first line was extended via Crabble Road to Minnis Lane in River in 1905.

By 1914 the much-used track was in a poor state of repair and lack of finance meant that only the most urgent and essential repairs were carried out. The start of the First World War aggravated the financial situation and also meant that spares and materials were hard to come by. By 1917 the whole system was in a very bad condition, with the track and overhead wiring needing replacement. Only about half the trams were in a serviceable condition with some of the earlier models having been cannibalised to provide essential spare parts to keep the others running.

It was while this regrettable state of affairs existed that the worst ever tram accident in the United Kingdom took place. On 19 August 1917 tram No. 20, on its way to River, went out of control at the top of Crabble Road and ran away down the 1 in 10 gradient, overturning at the bottom where there was a bend in the track. Of the passengers, ten were killed and sixty injured, which indicates that the tram was seriously overloaded since its seating capacity was twenty-two inside and twenty-six outside on the top deck – a total of forty-eight. As a result of this dreadful accident the use of the top deck by passengers was banned on Crabble Hill.

The descent of the Crabble Road gradient called for a degree of skill and experience on the part of the driver, even when the tram was not carrying any passengers. The main difficulty arose at the point where Crabble Road met Crabble Hill as there was no patch of level ground on which the tram could stop, after it had climbed Crabble Hill at full power, before descending the other side. It was the usual practice to bring the tram to a stop on the brow of the hill by cutting off the power as it approached and then applying the handbrake. The slipper brakes were then screwed down and the handbrake partially released to allow the vehicle to continue its journey down the hill, relying on gravity.

The steepest part of the route was the gradient between the first curve and the railway bridge, after which the road flattened out, although the handbrake was only slowly released after the lower curve had been negotiated and the slipper brakes taken off.

A Board of Trade inquiry was held a week later, presided over by Colonel Pringle of the Royal Engineers. The driver of the tram stated in evidence that the handbrake was not working and the emergency brake had jammed, although he admitted that the handbrake was working all right at the previous stop. An examination of the tram showed that the handbrake chain had become detached but, as there were no marks on the road made by the chain, it was reasonable to assume that it had come off as the tram overturned. The slipper brakes, although worn, were perfectly serviceable.

Attention was now turned to the emergency brake. This was not easy to operate as first the power had to be shut off, then the reversing key set to a special position and, finally, the main power control advanced to increase the braking power. Examination showed that the main power handle was full on but the reversing key was in its normal operating position, which meant that the tram was running down the hill on full power, rather than full emergency brake.

It was established that the conductress, who was to lose her life in the accident, had already told the driver that the tram was full and she could not take on any more passengers and it may have been that, intent on not stopping to take on any more passengers, the driver missed the mandatory stop at the top of the hill. When the driver realised that the normal brakes were incapable of slowing the vehicle, it seems he applied the emergency brake but omitted to set the reversing key and so, in fact, had switched to full power.

The inquiry found that the main causes of the accident were: (i) driver error due to inexperience; (ii) overloading; and (iii) lack of familiarity with the emergency braking system. It was noted that the driver had failed to make the compulsory stop at the top of the hill and had continued onto the hill without slowing. His mishandling of the controls meant that the tram descended the hill at top speed, the weight of the excessive number of passengers adding to the tram's momentum. Although the driver tried to brake, the weight, speed and condition of the braking system meant that, once the tram had started to run away, there was little he could do to stop it.

The manager of Dover Corporation Transport told the inquiry that he had had to use inexperienced drivers as the War Office had called up all the experienced men and the existing panel of drivers consisted of men who had suffered physically and mentally during their war service or others who were not considered fit for the Army.

The Coroner's inquest recorded a verdict of death by misadventure on the eleven fatally injured passengers without placing any real blame on the driver. Since the Corporation was seriously under-insured, the £14,575 compensation payable to the injured and the dependants of those killed had to be met largely out of the general rates as only £1,000 was recovered from the insurers.

After the war, the popularity of the trams began to wane with the introduction of motor buses and other forms of transport. The Dover

Corporation Tramway continued in use for almost another twenty years but the end was in sight and the last tram ran on 31 December 1936.

The Dock Road Disaster

In 1951, Chatham was still very much a naval and military town. The great dockyard, which had been operating for over two centuries, was still building and repairing ships of the fleet and many young lads admired the dashing 'matelots' and 'squaddies' who were to be seen in the town, proud to be wearing their navy blue or khaki uniforms.

And no youngsters were keener on such matters than the lads of the Royal Marine Volunteer Corps. Although an unofficial outfit, it was sponsored by Royal Marine officers and very smart these boys looked in their miniature Marine uniforms: miniature because they were aged between 9 and 15 and were therefore much too small to fit into a regular Marine uniform.

The cadets met regularly to drill and exercise, learn about life in the Royal Marines, study seamanship and generally prepare themselves for a possible career in that proud and ancient body. As a special treat, on 4 December 1951, they were going to watch a boxing tournament organised by the Royal Navy at HMS *Pembroke*, its Chatham shore station.

It was with considerable excitement that fifty-two cadets assembled at the Melville Royal Marine Barracks in Gillingham, ready to march to the tournament. Most were wearing their uniform of a navy blue battledress and beret, set off by a smart white belt and lanyard. The Corps adjutant, Lieutenant Clarence Murrayfield Carter, a regular Royal Marines officer, sorted the excited lads into three platoons, each under the command of a young cadet non-commissioned officer. Around 5.40 pm, when all was ready, the three platoons came to attention and marched out of the barracks, the first two platoons in columns of three and the third marching two abreast, all keeping to the left-hand side of the road. The rearmost platoon was composed mainly of newer recruits who had not yet been issued with a uniform, although the rearmost pair were in full uniform with white blancoed belts. Lieutenant Carter was the sole adult with the group and moved up and down the ranks as they marched while a cadet lance corporal had been placed in charge of each platoon and marched alongside it.

Although it was a dark and slightly foggy evening, the marching boys carried no lights; there was no official requirement to do so as they were marching along urban roads with street lights.

Between 15 and 20 minutes later the column had just passed the impressive entrance to the Royal Naval Dockyard and was marching along Dock Road. Although an important road, Dock Road was rather narrow – around 27ft wide – and poorly lit. The gloom was aggravated by the fact that one of the few street lamps had failed and it was like marching into a tunnel. As the marching boys reached the municipal swimming pool, a Chatham & District Traction Company double-decker bus approached from behind them.

Seeing the bus coming, Lieutenant Carter, who had been moving up and down the column, keeping to the pavement, ordered the column to keep in to the left, to allow the bus to pass them. But to his horror, instead of pulling out to pass the marching boys, it continued straight on and ploughed into the column before swerving to the left where it mounted the pavement, knocking him flying before striking a lamppost and coming to a halt.

Michael O'Hara, aged 13, was the lance corporal in charge of the leading platoon, walking in the gutter beside the marching boys:

> We were just approaching the swimming bath gate when I heard a bus roaring down the road from behind us. It was so close on top of me that I jumped onto the footpath. I then saw it flash past me on my right. As I jumped on the footpath, I saw Lieutenant Carter hit the wall on the left of the footpath. I then saw that a bus had passed by and saw it stop immediately . . . I looked round and saw the poor chaps lying in the road.

Michael's colleague, 11-year-old Bryan Harris, was in charge of the second platoon:

> I was about level with the third rank from the back. I happened to look back to the rear of my platoon to see if all my cadets were in step when I saw a bus. It was just running through the rear platoon so I jumped onto the pavement. I tried to grab hold of a boy named Stone but I missed him and fell backwards against the wall.

The third and rearmost platoon was under the command of Cadet Lance Corporal Alan Brazier, 12½ years of age:

> My platoon was marching in twos and there were about eight cadets in the platoon. The left-hand file was marching in the gutter; I was marching on the pavement on their left, level with about the centre cadet. I think it was Cadet Jarrett. I then heard a bus coming from behind us; I looked round and saw the bus nearly on us. It seemed to

be going fast. I shouted, 'Look out!' and I pulled Cadet Jarrett out of the ranks onto the path and the bus went right into my platoon. Three other cadets in my platoon jumped for it onto the path when I shouted and were uninjured. I told them not to look back at the cadets on the road. Six of the cadets in my platoon were dressed in civvies. The rear cadets in each file, Cook and Rose, were dressed in cadet uniform and were wearing white belts and white lanyards on their shoulders.

Other cadets showed great presence of mind in the face of disaster, such as 13-year-old James Solley:

I was marching in No. 1 platoon . . . towards Pembroke Gate. I was in the rear file of three and in the rank nearest the centre of the road when I heard a noise like the sound of a run-away steam-roller behind me. I ran forward, grabbed the two nearest boys in front of me and flung them towards the centre of the road and jumped myself to the centre of the road, landing on my knees on the road. I looked round and saw the bus run over about three cadets and come to a stand-still.

The driver of the bus, John William George Samson, 57, was an experienced bus driver and had completed forty years service with the company a year previously. The fine chiming mantle clock that he had been presented with occupied pride of place on his mantelpiece at home. He was known to many of the boys, who referred to him as 'Sambo', and he had driven this route – service 1 from Luton to Pembroke Gate – more times than he cared to remember. He was driving on sidelights only and later claimed that his speed was around 15–20mph.

There is no doubt that Driver Samson, for whatever reason, failed to see the marching boys. He felt the bus wobble and there was a series of bumps, which he later described as 'as though I had run over a lot of loose stones or something'. He put his foot hard on the brake pedal and stopped within a few yards, but not before the bus had mounted the kerb and struck a lamppost.

Thinking he had hit a car or something else in the road without lights, he went back to see what had occurred. There were terrible screams coming from behind the bus. 'What's happened?' called his conductress, Dorothy Dunster. 'I don't know,' Samson replied and, running to the rear, he saw the carnage he had caused. 'Oh, my God,' he cried. 'What have I done?'

What he had done was to kill or fatally injure twenty-four of the cadets and wound another dozen, the most casualties in any road accident in Great Britain at that time. 'I couldn't see them!' he kept repeating to anyone who would listen.

Petty Officer Stoker Mechanic Arthur Rainsforth of the Royal Navy was walking up Dock Road with a couple of colleagues when the incident occurred and was one of the first on the scene: 'It was dark, and suddenly I heard screams. It made me go cold because it was the high-pitched screams of children. I saw a bus stop and three of us ran blindly up the road. We saw the boys. They were spread out from one side of the road to the other.'

One of his companions took up the story: 'I picked up a boy and he cried, "Oh Mum! Oh Mum!" I put him on the side and went to two others. I cradled them but they died in my arms.' Of those that lost their lives, seventeen died on the spot and seven died later in hospital, all but one the same night.

One of those at the scene, Thomas Mitchell, asked George Samson to turn his bus round so that the scene could be illuminated by his one remaining headlamp so he drove it down to the Pembroke Gate to turn and come back to the scene. The fact that this was felt necessary is an indication of the lack of lighting in the area of the accident.

Once the injured had been taken to hospital and the seventeen pitiable young bodies removed to the mortuary, the scene was cordoned off and covered with tarpaulins until the next day when the police photographers and other officers could investigate the scene in daylight.

The bus was impounded by the police and kept under guard until it could be professionally examined. A brief inspection the same evening disclosed that the brakes and steering were in good working order and a fuller examination was carried out in the Chatham & District Traction Company's garage the following day by a senior vehicle examiner from the South-Eastern Transport Authority. There was, as might be expected, a degree of damage, consistent with the vehicle having been in contact with both human bodies and the lamppost. The front nearside wing was badly dented and torn, while that on the other side was slightly bent. The radiator shell was broken and the guard rail brackets on both sides were bent back, the rails having come off and been found in the road. The offside headlamp glass and bulb were broken. Perhaps more disturbing were the traces of blood and human flesh on the nearside front tyre (which, incidentally, was nearly bald), on the trackrod, the guard rail bracket, the chassis and under the rear platform.

The fatally and seriously injured boys had been taken to the Royal Naval Hospital in Gillingham where, on 6 December, the Coroner, Colonel Jervase Harris, took evidence of identification. 'You have seen body number 1?' he asked a red-eyed mother. 'Yes,' she whispered. 'And were his full names Raymond Peter Cross, aged 11 years?' the Coroner continued. Another answer in the affirmative. 'Thank you. Would you please sign here?' And so on to the next grieving parent.

At the back of the room stood Driver Samson, twisting his cap in his hand, distraught. As the twenty-third victim was identified, he collapsed.

The full inquest took place, also at the Royal Naval Hospital, on 14 December 1951, at which the testimony of the various witnesses differed considerably. The officer in charge of the cadets and the bus driver both obviously felt that they might be held culpable and so their versions could well have been coloured by this. Driver Samson stated that his speed was 15–20mph, while Lieutenant Carter, supported by an independent witness, estimated it at 40–45. Since the road was subject to a 30mph speed restriction, this latter estimate would seem to be exceptionally high, given the driver's experience and previous good driving record. John Samson agreed that he was driving on sidelights only, which was perfectly legal. Other bus drivers stated that, that night, they drove on dipped headlights while some of their colleagues defended Samson's action. Still other witnesses disputed whether the night was particularly dark, although at that time of day and that time of the year, there would certainly have been no daylight left.

Was the officer in charge of the cadets negligent in failing to ensure they carried lights, even though it was not an official requirement to do so?

In the end the inquest jury returned a verdict of accidental death. The Coroner thought Lieutenant Carter and the other witness, George Dixon, were mistaken in their estimate of the speed of the bus and felt Samson's assessment was nearer the truth. He stressed, however, that he did not hold either Carter or Samson negligent in law. The Coroner added that he wished to comment on the actions of Cadet Lance Corporal Brazier who had been in charge of the rearmost platoon: 'I think the boy's prompt action was undoubtedly responsible for saving at least two of them from injury or even death. He acted with great promptitude and remarkable steadiness for a boy of his age. Immediately after the accident he warned the boys not to look and he behaved in a most exemplary fashion.'

Despite the inquest holding that John Samson was not negligent in law, he was nevertheless charged with dangerous driving and found guilty at the Old Bailey. The jury made a recommendation for leniency and the judge,

Mr Justice Pilcher, fined him £20 and banned him from driving for three years. The judge added that the mental punishment Samson had undergone, and would continue to endure, far exceeded anything the law could apply. It is true that there was a great deal of local sympathy for the driver of the bus and his neighbours did their utmost to protect him from the media, both at the time and subsequently.

There was considerable agitation for a public inquiry into the accident but, in the end, the matter was considered by the Government Committee on Road Safety, which reported to the Minister of Transport, concluding that 'there were three main features of the accident; an inadequacy of the street lighting, the lack of proper safeguards for the marching cadets and the failure of the omnibus driver to use his headlights'.

As a result the street lighting in the Medway Towns was improved and all three services decided that a red light should be carried at the rear of any marching columns at night. The bus company accepted liability for the tort of negligence and paid a total of £10,000 to the parents of the victims. In a spirit of goodwill, the mayors of the three towns set up a public fund to which contributions amounting to nearly £9,000 were received. After £2,300 had been spent towards defraying the funeral expenses and assisting those boys who had been injured, there was confusion as to what the remainder should be used for. Following a protracted legal wrangle, the High Court decreed that this was not a charitable trust and its objectives were too uncertain and therefore the balance should be returned to the donors. In view of the difficulty in doing this, the money was held in an account and some of it used to restore the graves and erect memorials.

Motorway Massacre

It had been a fairly quiet night in the Operations Room at the headquarters of the Kent County Constabulary but the night shift were not sorry to be handing over to their Early Turn (6 am to 2 pm) colleagues and heading for their warm beds.

The early morning of 11 December 1984 was more like November than less than a fortnight to Christmas. It was cold, dank, with patchy fog covering much of southern England. Nevertheless, a police patrol car had made a normal run along the M25 London orbital road at about 5 am and had reported no thick fog and no need for the warning lights to be switched on. This was confirmed ½ hour later by another officer going off duty.

It was certainly not an ideal day for motoring and extreme prudence was called for on the part of any drivers who ventured out on the roads. But, unfortunately, prudence and her sister quality, patience, are unknown to some people who seem unable to drive within their capabilities and reasonable safety limits.

Kevin Richards was one of the many drivers who were using the M25 near the Kent/Surrey border just after 6 am that morning and he later told newsmen that, driving along the nearside lane, he suddenly ran into fog so thick that it was as if someone had thrown a blanket in his face. Overwhelmed by this loss of vision, he braked but his lorry ran into the back of a car which had also reduced its speed because of this sudden, thick bank of fog. A following lorry, in its turn, struck the rear of Kevin Richards' lorry, forcing it up the embankment. As he jumped out he heard an explosion, the sound of crunching metal – and people screaming, 'Let me out, let me out!'

'Flames twenty feet high were leaping from the wreckage. I couldn't get near to help. The heat was so intense that metal was melting,' he added.

Travel agent Mrs Janet Brown was caught in the tail end of the accident as she was driving to the airport to catch a flight to Iceland. 'I was near the back of the pile-up and am lucky to be alive. Suddenly the whole scene was chaotic. I drove into this terrible accident. The pile-up just seemed to go on and on. Cars were jammed nose to tail; it was horrific.' She suffered minor injuries which were treated at Bromley Hospital.

Another fortunate survivor was Mrs Deborah Hall from Seven Mile Lane. She was driving to work at Gatwick airport when she hit a sudden and impenetrable fog bank:

> There had been a clear stretch for four or five miles I suppose and suddenly there was this wall of fog. I could just see rubbish all over the road which turned out to be a load of toilet rolls from the lorry in front. Then something shunted me from behind and I was forced right past the lorry. I could hear other cars being hit behind. You literally could not see a thing. I couldn't see the cars or the grass verge at the side.
>
> It all happened so quickly. The whole accident must have taken five minutes. When I realised what was happening I thought, "This is one of those motorway pile-ups" and I didn't know whether to sit there, knowing a juggernaut could come behind and crush us all, or to cross the road to the verge and risk getting run over.

She decided on the latter option and made her way through the mangled wreckage to the grass verge where she joined some other survivors. She waited there for 2 hours before being taken to hospital with whiplash injuries. She later described to the *Sevenoaks Chronicle* the impotency felt by the survivors. 'There was nothing we could do,' she said. 'After about fifteen minutes the fire started and everything went up. There was one man trying to get hold of a fire extinguisher but it was futile. People were trapped in their cars and you could just hear their screams.'

In the Police Operations Room in Maidstone there was the usual good-humoured banter as the shift settled into their allotted jobs on the radios, telephones and teleprinters and prepared for a busy day. They had not long to wait. It was just after 6 am and Sergeant John Bell had scarcely sat down in his seat when the first call came in on the motorway emergency telephones. The initial report of an accident on the M25 motorway was quickly followed by several more and it soon became apparent that this was much more than a minor shunt.

Sergeant Bell immediately rang the Traffic Division garage at Sevenoaks and told them not to release their night shift as it seemed likely that every available Traffic patrol would be needed on the dark and foggy stretch of the M25 between Sevenoaks and Godstone. A similar call was made to the Traffic Division garage at Maidstone. Sergeant Bell instructed the Traffic patrols to close the M26, which led from the M20 to the M25, and to divert traffic onto the old A25 to reduce the inevitable jams that this accident was going to cause.

The other emergency services were also alerted and Dennis Sargant, a senior officer at the county ambulance station at Southborough, was on stand-by duty at home in Maidstone when he was directed to attend the incident. It took him just over 20 minutes to get there, little foreseeing that he would remain there for nearly 8 hours as the ambulance officer in charge:

> The full horror didn't strike me immediately, even though flames were shooting fifteen to twenty feet in the air. Only when dawn began to break did I see the full extent of what had happened.
>
> When I arrived it was clear that there was nothing more we could do for those people who had been trapped in their vehicles. All we could do was to get the injured to Bromley Hospital and everyone to safety. It was the worst incident I have attended in my twenty-four years of service and I hope I never have to attend another like it. It was absolutely terrible.

Constable Fred Harrison and his partner, Constable Bill Bowman, from the Traffic garage at Coldharbour near Maidstone, got the radio message at 6.10 am and arrived at the M20/M26 junction 10 minutes later. Donning their reflective jackets and putting out the necessary lights and notices, they managed to prevent any more vehicles from heading towards the scene of the accident. Fred Harrison remembers:

> The fog was extremely thick and our task to say the least was a bit 'iffy'. The traffic, as is normal in fog, was not slowing down too much. We had our usual complement of six collapsible signs ('Slow' or 'Accident') and twenty cones which were deployed (not to much use). We also carried fog flares. These were a long, pole-like firework which stood in a metal stand. They burned with a bright flame but probably added to the density of the fog. Bill and I were dancing about in the five lanes, trying to get the traffic to leave onto the A20. However, I don't think we were entirely successful in preventing every vehicle from entering the M25.

Constables Harrison and Bowman remained here for the next 2 hours, before being relieved for a short meal break after which they returned to try to control the traffic until 12.30 pm, by which time the Highways Authority had set up a proper diversion.

Despite the earlier weather reports radioed in by the police cars on the motorway, it seems there was what a police spokesman described as 'freaky fog'. The early morning traffic on the M25 was heavy when perhaps an incautious manoeuvre on the part of some motorist or other led to a horrific incident. We shall never know the true cause of the accident since any likely culprit perished with others in the holocaust that followed. But we do know that he or she was not the only incautious driver on the M25 motorway, near the Kent/Surrey border, that day. How else can one explain how a total of twelve heavy lorries and twenty-five private cars came to run into (or were shunted into) the original pile-up?

Survivor Deborah Hall ventured an explanation: 'As you went into the fog you instinctively braked, to slow down, and that is how the pile-up happened. The fog came so suddenly; it had been perfectly clear.'

There are no exits from or entrances to the motorway for 18 miles along this stretch, which seriously hampered the emergency services in their attempts to reach the scene to treat the injured and try to avoid any further escalation of the incident.

The crew of one of the many fire engines called to attend the accident couldn't believe how vehicles were hurtling past them, despite the fog and poor visibility. The driver of the fire appliance was travelling as fast as he felt was safe but still he was being overtaken. Knowing that the road ahead was blocked by the crashed cars, one of the firemen leaned out of the window of the fire engine, waving his high-visibility jacket to try to slow down the passing traffic but his efforts were ignored.

When the fire crews reached the scene they found that all the vehicles involved were on fire. Such was the heat given off that the fog in the immediate vicinity was burned off. One of the firemen described the scene as like a breaker's yard which had been set alight. The *Kent & Sussex Courier* reported that 'It was impossible to tell which cars had been involved as they had been squashed out of shape. Even a twenty-five ton lorry had been flattened . . . Sand from a lorry had shot backwards and submerged the cab of a lorry behind. Three lorry cabs were crushed together into the space of one.'

'We were greeted by a wall of flame,' said Leading Fireman Tony Willshaw. 'It was horrific. You can't visualise what it looked like. The fire situation was already well-developed and it soon became obvious there was no casualty we could do anything for. It was just pathetic – nothing we could do. I have never been to an accident like that before and I never want to again.'

With the fire eventually extinguished, the fire fighters joined the police and ambulance crews in the gruesome task of removing the trapped dead and injured travellers. Nine persons were burned to death in the flames and another was crushed to death in his car. In all more than 150 police, fire and ambulance crews were engaged on this incident, the work continuing round the clock.

Both sides of the motorway were closed so that the eastbound carriageway could be used for the emergency vehicles and a forensic scientist and the Coroner attended the scene. The stretch of motorway involved was closed for two whole days for an investigation into the causes of the accident and for the road to be repaired, the extreme heat having literally melted the tarmac.

Such was the intensity of the inferno that some days after the accident many of the bodies had still not been identified. 'Only two bodies are recognisable as bodies and they are so badly damaged identification is difficult,' said a Surrey Police spokesman. 'The rest were reduced to ashes.' Even identification through dental records was not possible and the police were compelled to rely on a process of elimination by sifting through the thousands of calls they had received from anxious friends and relatives.

Chapter 5

Aircraft Accidents

In these modern times, on the rare occasions that a Boeing 747 or similar airliner crashes there is almost inevitably a great loss of life. But things were rather different in the earlier days of aviation when crashes of passenger carrying aircraft where almost commonplace. But, given the small passenger capacity, the slower speeds and lower altitude, the fatalities were remarkable light. Nevertheless, they were seen as disasters in their time. Fortunately, Kent has been spared any Lockerbie-type disasters but has had more than its fair share of the earlier type of plane crash, a few of which are detailed below.

Crash Among the Cob Trees

The First World War led to flying evolving from an eccentric and hazardous pastime, indulged in by a few wealthy playboys and flying fanatics, to an accepted and fairly common form of transport. By the early 1920s flying had become generally accepted and those who could afford it delighted in using it to travel from and to various points in Europe. A particularly popular route was that between Paris and Croydon, over which regular, scheduled flights took place.

On 27 August 1923, a Farman F60 Goliath, registered number F-AECB and owned by the French Air Union, took off from Le Bourget aerodrome, Paris, on a rather dull and miserable day. These somewhat ugly machines had been designed as heavy bombers but the ending of the war in 1918 resulted in their being converted to passenger use. This particular aircraft had only been brought into service a little over a month previously and had logged less than 100 flying hours.

Having left Paris at 12.45 pm, it landed at Berck, on the French coast near Le Touquet, an hour and a half later to pick up further passengers. With the newcomers comfortably ensconced in their seats, the plane took off again at 2.45 pm with a total of nine passengers. Heading across the Channel towards England, the weather deteriorated and became particularly wet and windy – in other words, a typical British summer day.

The pilot, J J Denneulin, was a very experienced aviator who had flown military aircraft during the First World War with the French air force and had been engaged on the cross-Channel routes for more than two years. He knew that as he approached the English coast near Hythe at a fairly low level he would have to climb to clear the escarpment behind the Romney Marsh. As he began to increase altitude he noticed a change in the note of the engines and the instruments indicated that the port engine was overheating. Prudently, he decided to make a diversion and brought his aircraft down safely at Lympne aerodrome.

The engine was examined by a mechanic at the airfield who found that the radiator was leaking. This was not regarded as a cause for concern and, with a temporary repair effected and the radiator refilled with water, the plane took off again to complete its journey at around 4.45 pm.

Flying at the comparatively low altitude of 1,500ft because of the low clouds, Captain Denneulin headed for Maidstone, intending to continue over Biggin Hill to Croydon. Suddenly, without warning, the starboard engine stuttered to a stop, the propeller blades ceasing to turn, leaving the cumbersome aircraft to attempt to continue on just one engine. Even with the remaining engine running at full power, this was quickly found to be insufficient and the aircraft began gradually to lose height. An emergency landing was called for and the pilot espied a large and apparently suitable field near East Malling. The flight mechanic/wireless operator sent a message in Morse code to Croydon to advise the authorities of the problem.

The next task was to move the passengers to a safer part of the aircraft and the mechanic instructed the four seated in the front of the plane to make their way to the rear. Three of them obeyed the instruction without demur but the fourth, who had been suffering from air sickness and perhaps thought a quick death in a crash preferable to the misery of his malady, refused to move.

The aircraft was now down to a little above tree-top height and, turning it into the wind, the pilot prepared to put down in the field. As he throttled back, the tail dropped and he could do nothing to restore the correct landing attitude. The plane began to bank to starboard and then dived nose first into the ground.

It was now around 5.15 pm and the people of East Malling had been listening to the sound of the aircraft's sole remaining engine for some minutes and suspected all was not well. There now came the sound of a crash, followed by a deathly silence. The local representative of the Kent County Constabulary was alerted and, mounting his trusty bicycle, he rode off, through the rain, in the direction of the crash. On arrival at the scene he was shocked to see what appeared to be a major disaster with a number of people all very shocked and distressed, and in some cases seriously injured, either still in the wreckage or attempting to get out of it.

The aircraft had come down in a plantation of Kent cob trees, flattening several of them and severely damaging the nose and cabin portion. The rear of the plane appeared to have escaped comparatively lightly and it was the passengers who had been in this section who the constable found extricating themselves, nearly all of whom were injured to some degree or other. One passenger, a Mr L E A Gunther, was dead and the mechanic was in a very bad way. Captain Denneulin had escaped with only slight injuries but only one of the passengers was uninjured. Four were seriously injured and three were nursing less severe wounds. After making the passengers as comfortable as they could, the pilot and the constable headed off to East Malling village to arrange for medical assistance.

Once the passengers and crew had been attended to, experts from the Air Ministry's Accident Investigations Branch attended and examined the remains of the aircraft. It was found that the crankshaft of the starboard engine had sheared which accounted for the sudden failure of the engine. The actual crash was put down to the remaining engine being inadequate to provide enough landing speed to make the controls effective and causing the plane to become tail heavy.

Although this accident was only a minor disaster in terms of the number of deaths and injuries, it was one of the earliest aircraft crashes in the county and also awoke the residents of East Malling to the dangers they faced with the growth of the nearby West Malling airfield, which played such an important role in the Battle of Britain and afterwards.

Crash of the Flying Dutchman
Stiff upper lip, sangfroid, British phlegm – call it what you will, this characteristic seems to have been much to the fore in the early days of aviation. And was not confined exclusively to the British, as we shall see.

It was in August 1927 that a large Royal Dutch Air Line Fokker aircraft took off from Croydon airport and headed for Holland. The pilot, Evert Vandyk, takes up the story:

We left Croydon at 8.05 am, bound for Rotterdam and Amsterdam. I have been doing the return journey daily for some time. As we were passing over the hill I could feel a trembling in the tail and, at that moment, the machine went out of control. We were flying at

1,000 feet and the machine started to dive, but I managed to keep her nose up. It was a jolly lucky get-off. Had we been flying at any great height the machine would have spun and nose-dived. I kept low because of the clouds. It was our luck.

With great skill, Mr Vandyk managed to bring the monoplane down and crash-landed in a field at Underriver, near Sevenoaks, close to a large house known as St Julians. The aircraft, skidding along the ground on its belly, was brought to an abrupt halt by a great oak tree, the nose missing it by about 3in. Fortunately, the full force of the impact was taken by the wing; had the plane struck the tree nose-first, the death toll would have been considerable. As it was, the only fatality was the 25-year-old mechanic, Jacobus Brunklaus, who had been sitting beside the pilot, the nine passengers and the pilot all escaping with remarkably light injuries.

Superintendent Edwin Fowle, in charge of the Sevenoaks Division of the Kent County Constabulary, was driven to the scene by Constable Watkins, the latter being detailed to mount guard over the aircraft to deter souvenir hunters, while his superior went to St Julians to interview the survivors. Here they were being cared for by the occupants of the house, Mr R S Herries, JP and Mrs Herries, together with members of their household staff. The local GP, Doctor Crawford, and a surgeon who lived nearby, Mr Sichel, were already in attendance and were treating the various injuries.

Among the passengers was a Mr J E de Lengerke, who was a member of the London Aeroplane Club, and one of his first concerns after his injuries were treated was to find his club badge. 'I'm glad I didn't lose that,' he said, on finding it still in his pocket. His other concern was that the accident might deter people from flying. He was himself a very keen aviator and, only a couple of days previously, had been having lessons in a Moth aeroplane. He regarded this near-fatal crash as a mere hiccup in his flying experiences. His sister was similarly composed and apparently undisturbed by the accident. 'I'm quite ready to go up again,' she said. Other passengers seemed more concerned that their relatives might be worried about them, rather than their own injuries and discomfort and there was no hysteria or recrimination.

Evert Vandyk was equally blasé about the close shave they had all experienced. Slightly injured, he simply washed the blood from his nose and chin before putting on a clean pair of socks – provided by Mr Herries.

Robert Payne, a farm labourer, had heard the engine of the plane make a strange noise and then stop as it flew over. 'The rudder of the machine appeared to be wrenched off and twisted and twirled about in the air before falling to earth.' The rudder was in fact later found about a mile from the crash scene.

Although the weather at the time of the crash was very poor, it does not appear that this had any significant bearing on the accident, the loss of the rudder being purely a mechanical failure. An inquest later returned a verdict of accidental death on the mechanic, who it seems had been sitting where the side of the fuselage struck the tree and so took the full force of the impact.

Honeymoon Horror

Newly-weds Albert and Edith Hodge had been celebrating their nuptials and enjoying a honeymoon in France, but all good things must come to an end and it was now time to return to Britain to start their married life proper in Sheerness. But not for them the mundane travel by train and boat; they were going to fly home and had booked seats on an Air Union airliner. Once again, the aircraft was a Farman Goliath, the same type as in the 1923 crash, flying from Le Bourget to Croydon.

In these days of Airbuses and Boeing 747s, carrying literally hundreds of passengers, it may seem a little curious that airliners in 1930 only seated a handful of passengers, and this was the case on this occasion. In fact, the aircraft took off from the Paris airport at 10.40 am on 10 February 1930 with just three passengers and an equal number of cabin staff.

All went well as the somewhat primitive aircraft, identical to those used in the First World War, droned across northern France but, after just 15 minutes, one of the two engines began to misfire and the pilot returned to Le Bourget for it to be checked. No fault was found but the sparking plugs were replaced as a precaution.

Off again, the lumbering biplane arrived at the English Channel coast without incident but shortly after reaching the snow-covered shores of Kent, a sharp, snapping noise was heard from the rear of the aircraft, which became unsteady and difficult to control. Some eyewitnesses on the ground said that the starboard tail-plane was broken, although the pilot was unable to account for how this could have happened. The airliner lost altitude by some 2,000ft and the pilot, Monsieur Nevot, instructed that the three passengers should move to the rear of the plane to restore the balance.

M Nevot discovered he had no elevator control whatsoever but, knowing he was not far from an emergency landing field at Pagehurst, between Staplehurst and Marden, he struggled to bring the aircraft down to about 10ft, ready for a crash-landing. Cutting the engines, he began to glide in but the aircraft was suddenly lifted around a hundred feet by an air current and he lost all control.

The aircraft became so difficult to handle that the pilot had no option but to make a crash-landing at Marden, the plane ultimately nosediving into the ground and breaking up. Speaking of the circumstances preceding the incident, Hugh Curson, the third passenger, later said: 'I cannot say how long we remained like that but it seemed ages to me. Suddenly we dived. There was the noise of a crash and I did not remember any more until I found myself in the wreckage.'

Hugh Curson pulled the pilot and the two mechanics out of the wreckage and they all escaped with fairly minor injuries. Our erstwhile happy honeymoon couple were not so lucky and both died in the crash. So badly was Edith's body smashed up, her father was only able to identify her by her wristwatch and a ring she wore.

No explanation was forthcoming as to the cause of the crash; the plane was only a year old and well maintained. Because of the state of the wreckage, it was not possible to determine whether the tail-plane had in fact been broken or otherwise defective prior to the crash.

Double Disaster

The autumn of 1934 was a particularly dark period for Kent with not one but two aircraft crashes in a matter of days, both of which claimed a number of victims.

The first incident occurred on 29 September when an Airspeed Courier, owned by London, Scottish & Provincial Airways Ltd, crashed at Tiverton Bottom, Shoreham, killing the pilot and three passengers.

This particular aircraft had already made one flight to Paris that day, where it was inspected before its return, arriving back at Heston at around 4.15 pm. The pilot took it to the petrol pump to be refilled and handed it over to Horace Luttman, a ground engineer at Heston aerodrome, who taxied the aircraft to the take-off point where he gave it a superficial 'turn-round' examination of the wings, controls and undercarriage. Mr Luttman was present that afternoon when the plane took off again at 5 pm for a further trip to Paris.

The Airspeed Courier, a single-engined aircraft of wooden construction, was built to carry six people, including the pilot and, on this occasion, there were four occupants when it left for Paris. The load the plane was carrying was therefore well within its limitations and it had a full tank of petrol. The pilot, 26-year-old Ronald Maxwell Smith, was a former RAF flying officer with five years experience. He had clocked up 1,500 hours flying time and was a qualified instructor. On a previous occasion he had made a wonderful forced landing which several experts said was the best they had ever seen.

What happened next on the journey to Paris is something of a mystery. A witness, Percival Shannon, who lived in Shoreham, had been in the Air Force during the First World War:

> I was just finishing my tea when heard the sound of a plane and there was something which made me think the plane was 'stunting' but I knew that, with the clouds so low, the pilot wouldn't be doing this unless he couldn't help it. There was then the sound like a plane coming out of a loop. I ran into the garden and saw nothing but I could still hear the plane. There was a layer of cloud along the valley and the plane came out of this in a vertical dive. I noticed two dark masses which made the aircraft appear to be twin-engined. It turned over right-handed as though starting a spin. It was travelling exceedingly fast.

He added that he thought the formation of the land at that point might create curious air-pockets, particularly in hot weather. 'In view of the fact that the hills behind Shoreham are between five and six hundred feet high, I would consider clouds at 1,200 feet as very low.'

This version was confirmed by another local resident, Edward Swaisland, who said he had heard what sounded like a plane in trouble so he went outside and saw it nosedive.

Constable Reuben Mannering was called to the scene and found the aircraft lying partly across the road at Combe Hollow. It was completely smashed and the bodies were totally unrecognisable and had to be identified by belongings, such as jewellery, rings, keys, wallet and passports, found on the bodies. The wreckage had not caught fire. The constable found the body of the pilot just to the right of the engine and that of a passenger, Frederick Garrett-Read, to the left, just in front of the engine. The bodies of the two female passengers, 26-year-old Dr P Rose-Innes and her mother, both terribly mutilated, were found still in the cabin. Despite the somewhat remote location of the crash, a huge crowd soon assembled and the area had to be cordoned off by the police, who were still in the process of removing the human remains.

The Air Ministry carried out a full investigation into the crash and came to the conclusion that the pilot had become disoriented because of the low cloud cover which prevented him from navigating by visible landmarks.

Reducing his altitude to get below the clouds, he failed to clear a ridge of high ground. It has to be said that this verdict does not entirely tally with the evidence of the eyewitnesses who spoke of the plane 'nosediving'.

The second incident occurred on 2 October 1934 when a twin-engined de Havilland Rapide aircraft, G-ACPM, crashed into the sea off Folkestone, with the loss of all seven on board.

It was not a good day for flying, with considerable mist and fog and occasional heavy rain, when the aircraft, owned and operated by Hillman Airways Ltd of Essex, left the Essex airport at Abridge at 10 am, heading for Le Bourget. Its departure was witnessed by the owner of the airline, Edward Henry Hillman, who saw that the six passengers all answered to their name before boarding. An hour later the plane had just crossed the Kent coast when it plummeted into the sea.

The Southern Railway's cross-Channel mail boat, the SS *Biarritz*, which had left Folkestone harbour just before 11 am, bound for Boulogne, played a major role in the search for survivors and the recovery of the bodies. The steamer was just 4 miles out when the attention of Captain W Baker was drawn to the blowing of a siren on the German steamer the *Leander*.

> The first thing I noticed was the German steamer *Leander* about half a mile ahead soon after we had left Folkestone. As we got nearer it could be seen that the steamer had lowered a boat and there was another steamer approaching her. We were steaming at twenty knots at the time. The weather was bad; there was fog and heavy rain.
>
> At first I thought there was a man overboard, or the *Leander* was transferring someone to the other ship. The *Leander* was giving a series of short blasts on her siren and, in case of emergency, one of the *Biarritz*'s lifeboats was made ready for lowering. As we got within hailing distance of the German ship, her captain told me that there was an aeroplane down in the sea.
>
> Our boat was lowered and we took over, from two other small boats which were down, three bodies which had been recovered. Two more were picked up by our boat.
>
> While the bodies were being recovered, the *Biarritz* circled over a wide area but we saw nothing further except for pieces of wreckage at different times. After nearly an hour the *Biarritz* returned to Folkestone with the five bodies which had been recovered from the sea.

We heard nothing of the aeroplane after leaving Folkestone, but this is not surprising, having regard to the weather conditions at the time.

The bad weather and poor visibility hampered the search, although the sea was calm. No survivors were found – just the five terribly injured bodies that were recovered, together with the airliner's papers, the pilot's log, some baggage and clothing and various pieces of wreckage. A knife, which had been completely bent double, and a badly broken flask showed the force with which the aircraft had hit the water. 'If you hit the water, it's like hitting marble,' said Mr F Wymer, the Marine Manager at Folkestone. All this debris, together with the bodies, was left in the long boat that had taken them from the sea, which was then hoisted aboard the *Biarritz* and covered with a tarpaulin.

The *Biarritz* then returned to Folkestone where groups of officials and police silently awaited her in the pouring rain. The 136 passengers on the steamer were kept below while the bodies were transferred to stretchers and brought ashore by the harbour cranes (this being well before the days of roll-on/roll-off car ferries).

While the bodies were removed by corporation ambulance to the Cheriton Road mortuary, police and port officials interviewed some of the crew before the packet set sail again at 12.30 pm on its interrupted voyage to Boulogne.

Harold Kennedy from Windsor, who was on holiday in Folkestone and had decided to take a day trip to Boulogne, told the *Folkestone Herald* that, as soon as it was realised on board the *Biarritz* that something was wrong, all passengers were ordered below deck.

Through the windows of the saloon deck it was possible to look on at the grim drama in the sea below. I saw one body and then turned away. The body was almost stripped of clothing and horribly mutilated. There were a considerable number of women on board; some were on the verge of collapse, others were crying.

Everything possible was done on the steamer to help. The lifeboat was very quickly lowered and it was out for about forty-five minutes before being recalled. Rain was falling almost the whole of the time and there was a fog which seemed to be just above the sea level.

A railway official who was also on board the *Biarritz* gave his version of events:

It was a ghastly business. When we got to the scene two dinghies had already been lowered, one from the German steamer and the other from the small British coaster, the *Snowcrete*. Manned by two men in each case, these little craft were half full of water. They had already secured three bodies which they were holding to the side of their boats.

The German captain was a fine fellow; he did everything in his power to help. He told the *Biarritz* that he had heard an aeroplane, followed very soon after by a crash. At once he had started a search. As we approached the *Leander* signals were being blown on her siren.

The recovered bodies were eventually identified as being those of a chartered accountant from Glasgow, a children's nurse from Southsea, a French businessman and a young French woman, both from the Paris region, and a manufacturer from Philadelphia. The body of the pilot, Captain W R Bannister, and that of the sixth passenger, a Frenchman, were not recovered. It is not known what the cause of the accident was as the recovered wreckage was insufficient to determine with any degree of accuracy the true cause. This was, of course, long before the days of the 'black boxes' used on modern airliners.

Limping to Lympne

By 1947 the days of the lumbering biplane airliners was well over. The Second World War had provided the impetus to improve the planes, the aircrew and the facilities. A whole new breed of aircraft was now filling the skies and circumnavigating the globe while the pre-war Imperial Airways had been replaced by the British Overseas Airways Corporation (BOAC).

One of these more modern aircraft was the Douglas DC-3 or C-47 Dakota. Although having its origins in the mid-1930s, the ubiquitous C-47 Dakota was produced in its thousands during the Second World War when it became the Allies' most widely used transport aircraft. After the war, many of these found their way onto the civil market for use as both freight and passenger aircraft and a few new ones were built in the early post-war years.

The Douglas C-47A-1-DK, registration G-AGJX was one such aircraft and was employed by BOAC on several of its short-haul routes. On 11 January 1947, this particular aircraft had set off from London airport, bound for West Africa with a refuelling stop at Bordeaux in France. Of the crew of four operational members (that is, not including the steward), three were unfamiliar with the London–Bordeaux route, a factor that was to prove crucial in ensuing events. The captain had also failed to ensure that he had all the necessary navigational and landing aid details for that route.

Despite very poor weather, the plane arrived at Bordeaux airport where a problem with another aircraft, together with the fog, prevented G-AGJX from landing. Concerned about the depreciating weather and the low fuel situation, the captain decided to divert to Le Bourget airport at Paris but, for some reason, failed to determine the weather in Paris as opposed to that in London. According to the navigator, the aircraft would reach Le Bourget about half an hour sooner than if they headed back to London and the captain knew Le Bourget well. In fact, fuel was not yet a serious problem as the aircraft would have had enough fuel for a further ½ hour had they returned all the way back to London.

As the plane neared Paris, the captain called Le Bourget, giving the control tower there just 6 minutes notice of his impending arrival at a time when the airport was extremely busy with aircraft arriving under instrument-flying conditions because of the foul weather. The Corneilles air traffic control was unable to handle more than one aircraft at a time as it only had one radio channel (these were the early days of post-war civil flying) and so the Dakota was circling around without ground guidance for around ½ an hour before the captain decided to return to England in view of the worsening fuel situation, much of it having been used up flying round Paris while waiting to get permission to land.

By the time G-AGJX reached the English Channel around 4 pm, the fuel situation was becoming grave and an SOS message was sent out, saying that the plane was over Cap Gris Nez and only had about 5 minutes fuel left. In view of the situation, the captain decided to try to put down at Lympne airfield, near Hythe, rather than continue to London. Lympne airfield (which no longer exists) was also wreathed in fog and, being a small field, more suited to light aircraft, so there was another change of plan and the Dakota headed for the emergency airfield at Manston, where a flare path had been prepared for it and the emergency services alerted.

En route, however, due largely to the very bad weather and poor visibility, the aircraft struck a piece of comparatively high ground at the well-named Highfield Farm, Stowting, some 6 or 7 miles as the crow flies north of Lympne, and slithered into some trees. A number of locals heard the crash and rushed to the site but the darkness, steep slope and wet and muddy conditions hampered the rescue attempts. The ambulances that had been summoned could get no closer than 400yd and the injured had to be carried to them on stretchers.

David Hickman of Stowting told a *Folkestone Herald* reporter that he heard the plane go over the village. 'I could hear the engines but the fog was too thick for me to see the plane. The engines appeared to be running very unevenly but they revved up suddenly and then there were two explosions. That was the last I heard of the machine.'

A Mr Hammon was milking his father's cows when he saw a man appear on the brow of the hill, shouting for help.

I thought it was a huntsman who was in trouble with the hounds. I ran up the hill towards him and he told me that an airliner had crashed into a spinney at the top of the hill. When I reached the spot I saw a Dakota broken in two and completely wrecked. A woman was walking around in her stockinged feet and I could hear cries for help from people trapped in the wreckage.

My wife and Miss Long arrived and we set to work to release the trapped people, prising away at the wreckage with crowbars and pickaxes. One of the first survivors we reached was a baby girl about eighteen months old, Christine Saunders, who was lying in her injured mother's arms.

More villagers arrived on the scene, bringing with them blankets and hurricane lamps. The road was five hundred yards below us and we had to carry the injured on stretchers down the muddy slope of the hill to the waiting ambulances which had arrived from the surrounding towns.

The machine had crashed in a small field, the Nookett, on my father's farm.

One of the lucky survivors was Mrs Olive Andrews, who was thrown clear when the plane hit the hill.

We left Heathrow at 9.30 am and were to have put down at Bordeaux. When we arrived in that area the fog was too thick and the pilot flew on to Paris. During this time we saw little of the ground and by the time we reached Paris the fog had closed down there. I think the pilot then decided to return to England. Just before the crash he gave us to understand that the petrol was running short and he advised us to put on our parachutes.

The aircraft was completely written off and four of the five crew members, the pilot, Captain Goalen, the first officer, Bernard Ward, the navigator, D Laws, and the wireless operator, R D Sandford, were all killed in the crash, together with four of the eleven passengers. The remaining crew member (the steward) and seven passengers had a very lucky escape, although none came out of the incident completely uninjured. Station Officer Ernest Lewis identified the body of the pilot, Captain Ian Goalen, 39, who had been with BOAC since 1938 and whom he described as a pilot of great experience. The father of the radio operator said that his son had been seconded to BOAC from the RAF in the rank of flight sergeant some fifteen months earlier.

At the ensuing inquiry, the cause of the accident was put down to bad weather conditions, aggravated by bad crewing and poor decisions on the part of the captain.

Air Display Disasters

The location of Manston, set in the flat, open country of the Isle of Thanet, close to the English Channel, made it an ideal spot for early aircraft to land if they were in difficulties. The occasional, unannounced use of the farmland in the area led to the Admiralty setting up a proper airstrip there during the First World War, which soon became a training school and an operational flying unit.

With the birth of the Royal Air Force on 1 April 1918, Manston became one of the new body's major grass airfields and was very much involved in the Battle of Britain in 1940, when it was heavily bombed by the Luftwaffe. Later during the war, a hard runway, 2,752m in length, was laid, which meant it was then capable of receiving even the largest bombers and the pilots of many badly shot-up Lancasters or Stirlings gratefully put down there on their return from a raid over Germany.

After the war, there was a partial demilitarisation of the airfield, although the United States Strategic Air Command was very much in evidence there during the Cold War and further extended the runways.

Perhaps to celebrate the return to more peaceful times, a major air display was organised for September 1948, at which the public would be able to see the latest in military and civil aircraft being put through their paces. The newly introduced jet-propelled aircraft made a deep impression on the huge crowd that had come to enjoy the show, but a special welcome was reserved for the de Havilland Mosquito, a twin-engined fighter bomber that had a formidable war record. First coming into service in 1942, this unique warplane was made from birch-faced, balsa-cored plywood, the lightness of which made it faster than even the Spitfire. It fulfilled many roles: nightfighter, bomber, pathfinder, among others. Its speed made it ideal for the latter role, in which it would precede the heavy bombers, pinpoint the target by extremely accurate navigation before dropping flares on it so that the following bombers had a very clear view of what they were aiming for. Having completed its task, the unarmed Mosquito would head for home, relying on its speed, altitude and manoeuvrability to evade interception.

At the Manston air display, a lone Mosquito was demonstrating the aircraft's undoubted qualities before a delighted audience, the pilot performing breathtaking, low-level aerobatics. The pilot, the experienced Flight Lieutenant Geoffrey Hanson, had been instructed to dive down to 200ft and then climb up to 500ft before demonstrating a barrel roll. After a quick pass at normal altitude he duly returned to dive to little more than roof-top height as instructed. However, for some reason he failed to gain sufficient height before attempting to roll the aircraft, which struck a line of cars on the road to the airfield, hit the ground and exploded. Burning aviation fuel covered cars, cyclists and pedestrians alike and nine people were burnt to death on the spot, including Flight Lieutenant Hanson and his navigator. Another three died later in hospital. Many of these unfortunate victims were so badly burnt that they could only be identified by their clothing or tickets to the air display.

Among those on the road excitedly heading for the spectacular air show was 11-year-old Malcolm Andrews. He was riding his bicycle from Margate and was followed by his mother, the wife of an RAF corporal serving in Malta, and his aunt, Mrs Lawrence, both also on bicycles, his mother carrying his 2-year-old brother, Brent, in a carrier on the back of the bike. Malcolm later described the scene. 'I went on ahead and when I got past Margate, I looked back but could not see my mother. I watched an aeroplane and saw it crash in a sheet of flame.'

His mother, brother and aunt were among the victims, their badly burnt bodies not being identified until the Sunday morning. They had earlier tossed a coin to decide whether to go to the air display or to go and watch the cricket on the St Lawrence Ground in Canterbury. They made a bad choice.

Another witness was Cecil Chiesman from Chislehurst who was driving his car to Manston, followed by another car in which his son, Stuart (13), Frances Lewis and a Miss Anstell were riding.

As Mr Chiesman glanced in his rear-view mirror he saw, to his horror, the aircraft approaching and then strike the following car. 'I ran back,' he said, 'but I could find no trace of the car or its occupants.'

At the subsequent inquest, Wing Commander Gilbert Vivian, in charge of flying at RAF Manston, testified that Flight Lieutenants Hanson and

A Farman Goliath of the type that crashed at East Malling in August 1923. (Polska Iotnicza, Warsaw 1937)

A Fokker F.VII of the type that crashed at Underriver in August 1927.

The Farman Goliath that crashed at Marden in February 1930. Note the open cockpit for the pilot and his mechanic. (Marden Heritage Centre)

A de Havilland
Rapide of the type
that crashed off
Folkestone in October
1934.

A Douglas DC-3
Dakota in US Air
Force livery, very
similar to the
civilian version
that crashed at
Stowting in
January 1947.

A pair of de Havilland Mosquitoes similar to the one that crashed at Manston in September 1948.

A Gloster Meteor jet aircraft like the three that crashed at the Biggin Hill air display in 1951.

A Second World War Douglas A-26 Invader bomber like the one that crashed at Biggin Hill in September 1980 while attempting a barrel roll at low level.

A Bell King Cobra of the kind that was involved in the second crash at Biggin Hill in 2001.

A de Havilland Vampire jet fighter similar to that which crashed at Biggin Hill in June 2001.

The Shakespeare Colliery, Dover, scene of the flooding disaster in March 1897.
(Dover Museum)

The Faversham gunpowder factory explosion: inside one of the explosives storage sheds.
(Fleur de Lys Heritage Centre, Faversham)

Firemen line up to march to the funeral service for victims of the Faversham gunpowder factory explosion.
(Fleur de Lys Heritage Centre, Faversham)

Scene of the worst incident in the bombing of Folkestone in 1917. Where Stokes, the greengrocer's shop, once stood and where forty-four staff and customers were killed there is now just a bare site. The Brewery Tap public house, however, which was also very much involved, still stands, although is now boarded up and likely to be redeveloped in the near future. (Author)

THIS TABLET MARKS THE PLACE WHERE ON MAY 25TH 1917 A BOMB WAS DROPPED FROM A GERMAN AEROPLANE KILLING 60 PERSONS AND INJURING MANY OTHERS.

Plaque commemorating the sixty persons who lost their lives in Tontine Street that fateful day in May 1917. (Author)

St George's Street, Canterbury, reduced to rubble after the bombing raid in May 1942.

Wrecked cars outside
a garage in Ashford.
(Ashford Museum)

Street scene, Ashford,
March 1943.
(Ashford Museum)

Two lads inspect
the wreckage of
their shed,
Ashford, 1943.
(Ashford Museum)

More devastation in
Ashford, 1943.
(Ashford Museum)

Two boys rescue their
caged birds and whatever
else they can salvage from
their wrecked home.
(Ashford Museum)

Rochester, after a V1 had exploded,
killing eight people.

Milton Place, Gravesend, where a second V2 landed, killing eight people.

The Marines' Barracks, Deal, being demolished following the terrorist bomb that killed eleven bandsmen. (Dover Museum)

The simple wooden monument to the forty-three 'strangers' buried in East Farleigh churchyard, victim of the cholera outbreak of 1849. (Author)

Martin were detailed to fly in the Mosquito as the leader of a formation of three planes and then to give a display of aerobatics.

> I saw the aircraft dive down to a hundred feet. It started to climb and, at three hundred feet, began a roll to the right. When it was three parts of the way round the roll, the pilot appeared to lose control. The aircraft lost height, flicked over on its back and dived to the ground. It burst into flames on impact.

In reply to a question by the Coroner, Wing Commander Vivian said that the Station Commander had ordered that there should be no aerobatics below 500ft and that planes should not dive below 200ft. The roll was started below 500ft. He added that Flight Lieutenant Hanson was an experienced pilot with 2,270 flying hours to his credit, 650 of these being on Mosquito aircraft.

Asked by the Coroner if he could give any explanation for the accident, the Wing Commander said, 'I think it was probably due to the fact that the air speed was slightly low and that the aircraft was flying too low, probably due to an error of judgment.'

Summing up, the Coroner said, 'People might question whether there ought to be displays of this kind at all. Perhaps there is every reason that the Royal Air Force and the skill and bravery of its pilots should be made known in this country and abroad.' He was not to know that this terrible incident was to be but the first of several disasters at air shows in the county in the ensuing years.

Biggin Hill airfield, once a tiny centre for pleasure flying, became famous as the base for many of 'The Few' during the Battle of Britain. From this airfield, snugly ensconced on the Kentish North Downs, close to Metropolitan London, many sorties were flown by the young fighter pilots in their Spitfires and Hurricanes to meet and destroy the bombers of the Nazi Luftwaffe. With the end of the war, control of the airfield by the RAF ceased and it gradually reverted to civil aviation.

Despite the dangers, as exemplified at Manston three years earlier, the concept of air displays was well established by 1951 and the Biggin Hill event was becoming one of the most popular of these. This year the crowd of spectators, many armed with their binoculars and short-wave radios, included an eminent personality in the form of the Prime Minister, Winston Churchill (not to be knighted for another two years). As part of the RAF's contribution, seven Gloster Meteor jets – the earliest production jet-propelled aircraft in service with the RAF – took off to demonstrate their speed and manoeuvrability. A technical problem prevented one of these aircraft from gaining height and it tore across the main road at negligible altitude and struck a bungalow. The aircraft instantly exploded, destroying both itself and the bungalow. Fortunately, the bungalow was unoccupied and, apart from the pilot of the crashed aircraft, no one was killed or indeed injured.

The story does not end there, however. Of the other six aircraft that had taken off and gained height in a normal manner, two became aware of the drama unfolding below them and, naturally concerned for their unfortunate colleague, circled around to see what had happened. These were not slow-moving civil or training aircraft and, with their concentration focussed on the events on the ground, the two pilots evidently failed to see each other until it was too late and they were on an irremediable collision course.

The inevitable happened and these two fine, new, state-of-the-art machines collided in mid-air and exploded before thousands of horrified witnesses. Both pilots were killed and the burning wreckage was strewn over a large area, causing several small fires. Fortunately, none of the debris fell on the tightly packed spectators or these two separate but closely connected accidents could have resulted in a truly major disaster, killing possibly hundreds of people.

Despite the unsurprising calls for their abandonment, air displays continued to be held and continued to attract large crowds. Nearly thirty years after the tragic events of 1951, the Biggin Hill Air Display took place in September 1980. It was the fortieth anniversary of the Battle of Britain and so was an important date for aviation buffs and a crowd of 40,000 was soon in position. Although there were a number of the technically advanced, modern warplanes on display, much attention was focussed on the survivors of the Second World War, such as the Spitfire, the Hurricane and the Lancaster. Another contemporary aircraft was a lone Douglas A-26 Invader medium bomber which had given sterling service during the latter stages of the war. This particular aircraft was being piloted by the renowned daredevil Captain Don Bullock and was now licensed for survey work only.

True to his reputation, Captain Bullock had asked the organisers for permission to take off early as he wanted more time to perform a barrel roll before this appreciative audience but consent was refused. The 1943 twin-engined aircraft was never built for aerobatics and Don Bullock had only ever performed a roll in it once before.

Peeved at this rejection of his request, Bullock pointed out that once he was strapped in to the aircraft he was the master of his own destiny, a telling comment in view of subsequent events. With four British passengers and a pair of US servicemen on board, Bullock took off on the ill-fated flight, scheduled to last 8 minutes. Only 2 minutes had elapsed before Bullock started to perform the risky barrel roll during which he appeared to hesitate. The aircraft was much too low for any form of remedial action to be taken and the Invader crashed into the hillside beyond the airfield, killing all on board. Fortunately, the crash site was well away from the airfield and the shocked spectators, none of whom were hurt, although the plane narrowly missed a row of houses in Oaklands Road, Biggin Hill.

There has been much dispute over the years among aviation experts and fans as to the culpability of the pilot, Captain Don Bullock. As mentioned previously, he was a renowned risk-taker and one might wonder whether he was the sort of pilot who should be taking part in events like these, attended by thousands of spectators. There is no doubt he was putting an ancient aircraft through a punishing manoeuvre that it was never designed to undertake and which was to cost him, and six others, very dear indeed.

Another twenty-one years were to elapse, during which air shows were put on pretty well every year, before the next 'Biggin Hill Blunder' occurred, during the weekend of 2–3 June 2001. As usual, a large crowd had gathered to watch a variety of ancient and modern aircraft being put through their paces, thrilled to see the skill and daring of the very experienced pilots.

There was probably no more experienced pilot than 66-year-old Air Marshal Sir Kenneth Hayr, a distinguished former fighter pilot and deputy Commander-in-Chief of the Royal Air Force Strike Command in the late 1980s, and who was decorated for his work in directing the 1990–91 Gulf War. Listing aerobatics, paragliding and parachuting among his interests in *Who's Who*, the now-retired Air Marshal was indulging in the first of these hobbies by piloting a 50-year-old de Havilland Vampire twin-boom training jet plane. His co-pilot on this occasion was Jonathan Kerr, an electronics engineer from Bournemouth.

The huge crowd was delighted to see this venerable aircraft, one of the earliest jet fighters used by the RAF, as it zoomed overhead, taking part in the final display of the day with a similarly aged Vixen aircraft. It made four passes at low altitude and was attempting to turn at the end of the last pass when it suddenly spun twice before crashing into a ridge, only yards away from a row of houses, but fortunately missing them. Both men in the aircraft were killed.

The organisers of the event were in two minds whether the next day's show should be cancelled but they spoke to friends of the dead men who were adamant that the victims would have wished the event to continue. A subsequent statement issued by Mr Kerr's family confirmed this: 'Jonathan was a very special person, who lived for his passion and died living it. He achieved his ambition to reassemble and fly his own Vampire. When we as a family visited the crash site we thought it very apt as a Spitfire, Hurricane and a Lancaster flew overhead. I am sure that it was the most fitting tribute to both Jonathan and Sir Kenneth.' Consequently, as Nick Smith, a spokesman for the Biggin Hill International Air Fair, put it, 'The show must continue.' And continue it did.

The following morning's events went off without incident before the usual large crowd. It was during the afternoon that the next disaster occurred. Crash investigators were still clearing and examining the wreckage of the Vampire that had crashed the previous day when, at around 3.30 pm, a Second World War Bell King Cobra fighter aircraft 'dropped out of the sky', crashed into the ground and exploded in a ball of flames on the edge of the airfield opposite the public enclosure, around 200m from the 50,000-seat main stand. It appeared that the aircraft seemed to stall at the top of a loop.

At the subsequent press conference, Chief Superintendent Gerry Howlett of the Metropolitan Police said the pilot of the King Cobra was a very experienced 40-year-old whose plane was taking part in a display with two other veteran American fighters, a Sky Raider and a Thunderbolt. 'About five minutes into the sequence the third aircraft of the trio, the King Cobra, appeared to enter a vertical manoeuvre which was close to the centre of the display area. It failed to recover from that manoeuvre and crashed in clear ground to the north west of the runway.'

The event organiser, Jim Maitland, added, 'It's a unique thing that when there are so few accidents that two should actually take place here in a single weekend. This doesn't alter the fact that the air show as seen in this country is widely regarded as the safest and best regulated in the world.'

Richard Green from Crayford was filming the event when the aircraft crashed. He told reporters, 'I was filming the plane with my video recorder when I saw it lose control and turn over onto its back. It then fell to the ground and there was a huge explosion of flames and smoke. The pilot would not have stood a chance.'

Another witness, trainee pilot Ashley Pinney, 24, described the incident.

The aircraft turned over and he tried to recover but it just did not happen. He tried to pull back on the stick but the plane plummeted to the ground and exploded into flames. The whole place fell totally silent. Everything went quiet until the noise of the emergency vehicles rushing to the scene shattered the eerie silence. There's no way the pilot could have survived.

'It fell like a stone,' said Neil Shuttleworth. 'Everyone knew what was going to happen. There was a dull thud as the plane hit the ground and a big ball of flames went up into the sky.'

The air show spokesman, Nick Smith, said 'I can think of no other way to describe it other than it just fell out of the sky. I would not be prepared to comment on the possible cause of the crash at this stage.' He added that he felt the two crashes were 'extremely unfortunate', but defended the safety record of vintage air shows, saying the last fatality at such a show was in 1980, twenty-one years previously. He dismissed suggestions that the two accidents made the future of the show doubtful. Referring to the 1980 crash involving the Douglas Invader, he added: 'I have been working here since 1978 and since then we have only had one incident involving a fatality before these two.'

The remainder of the 2001 event was cancelled after this second crash but the Biggin Hill air show has continued to be held in subsequent years.

Chapter 6

Industrial Disasters

Although Kent, basking in its fame as the Garden of England, has always been primarily an agricultural county, it has for many years nurtured a number of thriving industries which tend to belie this image. There have been paper mills, cement works, brickfields, coal mines, shipyards and dockyards, motor manufactories and many more, bordering on the rivers Thames and Medway or nestling among the orchards, meadows and hop fields for which the county is better known. Some of these are still thriving, others are in decline and many have disappeared over the years. And all these industries – not excluding the agricultural industry – have had their share of disasters.

Fortunately, the scale and complexity of most Kentish industries has meant that any incidents that have occurred have mostly resulted in a comparatively small casualty rate – but not always.

The Erith Explosion
Around the middle of the seventeenth century – the time of Guy Fawkes and 'gunpowder, treason and plot' – the manufacture of gunpowder was growing apace in various parts of the country and under conditions that would horrify today's Health and Safety Executive. And Kent was a major provider.

Gunpowder is classed as a low explosive and was used mainly as a propellant for the balls fired from the flintlock pistols and muskets then used by the military and for similar firearms used by civilians, such as farmers and gamekeepers. It was, however, treacherous stuff and the slightest spark could set it off.

By the middle of the nineteenth century, there were important gunpowder factories in the little market town of Faversham, while stocks of this 'black powder' were stored in specially constructed magazines near Erith, being transported by barge up the River Thames from Hall's factory in Faversham.

On the morning of 1 October 1864, two of these sailing barges, the *Good Design* and the *Harriet*, were moored at the end of the 40yd-long jetty that projected out into the Thames from the south bank at a lonely spot known as the Plumstead Marshes. It was here that the magazines were located, around 2 miles from the town of Erith and a similar distance from Belvedere. Clustered around the magazines, and only about 70yd from the main one, were a number of cottages provided for the workers.

It was just getting light that autumn morning as the crew of the two barges set about unloading the 200 barrels of black powder that they had just brought up from Faversham. These operations were being supervised by the master of the *Good Design*, William Jemmett, and his mate, Luke Barker, both of whom had considerable experience in the handling of gunpowder.

What happened next is open to conjecture. Suddenly, both barges exploded with a tremendous roar that could be heard miles away. Apart from the cargo being unloaded from the barges, there were nearly 40 tons of explosives in the main Hall's magazine and a small quantity in the adjacent, less-important Low Wood store, and all this ignited sympathetically in a matter of seconds. Pieces of the barges were thrown high into the air, to return to earth scattered over a wide area. Of the two magazines, there was very little left and nine persons were either dead or dying. Unlike modern explosive stores and magazines, the two on Plumstead Marshes were simple, surface constructions and were not protected by earthen embankments such as those that are now used to ensure that the result of any accident is directed straight up and not horizontally where it would do most damage. Magazines are now also spaced well apart from each other to prevent sympathetic detonation of the type that occurred here.

Since all the four crew men on the barges were blown to pieces, there was no survivor to explain what had caused the initial explosion on one or other of the barges. What is certain is that the crews of the barges consisted of sober, industrious family men, who were well aware of the dangers that their cargo presented. One would have expected that the prohibition on cooking and the lighting of candles on board when carrying gunpowder would have been scrupulously respected but there is always the possibility that familiarity had bred contempt and someone had decided to cook himself some breakfast. Certainly the Coroner's jury made a clear recommendation that 'the practice of allowing stoves or lights of any description on board the gunpowder barges should be discontinued'.

Apart from the four barge crew members, the explosion also killed two men who were employed on the construction of a river wall nearby and had no connection with the barges or the magazines. They had, however, arranged to leave their tools in an outhouse belonging to Walter Silver, the foreman at the Low Wood magazine, and were in the process of collecting them when the explosion occurred. As for Walter Silver, he had a miraculous escape; he was straining milk just inside his cottage's back door when the initial explosion on the barge blew him over. Before he could get up, the second explosion, that of the magazine, destroyed his cottage, covering him in debris. He was uninjured other than a few bruises but his young niece was less fortunate and was killed outright.

The foreman of the other magazine, George Raynor, was also killed when his cottage was completely destroyed. His wife and daughter were wounded but survived. Elizabeth Wright, the 9-year-old daughter of one of the under managers, was also severely injured and, although pulled alive from the wreckage of her home, died later in hospital. The total death toll was therefore nine persons.

Damage and injuries were not confined to the two barges and the buildings near the magazines; James Girnes was heaving ballast on board a Trinity House lighter moored nearby when he saw a sudden flash. 'Why, there's a flash of lightning,' he said to his colleague, before he was lifted off his feet by the blast and deposited back on deck before finally rolling overboard. The cold water brought him to his senses and he swam to the shore, dazed and bloody but alive.

A great mushroom of smoke arose over the site and papers, documents and furnishings were scattered over a wide area. To most people in the Erith area the cause of the thunder-like rumble was still a mystery and many thought there had been a disaster at the great Arsenal at Woolwich. Others remembered that a Doctor Cummings had foretold the end of the world and believed that this was the beginning of Armageddon. The ancient Saxon church in Erith, the scene of a meeting between King John and the barons in 1215, suffered damage to its roof and ceiling, despite being nearly a mile away from the scene, and the newly constructed Belvedere railway station, a similar distance away, lost some of its walls. Another new, brick building collapsed, depositing bricks across the railway line and many buildings in Erith and Belvedere lost their windows. Debris was scattered as far as 2 or 3 miles away and the shock was felt in London, 15 miles away.

As the true situation became known, rescue parties cautiously made their way to the site where they discovered a huge crater and a wide breach in the river wall which had to be filled before the next high tide if the area was not to be flooded. Fortunately, there was a team of some 350 labourers, working on a main drainage scheme nearby, and these were pressed into action to assist, as were all the available soldiers at Woolwich barracks. By 10 am 1,500 soldiers – marines, horse artillery and engineers – had been shipped to the scene by train and were put to work building a temporary breakwater from such beams and spars as were available. These were supplemented by hundreds of sandbags.

Once the news had spread to the general public, the scene of the disaster became the latest public attraction and thousands took the train to Erith to gawp at the scene of destruction and death. Perhaps this morbid curiosity played a part in the imposition, over the ensuing years, of more stringent regulations concerning the storage and manufacture of explosives, although, as we shall see, this was not to be the last disaster of this kind in Kent.

Mining Mishap

Kent is not widely known as a mining county but for fractionally less than a hundred years there were a number of important coalfields exploited in Kent.

Geologists first began to speculate that there was coal beneath the rolling countryside of East Kent in the 1840s but it was not until 1890 that this notion was fully explored and the first mine was opened. Soon there were numerous workings springing up in the area but only four proved viable: Betteshanger, Snowdown, Tilmanstone and Chislet.

With no mining tradition in the area, there was a concentrated recruitment drive in South Wales, the Midlands and the North East and miners from these areas were encouraged to come south to work in the new Kent coalfields. Villages sprung up at Aylesham, Elvington, Hersden and Mill Hill in Deal to accommodate these 'foreign' miners, who were only too keen to come to Kent where the wages and conditions were good, not to mention the surroundings.

The very first Kent coal mine was called the Shakespeare or Dover Colliery and was sited in the parish of Hougham, near Dover, where boreholes had proved the existence of coal at a depth of around 1,000ft. The operators were the Kent Coalfields Syndicate Ltd, which was formed in 1896 to take over the old, abandoned Channel Tunnel workings at Shakespeare Cliff.

In June 1896 the first, No. 1 or Brady pit, was sunk and, over the months that followed the machines bored down into the earth for nearly 400ft until water flooded the workings. Being close to the sea it is often assumed that this was sea water but in fact it was fresh water from the vast underground lakes in the area. The company had not expected to encounter water but this was to prove a major problem in all parts of the Kent coal field as mining went on. For financial reasons, no funds had been allocated to the cost of purchasing pumps and so the first pit was abandoned and allowed to fill with water.

A second shaft, the Simpson, had been started in 1897, close to the first boring, and so the company concentrated on this. During the night of 6 March 1897 fourteen specialist workers, known as 'sinkers', were excavating the main shaft and, 300ft down, had reached the top bed of the Lower Greensand strata without any sign of the ingress of water. Since the trouble in the Brady pit had not occurred until this geological bed had been pierced, and when only a trifling amount of water had penetrated the workings, the operators were confident that there was no likelihood of flooding at this stage. A full 60ft of rock remained to be penetrated before any problems were likely to arise. Such was the confidence of the management that there was no concern that the pumps ordered to deal with any flooding would not be installed for another day or two.

This confidence appeared to be justified as the boring in the new shaft had been remarkably dry, with not the slightest sign of water either at the bottom of the shaft or in the deeper, exploratory boreholes sunk to investigate any likely problems or the presence of water. However, suddenly and without any warning, water poured into the shaft at a rate estimated at 40,000 gallons an hour, extinguishing the lights and inundating the workers. A hoppit or kibble loaded with rubble had just been raised to the surface so no assistance was immediately available from above. Some of the workers got into another hoppit, presumably believing that the ingress of water would not amount to much and hoping that the winding gear would soon be sent down to pull them up, but they were to be cruelly disappointed. Their passive hopes were soon replaced by horror as they realised the water and sand were pouring into the shaft. Despite the prompt and urgent action of the surface workers, before the winding gear could reach the men at the bottom they, and the hoppit, had been engulfed in the quicksand. In pitch darkness, their terror can only be imagined by those who have never been in such a nightmare situation.

In desperation, six of the men managed to scramble to the side of the shaft and start to clamber their way up the metal rings that supported the timbers used to shore up the sides of the shaft. But 300ft is a long way to climb, and the water was rising rapidly beneath them and lapping at their heels. A glimmer of electric light from the surface revealed a rope that had been thrown down and three half-drowned men relinquished their hold on the side of the shaft and swam for the life-saving rope to which they desperately clung. As the rope was pulled up, they managed to get onto the top of the loaded hoppit which was full of sand and water. Once the hoppit reached the top of the shaft, the three lucky survivors were led away to be dried off and given a hot drink to revive them.

Meanwhile, the hoppit was emptied and sent down again, this time with a flaming light in it. By the light of this crude illumination, those at the top could see three more men who struggled to get into the hoppit as soon as it reached them, upon which it was raised once more to the surface. While these further three exhausted men were being cared for, the hoppit was sent down for a third time but, this time, it returned empty.

Crestfallen, the workers surveyed the sight of the empty bucket but the Master Sinker climbed in and, accompanied by John Little, one of the first three to be rescued, was lowered down, carrying two torches. They carefully searched the surface of the water, which by now had risen some 40ft, but there was no sign of any further survivors.

George Holder, who, as the duty Master Sinker, had control of the pit, described the incident:

> I was on the pit bank when the accident occurred. We heard shouting and screaming from the bottom of the pit. Men were shouting for the hoppit. I knew that something had happened down below. I helped the men run the bridge off the pit and at once sent down the hoppit. I could hear there was water at the bottom of the shaft. We lowered the hoppit down and drew it up in a few seconds. When it came up three men were hanging to it and it was full of water and sand. We helped these men out and took them to one of the cabins. Two were rather exhausted.
>
> I then sent the hoppit down again with a flaming lamp in it, as there were no lights at the bottom. When it returned there were three more men in it. The next time I lowered the hoppit I went down myself, taking Little, one of the men who had been rescued, with me. We took flaming lamps with us but we could find none of the other men.

On their return, grappling hooks were lowered but no bodies, nor the spare hoppit, were felt. All that remained possible was to keep the winding gear running and use a water barrel to try to reduce the level of the water as much as possible. This patented piece of equipment held 2 tons of water and could draw 60 tons an hour, which, although significant, was infinitely less than the soon-to-be-installed pumps could handle and could just about keep pace with the level of the rising water.

Of the fourteen men at the bottom of the shaft, only six were rescued. The remaining eight workers were not so lucky and were drowned or suffocated in the shaft. As a large quantity of sand came in with the water, it seems likely that the trapped men were embedded in this and were unable to rise with the level of the water.

John Little, the plucky young sinker who went down again with his boss to see if he could help rescue any of his comrades, described the scene to the *Dover Express*:

> We never expected any water to come in as the pit was perfectly dry and we never had the slightest sign of water; in fact, the gault was so hard that three men were employed on the punches which were used for breaking up the bottom. The water came in upon us quite suddenly, without the slightest warning. We had had our boreholes sunk several feet down, but there had been no sign of water . . . The pressure of water seemed to burst in the bottom of the pit. It rose very quickly, a quantity of sand coming with it. The lights were extinguished by the water. We shouted at the top of our voices to direct attention at the mouth of the pit. I saw four or five men standing on the large hoppit to get out of the way of the water but, as it was of course, very dark, it was impossible to see much. I, and some others, climbed up the timber in the shaft as far as we could. I did not see the hoppit come down but, soon after we shouted, I caught sight of a rope dangling in mid-air, and knew that it had come down. I made a jump for it and swam to the bucket. Two others also got on the hoppit but I could feel there were some more who had hold of it, who must have let go their hold, as we did not bring them up. I afterwards found that one man who came up in the second hoppit had dropped off the first. I was not so exhausted as the rest of the men and, when we found the hoppit come back without anyone on it, after it was lowered the third time, I went down with the master sinker. I jumped in just as I was. We went down and searched the surface of the water to see if there was anybody floating about, but there were none and we returned to the surface.

A Dover man, William Bishop, who lost his brother in the disaster, also described the scene:

When the bottom rose up it was fearful and I hardly knew what occurred next. I climbed up the rings round the sides up to the brickwork, twice being under water. There are lighted candles all round the pit, but these all went out, of course, and the only light was from the electric light at the mouth which lit up the water . . . I thought I saw the rope in the centre . . . so I jumped for it, about fourteen feet I should guess, sliding down as I caught it. Having been a sailor for about fifteen years, I managed to hold on. A mate named Little had evidently done the same thing for I found him above me on the rope. He had also been a sailor.

The three of us on the rope were drawn up and our injuries attended to. I nearly had my neck broken, as well as my legs. The bucket then went down again and saved three more, who were nearly dead when recovered . . . I shall, you may be sure, now leave this kind of work, for a man has a chance at sea, but down in a hole there is none.

Divers from Sir John Jackson's Harbour Works were brought in around 4 pm the following afternoon and were lowered, with their equipment, on a bricking scaffold to within a foot of the surface of the water. A short iron ladder was put over the side and, his helmet securely screwed on, one of the divers stepped down into the water and disappeared, while two men worked hard on the air pump. After 10 minutes the diver returned to report that he had found nothing at the bottom but sand 'which seemed to be all alive'. From the description of the shaft lining that he was able to give, the mining experts reckoned there must have been twenty feet of this sand covering the bottom of the shaft. The diver made one more gallant attempt to discover the missing men but to no avail.

The water continued to rise to a depth of 80ft or more and, finally, the company managed to speed up the installation of the pumps in order to reduce the water level and reach the bodies of those who had drowned, an operation that took a month to complete. Four of the victims were young men in their twenties, two in their thirties and one of 54. No details are available for the eighth man. Some were local lads, others came from as far afield as Derbyshire, Woking, Shropshire and Nottinghamshire, all lured to Kent by the promise of well-paid work but found death instead.

Investigation revealed that the cause of the problem was the abandoned No. 1 or Brady pit. Left to fill with water, the wall between this shaft and the No. 2 shaft gave way under the hydraulic pressure, flooding the second shaft, the timbers used to shore up the sides being incapable of resisting this exceptional degree of pressure. As the water in the second shaft rose, so the level in the Brady pit fell until they were equally level.

The problem of flooding was not solved until five years later when a new process was introduced, using cast-iron tubes to line the shaft as it was dug, thus sealing it off from any water in the rocky strata. Using this method, known as 'tubbing', the shaft was sunk, lower and lower, until in September 1903, the first coal seam was encountered.

The workings were not a great success by any means. By 1907 the mine was producing 8 tons of rather poor quality coal a day – less than the colliery used to fire its boilers and fuel its machines. Only one commercial load of coal was ever produced, being sold to Leney's brewery in Dover. Disappointed with both the quality and the quantity of coal extracted, the directors arranged for several wagon loads of first-class Northumberland coal to be brought down and shown to the shareholders when they made an official visit to the site. Inevitably, the colliery closed in 1909 and the company placed in the hands of the official receiver. A further attempt was made to get it working the following year but the mine finally closed definitively in 1915, being sold for scrap in 1918.

Coincidentally, the site of this mine was obliterated in the 1980s by the workings in connection with the (successful) Channel Tunnel.

The Faversham Big Bang

The manufacture of gunpowder was such a thriving industry that by 1786 there were three factories in the town of Faversham supplying mainly this black powder, utilising the two tributaries of the River Swale – Oare Creek and Faversham Creek.

In 1846, Christian Schönbein discovered gun cotton, the first high explosive that, as such, could be used for its own destructive effect and not merely a propellant. One of Faversham's powder factories, the Marsh Works, became the first gun-cotton manufacturing plant in the world. This was not to last, however, as the very next year, 1847, there was an explosion in the factory that killed eighteen workers and injured many more. Only ten of those killed could be identified, the others having been literally blown to bits.

However, once the properties of gun cotton began to be better understood, production recommenced and the Cotton Powder Company (CPC) built a new factory on the waste land bordering the Swale, 3 miles from the town itself. There were a number of advantages in using this site; access to the river for transport and the distance from the town being just two. But there was also a disadvantage in that the saltings on which the factory had been built were unsuitable for the growing of the trees and shrubs that were normally planted around such factories to reduce the effect of blast in the event of an accident.

By the start of the First World War in 1914, this 'Cotton Powder' factory, as it was known, was turning out detonators, distress rockets and compounds such as cordite, gelignite and dynamite as well as gun cotton. Workers came from far and near, encouraged by the extra 2s a week danger money offered and the fact that any male employees were exempted from military service. For an extra 2s a week, the potential danger of an accident in the powder factories seemed infinitely preferable to being paid a mere shilling a day to wear khaki and face the very real dangers and horrors of trench warfare and there was no shortage of young men volunteering. Indeed, the *Kentish Gazette* of 5 June 1917 commented on the strong feelings that existed in Faversham at the time about the 'hundreds of young men hiding away at the local munitions works'. These feelings appear to have had little or no impact on the Minister of Munitions, David Lloyd George.

The simple, primitive gunpowder factories of the eighteenth and nineteenth centuries had by now given way to quite sophisticated works which were furnished with electricity by their own generators, boasted their own coal-gas plants, modern boilers and compressors. The jetties and berths on the river and creeks meant there was little or no need for explosives to be carried through the town – much to the relief of the inhabitants. There was no public transport to the factories and the workers either walked or cycled from their homes or from the railway station to get to work.

Another company, the Explosives Loading Company (ELC), had arrived in 1912 to set up business alongside the CPC's plant and apparently worked closely with the latter, concentrating on the compression of TNT (trinitrotoluene) into charges for mines, shells and torpedoes. The TNT, being expensive to produce, was later 'stretched' by the addition of ammonium nitrate, the resulting mixture being known as 'amatol'.

Because of the volatile and highly explosive nature of amatol, the ELC's buildings were light, wooden constructions, spaced well apart to minimise the spread of any accidental 'blow'. The whole complex was closely guarded by a military detachment of 128 troops, as well as two-dozen civilian security patrols. The firefighting arrangements, however, left something to be desired. The CPC had its own small fire brigade, working on a call-out basis, with ample hydrants and hoses, but the ELC was less well equipped and only had a manual, hand-operated pump and a number of chemical extinguishers. Water could be obtained from nearby water drainage ditches but there were no mains water hydrants, although some hydrants had been supplied, but these were awaiting installation at the critical time. The Chief Inspector of Explosives, Major A Cooper-Key, had also commented on the lack of fire buckets only three days before the 'big bang'.

In Faversham town there were three fire brigades: the Volunteer Brigade, the Kent Brigade and the Norwich Union Brigade, the latter two being provided and maintained by insurance companies, primarily to deal with fires on properties covered by them. These were small, poorly equipped brigades (if that is not too grand a description for these amateurish units), the engines or pumps of which had to be harnessed to one or more horses or towed by one of the rare and somewhat unreliable motor-lorries to be found in the town.

In 1916 the whole munitions industry was going flat-out to provide enough ordnance for the over-stretched armed forces. The Faversham works were no exception and the workers were putting in a lot of overtime and the normal regulation limits had been 'stretched' in order to accommodate all the raw materials that had been supplied to the sites. On the ELC site, building No. 833 was licensed for the storage of TNT but, because of the pressures of war, it was now being used (without any official authorisation) to store about 150 tons of ammonium nitrate as well as around 15 tons of TNT.

This matchboard building was surrounded by cases of TNT lying in the open and a number of empty linen sacks, used for TNT and awaiting return for refilling, were resting against the wooden walls. The building was located some 50ft from a boiler house, the three flues of which were only 37ft high. They had been fitted with spark-arresters to prevent any embers from escaping into the atmosphere but these were apparently not 100 per cent efficient as the security patrols had reported seeing sparks emitted and had in fact already extinguished a small fire that had broken out in the dry undergrowth.

According to a witness, Sunday, 2 April 1916 was 'a glorious day'. Work was in progress as usual but most of the staff broke off for lunch around noon. Some 10 minutes later, Mr Underwood, the clerk of works for some building contractors working on the site, noticed that some of the empty TNT sacks resting against the walls of Building No. 833 had caught fire. He ran to the office and informed the Assistant Manager, Mr Palowker, who was 'holding the fort' while the Manager, George Evetts, was at lunch, and Mr Palowker called out the works fire brigade and also asked the CPC to send their engine to assist.

The CPC engine was routinely manned by the firm's charge-hands who wore a badge with 'FB' on it to identify them. On this day, one of the charge-hands was a young, recently married man, Steve Epps (who was later to be awarded the BEM). Steve had previously been the driver of a horse-drawn brewer's dray but the money had been poor and so he had transferred his allegiance to the CPC factory where he soon became a charge-hand and, in accordance with custom, a member of the part-time fire brigade. When the call-out hooter sounded, he abandoned his lunch and ran to join the engine and go to the fire but, as he later recounted to a member of the Faversham Society, 'By the time we got there, the stuff inside the shed was already alight.' The problem now was to remove the tons of TNT that were stacked near the shed in 56lb boxes as, unless they were soon moved, the fire could spread to the other buildings.

Steve Epps takes up the story: 'We was chucking it to one side, handing it down – it kept falling all round about you. They were slamming it round and one old chap – he could see I was a bit nervy – he said – "That won't go off unless it's detonated, old chap." I said, "Right, I feel safe enough."'

The nineteen members of the CLC fire brigade at the scene then resumed the task of fighting the fire. There being no fire hydrants, they had to take water from a dyke and pass it in buckets along a human chain. Before long there were around 200 factory workers and military personnel either fighting the fires or removing boxes of TNT to a safer location. Apart from these, there were a large number of factory workers who, despite being told to move away, hung around to watch what was going on. They were probably aware that small amounts of TNT will simply burn and that ammonium nitrate is not easy to detonate and the excitement of the fire enlivened their Sunday lunch break.

But the fire was quickly getting out of control. A call had been made to the Faversham fire brigades but, although these set off very promptly, the poor roads between the town and the munitions factories made progress very slow. At best, the roads were mere winding, narrow country lanes; at worst the stretch from Oare to the works was a deeply rutted, flint-surfaced muddy track.

A little over an hour after the discovery of the fire and before the arrival of the town brigades, the works' fire brigades had finally located enough hose to run from the seat of the fire to the nearest CLC hydrant, some

¼ mile away, but this proved to be too little, too late. 'We'd just got the water on it and up she went,' said Steve Epps.

Another employee, George Goldfinch, was assisting at the scene with another man and was running beside the dyke towards Building No. 833 when there was a great explosion. According to information given to the Faversham Society by his niece, the next thing Gorge Goldfinch remembered was 'finding himself on the other side of the water and seeing the other man quite near him with all his clothes blown off him, and just his shoes and socks, and his collar at a strange angle around his neck'.

George Goldfinch's own clothes were in tatters and his arm was broken. He had a number of other, minor injuries and remained partially deaf for the rest of his life.

Just why the combination of TNT and ammonium nitrate suddenly exploded after burning for so long is not clear, although it was suggested that oxygen given off by the burning ammonium nitrate coming into contact with the TNT could, according to an official report, have resulted in 'a reaction of unforeseen and exceptional violence'.

Among the other eyewitnesses interviewed by the Faversham Society in the 1960s was Sydney Wilson, the town clerk of Faversham from 1943 to 1957, who was a member of the town's Volunteer brigade during the First World War:

> Before we could get started, the first big explosion took place. We had an American-type petrol engine, horse-drawn, but on this occasion we had lashed it to the back of a Shepherd Neame lorry, and I stood in the lorry looking over the bonnet, signalling to the fellow who was steering the engine behind. As we passed through Oare village and came up on the Uplees road overlooking the factories, a second terrific explosion occurred and my only recollection of it really is seeing a fan of flame, the lorry momentarily pausing and the engine behind cracking into it.

It later became clear that, apart from a number of comparatively minor explosions, there were three major ones which were heard and felt as far away as Norwich and Great Yarmouth. In the first explosion, when the burning Building No. 833 blew up, another two process houses, about 100m away on the CPC site, immediately exploded in sympathy. These were new buildings, used for the washing of nitro–glycerine, of which there was an estimated 1,000 tons in the two buildings. After this first, combined explosion there were two more. The second explosion, referred to by

Sydney Wilson above, occurred around 1.40 pm when one of the ELC buildings, used for making amatol charges, went up. About 20 minutes later, another ELC building, which contained primers for sea mines and had been set alight by falling burning debris from the two previous explosions, also went up.

The scene on both the ELC and the CPC sites was one of complete devastation. The five sheds in which the explosions had occurred had simply disappeared. Where Building No. 833 had been there was now a crater 150ft across and between 10ft and 15ft in depth. Every one of the light buildings in a 200m radius from the explosion was destroyed, 6 of which were on the CPC site, and up to 200 sheds suffered some damage.

The ELC Manager, George Evetts, having been alerted by his assistant, Mr Palowker, had abandoned his Sunday lunch and hurried to the scene where he took charge of the situation in a very competent manner, organising the removal of the empty and burning TNT bags. When the shed exploded, he was around 40m away and was knocked unconscious, his jacket being torn from his back. When he regained consciousness, he found his office was on fire so he hastened to try to save the firm's books and papers. Despite the walls and roof of the office falling in on him, he went on to summon the very urgently required medical assistance. Together with his counterpart from the CPC factory, William Bethell, he returned to the scene of the initial explosion, arriving just in time to be met by the second and third explosions. The roof of a TNT magazine was seen to be alight but no one appeared willing to do anything about it so the two managers set about extinguishing it themselves, thus averting a further major explosion. The tireless work of these two was recognised by a subsequent award of the Edward Medal (Second Class) to each of them, as well as to a few others, including Steve Epps. (This medal, awarded for outstanding gallantry in industrial situations, has been replaced by the George Cross.)

The part-time fire brigades worked heroically pending the arrival of the town brigades. The CPC brigade dashed from place to place, endeavouring to put out the fires started by the explosions. Of the nineteen members of that brigade, seven lost their lives that terrible day and most of the others were injured, more or less seriously. Steve Epps was in a party of seven firefighters when Building No. 833 went up. His colleagues all lost their lives and young Steve was blown into a dyke and for some time was left as dead. Fortunately, someone noticed signs of life and he was carted off to hospital where he was to remain for nearly five months.

When my wife came to the hospital for the first time, she didn't recognise me. My sister went to the hospital that Sunday night – and the Monday and the Tuesday and the Wednesday – and she didn't recognise me either. She thought to herself, 'My brother's dead.' Then she realised that there was one who might be me, and she told my wife that the nurses wanted her to go to the hospital to make sure. So she went . . . Of course, I'd got a broken thigh bone, a broken jaw and four broken ribs, and I'd lost the use of my arm and hand on the side where my ribs had been broken. And my wife kept looking at me and kept thinking, 'Is it Steve or isn't it?' because she couldn't really recognise me properly. And then at last she looked again, and she said, 'Yes, that's him.' And they said to her, 'We're ever so sorry but we haven't touched him yet because we didn't expect him to live'.

Eventually the three Faversham fire brigades arrived and the twenty-nine members of these showed great courage and devotion to duty in a dreadfully perilous situation. Their leaders, Guy Tassell, the Town Clerk and Captain of the Volunteer Brigade, Charles Semark, a local engineer and Captain of the Kent Brigade, and James Goode, a builder and Captain of the Norwich Brigade, all got their hands dirty and showed great fortitude, moving cases of TNT from threatened buildings and rolling hot shells into a dyke. All three were later awarded the Medal of the Order of the British Empire (the forerunner of the British Empire Medal). Sydney Wilson of the Volunteer Brigade recalled being engaged until the evening, damping down the fires but mostly 'picking up whatever we could find to lead to the identification of the victims'.

Conspicuous at the scene were two small military detachments, one of which, consisting of a corporal and nine other ranks from an anti-aircraft battery at Oare, arrived just as the first explosion occurred. Fortunately uninjured, they were soon joined by another, slightly smaller squad under a young officer. Together these troops performed sterling work, rescuing survivors and removing or extinguishing their burning clothes or digging them out of the mud and debris.

The risk all these brave men took is illustrated by the fact that there were some 3,000 tons of gun cotton stored close to where the explosions occurred and, according to local GP and Medical Officer of Health, Dr Charles Evers, who was quickly on the scene, 'If that had gone off . . . it would have wiped out all the works, doctors, patients, soldiers, helpers and all'.

Dr Evers later wrote that he was driven to the scene by his driver after the first explosion but before the second and said he could see a tremendous volume of flames and smoke. As he reached the factory gates, where there was a sizeable crowd gathering, there was a

> . . . tremendous burst of flame, followed by, at what seemed ages long, an appalling report. The crowd fled for their lives.
>
> A continuous stream of injured men were dribbling in – pitiable objects. Some had been blown into dykes and were wringing wet and shivering with shock; many were shaking all over. Some were brought on trolleys, some carried, some helped along. One man cheerfully proclaimed that he had a broken leg, which I set Amos on to put up (it was not compound). Others were bleeding and some had half their clothes torn off or burnt off – an awful procession . . .
>
> Even then we did not realise the full extent of the disaster, as we had not penetrated to the heart of things and could do no more than attend to those who kept coming up faster than we could deal with them. We had not time to realise that behind that curtain were the worst stricken men, who could only be moved very slowly, and a number that need never be moved at all, for no help could restore them . . .
>
> Five of the national reserves who were on guard were killed instantly: of one, nothing but his rifle was ever found. . . . The vagaries of the explosion were many: two men side by side – one killed instantly, the other hardly hurt; a number of men between 30 and 40 yards away from the explosion unharmed, while men 100 yards away were blown to pieces . . .; men had all their clothes blown off them and were yet unhurt.

Also quickly on the scene was another local doctor, Prideaux George Selby from Teynham who was accompanied by his formidable wife, Elizabeth, who was the Commandant of the Sittingbourne VAD Hospital. Mrs Selby bustled around, intending to assist in particular any women who had been injured. As it happened, being a Sunday, there were no women on the site but this did not prevent Mrs Selby from hitching up her skirts and getting stuck in.

A small town of just 10,000 inhabitants, Faversham only had a small cottage hospital with 10 beds which was obviously totally incapable of handling all the injured from a major disaster. As the Medical Officer of Health, Dr Evers instructed that any military patients already in the cottage hospital who could be moved should be found alternative accommodation and the staff there managed to double their normal bed capacity. Other patients were taken to the infirmary at the town's workhouse, the Salvation Army Hall (furnished and equipped by local residents) and the two local houses that had been converted into military hospitals for the duration of the war. Dr Evers recalled, 'When one considers that at one o'clock there were about twenty-five hospital beds in the place . . . that by five o'clock about one hundred cases had been treated and accommodated in the hospital and not at all in a makeshift manner'.

Doctors and nurses began arriving from all over the county – as far away as Margate and Ramsgate, which, considering the lack of telephones or radio and the limited means of transport available at that time, was a remarkable achievement.

All sorts of vehicles were being pressed into service as ambulances, both civilian and military. Some of the injured were even shipped by barge to Sheerness. Dr Evers having decided he would be of more use in Faversham and being unable to find his driver, drove himself, with an injured man in the back of his car, propped up by a soldier. The journey back along the narrow, rutted road was a nightmare with a stream of oncoming vehicles trying to get to the scene of the disaster.

Dr Evers' account continues,

At last the rush ceased and we began to tackle the poor men in earnest. They were dirty, wet, cold, bleeding, groaning, insensible, and every bed and linen was immediately of course stained the minute they were placed in them. . . . Their clothes had simply been thrown out into the garden: those of the eight men in Ward 2 would not have made one decent suit amongst them.

Dr Evers and his qualified colleagues were ably assisted by the ladies from the Faversham and Whitstable Voluntary Aid Detachments (VADs), one of whom, Miss Melice Telfer, later told the Faversham Society's researcher that,

They set to work like professionals and did *anything* and did it well and coolly. . . . One man had been thrown through a window and Mrs Andrews, the Surveyor's wife, spent practically the whole afternoon taking small pieces of glass out of his face. [With] others we were told to do just whatever we could. We took our scissors and slit up their clothes to get them out. One man had been thrown straight into water, so you had to get him out of his very wet clothes, in which he was shivering. . . .We were given more or less carte blanche to do whatever we could for them . . . and we were just busy, oh, until quite late at night.

With the injured being cared for, the next task was to take care of the bodies of the unfortunate men who had lost their lives in the disaster and this gruesome work began in earnest on the Monday morning. Sydney Twist, a 17-year-old apprentice fitter and turner at the CPC factory, told the *Faversham Times*:

> The bodies . . . were on wattle gates, filling the cycle shed, with others in Dan's old tile works. At dinner time I walked over to the ELC. . . . The boiler house had disappeared, one boiler lying on its side just outside where the boiler house had stood and the other lying in the dyke about twenty-five to thirty yards away.

The precise number of fatalities will never be known as some bodies were not found, many were too badly mutilated to be identified and the fact that the factories kept no accurate records of who was on their sites; the best estimate is somewhere between 108 and 116. Although around forty victims were buried other than in Faversham, a mass grave had to be prepared in the town's Love Lane cemetery to take another sixty-nine and a number of others were buried in private graves. One body was found in a dyke a week after the disaster. Among the dead were two ambulance men, and another one was so distressed by his experience at the site that he hanged himself the next day. The burial service at the mass grave was conducted by the Archbishop of Canterbury, Dr Davidson, and was attended by hundreds of mourners and military guards of honour as well as ministers from all religious denominations. Of the sixty-nine interred in the mass grave, only thirty-four could be definitely identified, the remainder simply recorded as 'a male person unknown'.

The Coroner's inquest jury recorded a verdict of 'accidental death caused by shock and injuries received in an explosion due to an accidental fire, cause unknown', but details of the evidence given to the inquest were kept secret because of the demands of national security in time of war and the information remains embargoed to this day.

It is not possible to say precisely what caused this terrible disaster other than that the ignition of the empty TNT bags was the primary cause. How these caught fire is open to conjecture: a carelessly discarded cigarette butt, arson/sabotage, spontaneous combustion or sparks from the boiler house. The first two possibilities were quickly ruled out on the grounds of the strict rules regarding smoking and the carrying of matches on the one hand, and the security and military patrols on the other. Spontaneous combustion was thought most unlikely and so the investigators plumped for the final choice: sparks from the boiler house chimney. The storage of both TNT and ammonium nitrate in the same building provided a situation in which a small fire could result in a devastating explosion and 'the practice was to be strongly discouraged'. The inadequate fire prevention and extinguishing equipment available was also criticised.

This war-time disaster resulted in more stringent (albeit fairly self-evident) precautions being recommended by the Standing Committee formed to inquire into the causes of explosions at government and state-controlled factories – a typical case of shutting the stable door after the horse has bolted. The two explosive factories (and several others) were taken over by a new company, Explosive Trades Ltd, in November 1918 and the sites continued in declining operation until the 1930s and had closed completely by 1936. The site is now completely clear and has reverted to pastureland.

Very Dangerous

Despite the improved national safety measures imposed following the Faversham explosion, Kent was to suffer a further, similar incident less than a decade later. This time the factory was not under pressure because of a major war being fought at the time, as was the case at Faversham in 1916.

The incident occurred at the Slade Green Filling Factory near Erith where Very lights were being broken down. On 18 February 1924, the assistant manager of the factory, Mr Pepler, was outside one of the isolated sheds when he saw smoke issuing from the roof. He knew there were twenty-six workers inside and he was about to investigate this worrying phenomenon when the shed blew up before his eyes. Running towards the virtually demolished building, from whence he could hear the cries of injured workers, he saw a girl standing in the doorway, her arms outstretched and obviously blinded. 'Keeping my coat in front of me, I gripped her on the arm and pulled her towards me, partly dragging and partly carrying her to safety. The impression I had then was that the whole interior was one red flame. This poor girl was standing in the flames and was on fire from head to foot.'

The grievously injured girl was taken to hospital with a number of others but later died from her wounds. In all, one man and twelve young women lost their lives in the explosion, their corpses being unrecognisable. One of the dead girls had only started work at the factory an hour before the shed blew up.

The subsequent inquiry learned that the task of the workers was to empty the explosive material out of unwanted Very light flares. This was poured into a shallow tray which was removed almost instantaneously. The official verdict was that there was either an unstable rogue cartridge among those being handled, or a cartridge had been dropped on the concrete floor, thus igniting it, or that the rims of two cartridges had struck each other, causing a fateful spark. No one survived who could have shed any light on the matter.

Walkway Found Wanting

The seaside town of Ramsgate has been a haven for ships for centuries and the construction of its harbour in the 1760s increased its importance for maritime trade. Never a major port like Dover or Gravesend, Ramsgate's position to the extreme east of the county favoured certain types of shipping and, coupled with its popularity as a seaside resort even before 1800 when sea bathing was becoming fashionable, the sea, in one way or another, has ensured Ramsgate's continued prosperity.

In more recent times, the trend towards foreign holidays has hit Ramsgate hard – as it has so many seaside towns – and more and more emphasis has been placed on shipping and cross-Channel ferry business. Several companies have run ferry services from Ramsgate to France, Belgium and Holland, not always successfully. These have included P & O, Sally Line and, more recently, TransEuropa Ferries, which provided a service between Ramsgate and Ostend. The cross-Channel ferry service suffered a serious set-back in September 1994, when a serious accident, described as 'Thanet's worst-ever peace-time disaster' (*Isle of Thanet Gazette*) occurred.

Access for foot passengers to the ships in Ramsgate harbour had always been, as elsewhere, by means of covered, zigzagging walkways which conduct pedestrians from the berth side to the appropriate level on the ship where they can gain access to and from the passenger decks. Shortly before 1 am on Wednesday, 14 September 1994, such a walkway was in use at No. 3 Berth as passengers for Ostend embarked on the ferry, the *Prins Filip*. With a crossing lasting the best part of 4 hours before them, they were all keen to get on and get their heads down.

Suddenly, however, one end of the walkway came away and dropped 10m to the deck of the pontoon which supported the walkway on the seaward side. There was panic and screams as the whole of the walkway shuddered and, with a resounding crash, the end of this great metal structure embedded itself in the pontoon 40ft below. All the passengers who happened to be using the walkway at the time were shaken up but the thirteen who were using that particular section at the time were catapulted forward to fall 40ft onto the pontoon. As a result, six were killed and the other seven all received multiple injuries.

Probably the last passengers to cross safely from the shore to the ship were Michael Hedges and his wife, Katherine. He told the *Isle of Thanet Gazette*:

> As I went over the gangway I could see a six-inch gap between the two sections. I jumped over it, which was difficult because I was wearing a back-pack. I didn't think anything of it at the time. I had just got into the foyer area when I heard people crying and some people panicking. I must have been the last person on board. I may be the luckiest person alive.

Another witness said, 'There was a fearful metallic screeching noise and a horrendous crash. We turned the corner just as the other end landed and the bodies were flying. They were all piled up, tangled with each other. You couldn't get through without having to climb over a pile of bodies.'

'I heard a bang,' said another would-be passenger, 'and saw it was the tunnel that had crashed onto the floor. It was terrible. We saw people lying on the floor and screaming.'

On hearing of the accident, security officers, stevedores and office workers rushed to lend a hand, while fire and rescue personnel, police and ambulance crews rushed into the port. Paramedics were joined by doctors and nurses from the Thanet Hospital and the harrowing job of extracting the dead and injured from the mass of bodies commenced in the rain and darkness. Lack of suitable facilities at the nearby Thanet Hospital meant that the injured had to be taken by ambulance 17 miles to the Kent and Canterbury Hospital in Canterbury for treatment, a matter that incensed local residents who had been campaigning for some time for the local hospital to have a full, 24-hour emergency service.

Around 400 passengers had already boarded the ship before the accident occurred and had to remain on board, in the harbour, throughout the night and well into the following morning as teams of police investigators came on board to take statements and make other inquiries.

Other police officers, from the Sussex Underwater Search Team, were soon on the spot and made an exhaustive search of the sea in the area of the gangway and recovered a large metal pin, which was to prove a significant find.

In the aftermath of this terrible accident – one of the most serious onshore incidents in the recent history of the ferry industry – the collapsed walkway was subject to intense scrutiny by experts and the Health and Safety Executive. The walkway had been supplied by two Swedish firms, FEAB and FKAB, only four months previously and was reasonably expected to last for years. Although FEAB had thirty years pontoon experience, this was the first gangway of its kind that company had manufactured. Economic Director Christen Utgren said, 'There was nothing unusual about the design. It is quite standard in its specifications, a very ordinary design for us.'

The structure had been in use for about six months and had been subjected to stringent safety tests before being granted a Lloyds of London certificate. These tests included placing heavy weights on the walkway to test its strength. Although the link has to move with the swell and 5½m tide, officials from the Port of Ramsgate said there was nothing out of the ordinary in the early hours of that fateful Wednesday. 'We never ever dreamed that anything like this could happen,' said the managing director at the Port of Ramsgate, Reginald Cooper. Similar walkways were in use on other berths in Ramsgate Harbour and the managing director said he saw no reason to take them out of service.

However, examination revealed that welds on a stub axle that connected one of the support feet to the walkway had failed, bringing the whole structure crashing down. The primary cause of this failure was shown to be fatigue cracking but it was held that the real problem was the totally inadequate design of the walkway. The walkway had to allow for movement of the landing pontoon due to the action of waves and the designers had completely failed to appreciate how it would behave while in use. As a result, they had grossly underestimated the stresses to which the support bearing would be subjected, leading to its failure.

Because of this finding, the two Swedish companies and other bodies involved in the design, construction and installation of the walkway, including the Port of Ramsgate, were convicted of corporate manslaughter and heavily fined.

Chapter 7

War and Terrorism

U ntil around a century ago, the many wars and skirmishes in which the British armed forces were involved did not directly affect the inhabitants of 'this sceptred isle'. It was not until the military use of aircraft became commonplace and the surrounding seas ceased to protect the country from attack that the awful realities of war were brought home to Britains.

Once this situation had arisen, countless incidents occurred in Kent that could quite properly be described as disasters. The wartime calamities described in this chapter should be seen as merely indicative of the sort of catastrophe that affected the county, especially during the Second World War.

Folkestone Under Fire
Although the military use of aircraft reached its apogee in the Second World War, this is not to say that Kent was not affected much earlier. The first time enemy aircraft attacked the county was on 16 April 1915, when a solitary Albatros BII dropped bombs on Sittingbourne and Faversham, causing some damage and killing a blackbird. Other strikes were made, by both aircraft and Zeppelin airships, on Ramsgate, Sittingbourne, Gravesend, Dover, Margate and other places, causing damage and a number of casualties, including several children killed in Ramsgate.

But the most disastrous of these incursions occurred on Friday, 25 May 1917 when twenty-three Gotha bombers took off from their airfields in Belgium heading for London via the Essex coast. On arrival over London, the raiders found, to their great disappointment, that the capital was under heavy cloud cover and they were unable to see their targets.

Frustrated, they turned for home and, flying at an estimated 14,000ft, found that the cloud cover disappeared as they flew southwards. Following the main railway line to the Channel ports, the bombers dropped high explosives at various points along the way: Luddesdown, Linton, Marden, Pluckley, Smarden and Bethersden, causing little damage in these country parishes and killing just one sheep.

Ashford offered a much more tempting target: the extensive and important railway works. They dropped six bombs but all missed the railway, although one girl was killed – the first fatality of the raid.

Having split into two wings, half the Gotha bombers dropped their load on Kingsnorth, Shadoxhurst and Mersham, while the other half attacked the Royal Military Canal and dropped several bombs on the Romney Marsh and then turned its attention to Lympne airfield. Little damage was caused and the planes droned on over Hythe where two more fatal casualties were caused.

Following the coast, the aircraft dropped further bombs on Sandgate before heading inland a little to attack Shorncliffe military camp. Here matters took a more serious turn as the German bombs killed seventeen Canadian soldiers and one British 'Tommy'. Their bodies, some terribly mutilated, were buried with full military honours in Shorncliffe Military Cemetery and local children later came to place flowers on their graves at a solemn and moving ceremony. This practice was continued ever after and became known as 'Canadian Flower Day' with up to 3,000 children attending, together with local and Canadian dignitaries. Although reduced in scale since the Second World War, the ceremony continues to this day.

Moving on to the nearby Folkestone suburb of Cheriton, bombs killed a further three people. And now it was the turn of Folkestone – the climax of the raid.

Unlike during the Second World War, this country was ill prepared for air attacks and no warning system had been set up. Communications were poor, relying on manually operated telephone switchboards and telegraph systems, and so no one in Folkestone was aware of the drama that had unfolded over the county in the previous hour or so. The responses made by Harry Reeve, the Chief Constable of the Folkestone Borough Police, to questions put to him during the inquest after the raid are extremely revealing:

The Coroner: 'In the case of a military, naval or aircraft emergency, who would control the inhabitants?'

The Chief Constable: 'I would act, under the direction of the military authorities.'

The Coroner: 'In the case of air raids, do the military authorities acquaint you of it?'

The Chief Constable: 'That is the arrangement.'

The Coroner: 'Do they acquaint you?'

The Chief Constable: 'They did not last Friday.'

The Coroner: 'As a rule, do they?'

The Chief Constable: 'Yes. I am informed from the Headquarters of the Eastern Command in London.'

The Coroner: 'Then I understand that on Friday, you received no warning?'
The Chief Constable: 'Not a word. We knew nothing about it till we heard them over the town.'
The Coroner: 'They were hostile aircraft?'
The Chief Constable: 'Not a doubt of it!'

The Chief Constable went on to add that when notice of air raids was received from the military, the police immediately informed the fire brigade and the ambulance brigade who stood by for duty. If the aircraft were believed to be in the area, the public were warned to take shelter, although there was 'no public hooter or anything of that kind to give warning'. At night, the lights on all vehicles are put out and the town 'made as dark as possible'.

The day in question being Friday – pay day – the town was busy with shoppers, window shoppers and people who were just strolling around the town, enjoying the warm early summer evening. A few distant explosions had been heard but these were put down to the troops training at Shorncliffe camp. These gradually came nearer until the Gothas came overhead and the true horror began.

The first bombs fell in Shorncliffe Road, the west end of the town, and around the Central station, killing a total of four people. The second salvo fell on the Radnor Park/Foord Road area and killed another man. In the Bouverie Road East area eight bombs were dropped, killing a further six. A boot-maker's shop, owned by Mr J Burke, suffered the most damage in this road, as described by a reporter from the *Folkestone, Hythe, Sandgate and Cheriton Herald*:

> The pavement was blown into the basement of the shop [which] presented a scene of indescribable wreckage. Broken furniture, bedsteads and fragments of bedding, wicker chairs and stores of all kinds lay mixed with the twisted and punctured ends of gas and water pipes, and the torn remains of electric wires. A bicycle . . . bore eloquent testimony to the force of the shock, its frame being bent in all shapes and its tyres torn bodily off the wheels. Mr Burke, who was in his shop at the time, was thrown out into the street and killed instantaneously.

In the early part of the twentieth century, the main shopping area of the town was in and around Tontine Street, the present commercial centre based on Sandgate Road not becoming the hub of the town until some years later. And so, Tontine Street that Friday evening was the busiest part of town and the street was crowded. Just two bombs fell in Tontine Street, one of which failed to explode (like many others during this raid). The other bomb, however, was a very different matter and took the lives of no less than sixty-one people.

With the war in its third year, Britain was suffering many shortages and several shops had queues outside them, with housewives hoping to be able to purchase some rare commodity, such as the potatoes that were reported to be available at Stokes' large greengrocer's shop. In those days it was normal for shops to be open well into the evening and so, when the bombs dropped at 6.22 pm, the scene was set for a catastrophe.

The first bomb scored a direct hit on the greengrocer's, the roof of which collapsed, killing forty-four customers and staff instantly, while a further seventeen later died in hospital. The victims were almost all women and children whose bodies were horribly mangled, some simply blown apart; severed limbs jostled with the carcases of horses among the rubble and debris, while the pathetic cries of mortally injured animals added to the horrific turmoil and uproar. Chief Constable Harry Reeve (whose only son was killed in France that same year) described the scene as: 'The most appalling sight I have ever seen. The memory of which will remain with me until my dying day.'

The excellent book, *A Glint in the Sky*, by Martin Easdown and Thomas Genth, includes a number of personal reminiscences by those who witnessed the devastation in Folkestone that day:

> I remember coming up the steps of my house and standing there to watch a line of buses coming along with lots of wounded people laid on the seats. They were taken to the hospital around the corner from us. I also remember seeing a man running along towards the hospital with a baby in his arms, and the baby was covered in blood. (Wyn Knowles)
>
> . . . I was walking in Tontine Street with two friends of mine, two little girls, and suddenly the planes came over and a man grabbed me by the arm and pulled me into the Clarendon pub, and just then the bomb fell and my two friends were killed. There were babies in prams outside the shops and some of them had their heads blown off. It was an awful sight. . . . Eventually I ran home and I was sobbing all the way. (Edith Vye)
>
> I recall seeing the planes through my bedroom window . . . and they looked beautiful with the sun on their wings. But they did terrible damage when they dropped their bombs. (Edith Cole)

Another, unidentified boy was playing cricket in the park when the planes came over and a bomb exploded 'not twenty yards in front of us'. His account, as quoted in the book, continues:

> Tearing for home . . . at last we came to our street, Tontine Street, and I shall never forget the scene. Squeezing my way through a barrier, . . . I saw my home, our business home, practically in ruins. Mother was in a state of collapse and father had shrapnel in his lung. Customers in the shop had been decapitated. Others were wounded beyond recognition and they lay everywhere. There was a terrible amount of blood about. Two horses lay dead, shockingly mangled and a fifty-foot gas flame from a penetrated main added to the horror.

Albert Taylor was the 16-year-old son of the licensees of the Brewery Tap public house in Tontine Street and said that the most tragic thing he remembered was the curly, fair-haired head of a small child on the saloon bar doorstep. Later, when he had taken over the licence himself, he would scrub and whitewash the step every morning as he could still see the stain where the small head had lain.

A Mrs Coxon described the scene fully in her husband's book, *Dover During the Dark Days*, and concluded, 'I do not think many people will be likely to forget the first visit the cultured Hun paid to us on the then undefended town of Folkestone.'

The German planes moved on towards their prime target, Dover. Here a warm welcome awaited them: six Army gun batteries opened up on them, as did a number of naval vessels in the harbour, and three planes from the Royal Naval Air Service took off to do battle with the 'cultured Hun'. The raid on Dover was abandoned and the Gothas headed for home, harried all the way by British aircraft and shipping, a number of the raiders being destroyed or damaged on the way.

In all, 96 people, mainly civilians, were killed during this raid and nearly 200 seriously injured; 72 of the fatalities occurred in Folkestone alone.

The Coroner, the respected local solicitor Mr G W Haines, warmly praised the people of Folkestone, saying that the town had furnished its proportion of men for the front, and the husbands of some of the women who were killed were fighting in France at the time. They would be glad to know their women could show that strength and determination and could give their lives in the way they had done:

> These women had to stand there without any defence, open to the enemy's attacks. Just as the men had to do at the beginning of the war when they were out-gunned and out-manned . . . These raids were

done to terrorise the people, but the women of Folkestone showed they were not to be terrorised and held out to the last as their men were doing.

The jury returned a verdict of 'Death by bombs from hostile aircraft, Great Britain being in a state of war, and the deceased at the time being a non-combatant.' It added a rider to the effect that they regretted that the competent authorities did not give notice of the approach of the aircraft, and were also strongly of the opinion that, in future, the town should be warned by a siren or other such device.

Little more than two decades later, Great Britain was again at war with Germany and the quiet little seaside town of Folkestone was to suffer once more. A total of eighty-three enemy attacks were made on the town during the Second World War, resulting in considerable loss of life, but no single incident created as much death and destruction as this one raid in 1915.

Canterbury Catastrophe

The year 1942 was a dark one for Great Britain. Supported by her Empire, she had been standing alone until the United States entered the war at the very end of the previous year and even then the Americans played only a small part in the European theatre of war. The threat of invasion by the Nazi forces was still very real and on everyone's mind. Following its failure to destroy the RAF in the Battle of Britain, the Luftwaffe had been concentrating on London and other major cities, including Coventry, all of which suffered enormous damage and loss of life.

The RAF was not standing idly by, however, and its bombers were attacking the German homeland regularly and in force. The Luftwaffe's use of incendiaries on Coventry alerted attention to the value of fire when used against primarily non-industrial targets and a heavy raid, using this type of weapon, was made on the historic and marginally important target of Lübek in March 1942.

In April, the Germans retaliated with a heavy raid on Exeter – a city very similar to Lübek – and the Nazi propagandist, Baron Gustav Braun von Sturm, referring to the well-known German guide books, declared that 'We shall go out and bomb every city in Britain marked with three stars in the Baedeker Guides.' This was no idle threat and further, similar raids were made on Bath, Norwich and York.

The RAF responded on the night of 30 May with an extremely heavy and destructive raid on Cologne using a thousand bombers for the first time. As a result, 85 per cent of that great city was destroyed and the people in historic towns and cities on both sides of the North Sea were on tenterhooks, wondering who was going to be next. Would it be Canterbury? That infamous traitor, Lord Haw Haw, had already warned that, should Cologne be attacked, Canterbury would be next. So far the city had escaped any serious attacks but how long could this last? The answer was soon forthcoming.

Sunday, 31 May 1942 dawned a bright, warm early summer's day in Kent and the good people went about their business and attended services in the great cathedral and other churches, unaware that, at that moment, a large force of Luftwaffe bombers was being armed and prepared for a major air raid. With the news of the attack on Cologne having been made public, there was a sense of impending disaster as the day ended and slipped into Monday, 1 June. Wardens and firewatchers had been reinforced and were especially alert that night and, sure enough, soon after midnight, the sirens began to wail.

The South East in general, and Kent in particular, had experienced so many air-raid warnings as the bombers flew overhead on their way to bomb London and other targets that the populace no longer took much notice of them. A secondary warning had therefore been introduced and sounded whenever there were 'raiders overhead'. This took the form of an interrupted siren sound, known variously as the 'cuckoo' or 'Tugboat Annie' air-raid warning and, not unexpectedly, shortly after the first air-raid warning had sounded, the second, more-urgent alarm was heard. This must be it! And sure enough, the pulsating drone of the German bombers could be heard, coming closer and closer.

It was a clear, cloudless night and the first few aircraft dropped flares – bright yellow and blue lights suspended in the air by their parachutes, lighting up the city as if it were day.

Approaching from the north east, three waves of bombers dropped a mixture of high-explosive and incendiary bombs on the city. One raider, at little more than rooftop height, dropped a shower of incendiaries on the roof of the cathedral but the firewatchers were ready and swept them off to the ground below where they burned fiercely but harmlessly on the ground. The cathedral was lucky but so many other buildings were hit that it was impossible to save them all. Soon the dying light of the flares was replaced by the ruddy glow of a myriad of fires which could be seen for miles. Fire crews from all over Kent and London attended and fought valiantly but all too often in vain.

For a full hour and a quarter the bombardment continued until finally the bombers, their task complete, headed for home. Subsequently three of the raiders were shot down by anti-aircraft fire and nightfighters.

In the hush that followed the storm, people began to emerge from their shelters, cellars and even from the surrounding countryside whence they had fled when the raid started. Firemen continued to battle against the flames and rescue parties were busy extricating those unfortunate souls who were buried in the rubble. Some hardy residents were determined not to let a little thing like an air raid spoil their beauty sleep. One gentleman ignored both the warnings and slept on in his bed until an incendiary bomb came through his roof and bedroom ceiling. He then got up, fetched a sandbag which he placed over the burning device and went back to bed.

The city was devastated and whole streets had been destroyed but, towering over the ruins, as a symbol of hope and courage, stood the great cathedral, much as St Paul's had done during the London Blitz. The centuries-old building was largely undamaged – thanks in no small part to the efforts of the firewatchers on its roof who had undoubtedly saved the day.

When the final tally was made, it was found that fifty people had lost their lives during, or as a direct result of, the raid. This included the town clerk and ARP Controller, George Goodfin Marks, and six children. The reason there were so few children, proportionally to the number of adults, is no doubt due to the fact than many children from Kent had been evacuated to Wales and other safe places back in 1940.

The weary but unvanquished citizens of Canterbury readied themselves for a return visit by the raiders and the authorities, obviously of the same opinion, rushed barrage balloons and anti-aircraft guns to the city. Fortunately, such preparations proved unnecessary since the city had a temporary respite and the inhabitants set about clearing up and trying to conduct their affairs and businesses in as normal a way as possible under the circumstances.

The city was honoured and delighted to receive visits from various dignitaries: the Duke of York (soon to lose his own life in a plane crash) arrived during the week following the raid; and Mrs Churchill and Mrs Roosevelt came together on 30 October 1942. By this time the city was, despite the devastation, getting back to a sort of wartime normality – a situation that was soon to be shattered once more.

The next day, 31 October, the barrage balloons – which had proved unnecessary – were removed for essential repairs while the city was busy with shoppers, both from the city and from surrounding towns, who were making their weekend purchases that Saturday afternoon.

Meanwhile, RAF fighters were combatting a group of Luftwaffe aircraft, both bombers and fighters, over the English Channel. A total of nine of the enemy aircraft were shot down but around twenty broke away and headed at low level for Canterbury, where they arrived around 5 pm. On the Sturry road they shot up an East Kent Bus Company's bus, full of homeward-bound shoppers, seven of whom were killed, as was the conductress. Another bus was strafed and the driver killed, while a train also received unwelcome attention, killing the fireman and a small boy.

When they reached the city centre, the raiders embarked on an orgy of terror and destruction, shooting and dropping bombs indiscriminately. With no real warning, the townsfolk had little chance and many fell, mortally wounded, in the streets or in the rubble of bombed buildings.

This final, brief but bloody encounter took the lives of thirty-two more people, mostly ordinary citizens going quietly about their business on that bright, autumnal afternoon. Fortunately many folk had moved out of the town completely or had adopted the habit of sleeping in the fields or seeking shelter at night in places such as the Tyler Hill railway tunnel, and so the death toll was less than it might otherwise have been. Apart from an occasional minor incursion, this was the last time Canterbury was to suffer at the hands of the Nazi war machine.

Ashford Attacked

The scenario that unfolded in the second major raid on Canterbury was to be replicated a few months later in another Kentish town. This time it was Ashford that felt the full brunt of the Luftwaffe on 24 March 1943.

It was mid-morning on a pleasant, sunny spring day and business was being carried on normally with shoppers patiently queuing for their meagre wartime rations, or simply chatting and passing the time of day with friends and acquaintances in the street. In the great railway works and other factories, shops and offices, men and women were 'doing their bit' towards the war effort. Little did they know that, just across the Channel, the Luftwaffe Staffel JG26 based at St Omer in France was preparing for a raid that was to inflict more casualties than any other single raid on Kent. Just before 10 am the fifteen fighter bombers were skimming the waves in an endeavour to get under the radar screen, then climbing slightly to get over the Aldington Ridge where anti-aircraft fire caused the group to split up.

Ashford was not complacent, however, and watchers at various points were on the lookout for any signs of enemy activity. None more so than the two spotters on the top of the Newtown bath-house tower which, between the locomotive works and the wagon sheds, contained thousands of gallons of water for use in the railway works. From their high viewpoint, these two volunteer railwaymen had a 360-degree view and were the first to spot the raiders, coming in very low at 350mph. One of these planespotters, Joe Knowler, described the scene to the *Kentish Express*: 'The planes had already broken into three groups as they came in low from the Mersham direction. Three came over the top of Colliers Hill with six on either side. Each group was aiming for a different target: the rail works, REME [Royal Electrical & Mechanical Engineers] and the [railway] station.'

Kent was by now well accustomed to meeting the brunt of Adolf Hitler's spleen – so much so that the ordinary air-raid sirens no longer made much impression on the inhabitants, and a special secondary warning was sounded whenever raiders were 'overhead' or there was 'immediate danger'. When this signal – variously known as the 'cuckoo' or 'warbling Minnie' – was heard people wasted no time getting off the streets. Without hesitation, Joe Knowler hit the button to sound this alarm in the railway works, while the ARP wardens in the town followed his example.

There was no time to lose; at the speed they were travelling the fifteen Messerschmitt 109s and Focke-Wulf 190s, led by Oberleutnant Paul Keller – 'Bombenkeller' as he was admiringly known to his young pilots, were over the town seconds after they were first spotted.

Joe Knowler takes up the story once more:

> Our only warning by field telephone was to 'stand by'. The next thing I knew they were coming over Colliers. It was impossible for the Bofors [anti-aircraft guns] to shoot at the planes. They were too low and if they had fired they would have hit the houses. Our men on the coast completely missed them and our fighters, which wanted to chase them into Ashford, were commanded not to. They would have been shot at by the town's armaments as well.

The alertness and prompt action taken by the roof-top spotters meant that many of the railway workers were able to take shelter in the few seconds between the warning and the first of the bombs. Not all made it but a good few did. The raid only lasted 3 minutes but caused a terrible loss of life. Machine-gun and cannon fire swept the streets and thirteen small bombs were dropped on schools, shops, garages and the railway works. Three workers were killed when two bombs (one of which failed to explode) hit the railway running shed and another eight were killed by another three bombs which hit the railway works. Robert Barham was one of those working in the running shed when the air raid started. On the fiftieth anniversary of the raid, he told the *Kentish Express*:

As I ran out through the doors towards the shelters all hell broke loose . . . There was a stuttering roar of aircraft engines, cannon guns – loud and getting louder. Bloody hell, five of the bastards head on, very low, big radial engines, FW 190s – a big black bomb dropping from the belly of one.

It all happened in slow motion as I flung myself to the ground. Heavy explosions, the ground kicks me in the stomach, engine noise now deafening as the planes sweep over at rooftop height.

Then they're gone. I get up and race for the nearest shelter because I can hear more of them coming. . . . The second wave sweeps over . . . Ack-ack firing back now; the rattle of light machine guns and the slower bark of the Bofors. In the background the mournful wail of the public air raid warning sirens start. Yet a third wave comes in, their bombs further away. . . . As I emerged from the shelter I saw a great pall of black smoke rising above the [Running] Shed roof. People were running. I joined them and later wished I hadn't. A thousand-pound bomb had hit an E Class locomotive just in from Tonbridge, tearing open the riveted boiler seam then exiting in front of the engine. Its delayed action fuse set it off twenty seconds later. The explosion turned the fifty-five ton loco on its side, trapping the fireman under two tons of coal. Boiling water turned instantly to steam, searing the man's flesh. He was screaming in agony, asking God to let him die. Mercifully, heavily sedated by morphine, he succumbed to his injuries three hours later.

The driver, who initially appeared not seriously injured and urged workmates to help the fireman, died before first-aiders could deal with him. Although there was no outward sign of injury, the blast had caused fatal lung injuries.

A roll call revealed one person missing . . . His body was found later buried under ashes in the disposal pit. . . . I wondered about my home. Amazingly the bus service from outside the Running Shed was still operating and on the journey home it was obvious that the damage was widespread. In Star Road I met my father who told me the house was still standing – just! I was shocked to see the roofless ruin that was our home, its roof timbers and rafters bare of slates. All the glass had been blown in. Inside every ceiling had collapsed.

A passer-by told us that the landlord had just opened The Flag. Still wearing our dust-laden overalls we went in and the pub was crowded with others similarly dressed. The dust in our parched throats was washed down with the best couple of pints of bitter I have ever tasted.

Fred Wade was a young fitter employed in the railway works and was working in the erecting shop when the warning was sounded.

> Climbing out from the pit underneath the locomotive I was working on, I ran to the large doorway to get outside to an air raid shelter. As I ran to the door the pilot was firing his guns and you could see the tracers in the doorway. I dived against the shop wall for protection as the bomb came through the wall, part of which hit me on the head. I was unconscious for a while . . . The loco I was working on was blown across the Erecting Shop. I had a badly cut head and shrapnel in the arms, legs and body. It was nine months before I returned to work.

Outside the railway works, five townsfolk died when a bomb demolished several houses in Star Road and another four when the tannery in Dover Place received a direct hit. Six lost their lives in Hardinge Road and seven in Kent Avenue. In New Street, a bomb hit Hayward's Garage where the petrol in the underground tanks ignited and burning escaping petrol created a scene reminiscent of Dante's *Inferno*. Most of the properties in New Street were very old and of lath and plaster construction. They collapsed like a house of cards when the bombs fell and two of the residents lost their lives there. Other fatalities occurred in New Rents and Milton Road. The Victoria Road School was hit but the 300 or so pupils had already quietly rushed to the shelter and all escaped unscathed.

Bob McNae was a schoolboy at the time, recalls that one of the bombs hit the town abattoir and large pieces of animal flesh added to the gruesome scene. The First World War tank that stood as a memorial in the centre of the town was close to another explosion, but the electrical transformer that was housed inside it was well protected from harm by the strength of this old war-horse.

The sole satisfaction that the Ashfordians could draw was the knowledge that the leader of the German aircraft, Oberleutnant Paul Keller, was himself shot down and killed. A regular soldier with a twin-gun Vickers in the timber yard at the back of Kimberly Works claimed to have brought him down, although there were several other claims.

Unfortunately, when the plane was hit, it exploded at roof-top level, causing much more damage than a simple bomb would have done, resulting in forty-five casualties, eight of whom were killed. Michael Harris was a 14-year-old apprentice working in the Stanhay Workshops at the time, and

owes his life to the fact that he was employed on piecework. He told the
Kentish Express:

> In order to finish the drilling operation on a piece of casting, I had
> delayed my visit to the canteen for a tea break. This played in my
> favour in two ways: one, the route to the shelter via the forge was
> direct; two, the wall behind the bench on which I usually sat in the
> canteen was raked by a row of cannon shell rounds. The other chap
> left in the workshop did not follow me to the shelter and he was killed
> near the canteen . . . I believe that the fatal shots were fired from a
> twin Oerlikon 20 mm cannon mounted on the railway bridge near the
> Drake and Fletcher works.

Another worker at the Stanhay Works was 17-year-old Trixie Godden from
Hamstreet. On that fateful day, she met her boyfriend, Sammy Milton, at
the railway station and they went, hand-in-hand, to the workshop where
they were both employed. When the 'immediate danger' warning was
sounded later in the day, she ran with others to the shelter.

> There was pandemonium, with people killed and injured. I saw a girl
> running in front of me and her head was blown off. It was all over so
> quick. In the factory there was absolute devastation. . . . Jimmy
> Stevens was dead. And Sammy was dead . . . I was so shocked I
> collapsed with my mother when I got home. Then I walked through
> the woods and my dear mum just plodded along behind me.
>
> I went back to Stanhay next day . . . Everyone was trying to clear
> up. Johnny Burden, the manager, said, 'Have a cigarette.' That was
> the day I started smoking and I am still smoking now [fifty years
> later]. Sammy's parents asked me to go and identify him and I went
> to the old cemetery in Canterbury Road where they lay, tier upon tier.
> They pulled back a blanket and I brought his possessions away with
> me. I picked primroses in the woods where we used to walk at
> weekends and made them into a coat-hanger wreath which went into
> the grave with him.

Many people believed that this raid was a reprisal since RAF Mosquitoes had
bombed the St Joseph's railway works in France the previous day. In all, the
raiders left fifty people dead and another seventy-seven seriously injured.

Hitler's Last Fling

By 1944 the war was going badly for the Nazis. They had suffered heavy
losses on the Eastern Front and an invasion of occupied France was

expected at any time. Reports were coming in of a massing of barges and landing craft in the Dover area, giving strength to the expectation of a landing in the Pas de Calais region. It was not until Allied troops began landing much further down the coast, in Normandy, that the truth dawned: the 'landing craft' that spotter planes had seen along the Kent coast were in fact dummies, designed expressly to deceive the enemy.

By this time, Hitler's ordnance had produced a new weapon (and his experts were preparing a second) and the time was right for him to unleash the first of his *Vergeltungswaffen*, or vengeance weapons – the V1. These bombs were unguided and too random to be used for precision attacks on military targets; their whole purpose was to strike terror in the hearts of the civilian population and disrupt military operations.

During the night of 12/13 June 1944, the long-range guns on the French coast fired several salvoes at Folkestone, some of the shells reaching as far as Otham and Maidstone. Attacks on the Kent coast by these guns were not uncommon, as the residents of Dover and Folkestone could testify, but it was unusual for the shells to reach as far inland as Maidstone. As matters transpired, these were clearly a deliberate diversion to draw attention away from what was about to occur.

As dawn approached, the Observer Corps watchers at Dymchurch heard a strange sound, described by one of them as 'a Model T Ford going uphill'. They then saw what first appeared to be an aircraft on fire but which they later could see were flames coming out of the rear of the machine. This must be one of the new German weapons they had been told about. Observer E E Woodland wasted no time in telephoning the Observer Corps headquarters in Maidstone. 'Diver, diver, diver,' he cried down the phone, using the pre-arranged code word. The sirens were immediately sounded and the county and London braced themselves to receive the first of these new terror weapons. In the event, this first 'doodlebug' or 'buzz bomb', as they came to be called, crashed harmlessly at Swanscombe, near Northfleet.

To the many Kentish people who came out of their homes to see what they thought was an aircraft in distress as it passed overhead, flames shooting out of the rear, this was yet another 'Hun' that 'Our Boys' had successfully intercepted and there were cheers from those who saw it hit the piece of wasteland and explode around 4.20 am. They began to have doubts when yet another such machine came over ¾ hour later and fell to earth at Crouch, near Sevenoaks. Their doubts were reinforced over the next few days as thousands of these vengeance weapons were launched over a period of 80 days, of which no less than 1,422 fell on Kent and another thousand in the sea just off the coast – 200 more than reached their target in London.

Anti-aircraft guns got some, fighter planes shot down many more or, as the Allied pilots became more skilled at dealing with these pilotless machines, diverted them by the simple expedient of flying alongside and tipping the wing of the bomb to turn it away towards the sea.

Despite their random, unguided approach, these devices did cause a great deal of damage and loss of life: 47 soldiers were killed when one came down on their camp at Charing Heath, 22 children and 8 staff died at a nursery school in Crockham Hill, 11 died when one came down on an Army camp in Marden, 7 in Dartford and 13 at Swanscombe. A doctors' surgery was hit in Snodland resulting in 12 people losing their lives. The 2 doctors, although badly injured themselves, continued to treat the other victims until help arrived. In all, 152 people were killed by these weapons in the space of 3 months and many more were injured.

As the British and, more particularly, Canadian troops advanced along the coast of northern France, towards the critical ports of Boulogne, Calais and Dunkirk, in the early autumn of 1944, so the attacks increased but these were short-lived as the Allied troops overran the launching sites in September.

The Nazis were not done, however, and around this time they launched their second terror weapon, the V2 rocket. Launched from new, mobile launch pads in The Hague, it was more accurate than the V1. Designed by Werner von Braun, who later played a leading role in the United States' space missions, it was also silent so far as the intended target was concerned. There was no warning when one was about to drop out of the skies and the explosive power of this rocket was infinitely greater than that of the V1.

Because of the vastly improved aiming of these devices and the impossibility of shooting them down because of their height and speed, most reached their target in London. However, sixty-four fell short in Kent causing death and destruction. By 10 November 1944, when Winston Churchill announced the use of these weapons, sundry places in Kent had already had first-hand experience of them: Borough Green, Chislet, Ditton, Eastchurch, Knockholt, Lullingstone, Penshurst, Yalding – all small towns and villages of no military importance. Gravesend had a 'double whammy' when two fell on the town in November 1944, killing a dozen people between them. Sevenoaks was also hit by two rockets. Other places to suffer included Sutton-at-Hone (ten killed), Swanscombe (eight fatalities) and there were further victims in Strood, Whitstable, Westerham and elsewhere, especially metropolitan Kent.

Once again, the advance of the Allied forces meant that the launching sites of this last 'Vengeance' weapon were overrun and Kent's trials and tribulations were finally at an end.

The Grim Total

In the course of the Second World War, 1,608 civilians were killed by enemy action in Kent. Of these deaths, 199 were in the Dover area, 115 in Canterbury and 103 in and around Ashford. A total of 29,272 high-explosive bombs were dropped and 727,784 incendiaries. To these figures must be added the 1,422 V1 'Flying Bombs', 64 V2s and a considerable number of shells fired from heavy batteries on the French coast.

Marine Bandsmen Blasted

With the end of the Second World War, Kent settled back to the more peaceful, bucolic life it had led before. But not for too long: in the 1960s and 1970s the Provisional IRA began to make its presence felt, both in Northern Ireland and in Great Britain. Kent was once again to be a target, first with a make-shift bomb at the Hare and Hounds public house in Maidstone and then, more seriously, when the Royal Marines in Deal were targeted.

The Royal Marines School of Music is a professional training centre for musicians serving with the Marines or the Royal Navy. It recruits school-leavers from the age of 16 who undergo nearly three years of intensive training in both music and combat first aid before being posted to one or other of the Royal Marine bands. Originally located in Portsmouth, it moved to Deal in 1950 and soon became something the townsfolk were immensely proud of. To see these young men practising their music and marching through the town was enough to gladden most hearts.

At around 8 am on 22 September 1989, a group of thirty or so bandsmen finished their pre-breakfast practice with a stirring German march, which they were going to play the following week on a visit to Strasbourg. As they gathered up their instruments and music, exchanging the usual rough military banter with their comrades, and began to straggle back to their barrack rooms an enormous explosion occurred. In the shadow of the camp's chapel a 15lb, home-made bomb had been detonated in the single-storey recreation centre. The explosion could be heard 2 miles away but the repercussions were to have a much wider effect on the school and the town.

The recreational centre and the adjacent accommodation block, in which twenty-six young bandsmen had just been billeted, collapsed like a house of cards, burying all those inside. Other Marines who had been drilling on the parade ground witnessed the devastation and many of the teenaged trainees were in a state of shock for sometime afterwards.

Would-be rescuers rushed to the scene and tore at the piles of masonry and dug in the rubble with their bare hands to try to reach any survivors. Adam Stacey-Clear, the surgical registrar at the Kent and Canterbury Hospital, was among the first medical professionals at the scene: 'There was a lot of emotion,' he told a *Daily Mail* reporter. 'There were plenty of pairs of hands removing the rubble, but it was a very emotional atmosphere. The first thing that struck me was the smell of cordite. There was mayhem, rubble and destruction. We did what we could, putting up drips and giving pain-killing injections.'

Other off-duty hospital staff rushed to the scene and the ambulance crews, who were operating a ban on overtime, waived their principles in order to assist. Dozens of firemen and service personnel were frantically trying to remove the piles of debris to get to trapped victims. From time to time there was a break in the hubbub as a call for quiet was made so that the rescuers could listen for any signs of life and calls for help. High-tech listening equipment was brought into use and the three helicopters hovering overhead were waved away as the sound of their rotors interfered with the listening equipment. Such was the scale of the devastation that a couple of heavy cranes from the nearby Channel Tunnel workings were drafted in to assist.

Eventually it was found that eleven Marines, aged between 20 and 35, had lost their lives and a further twenty-one had been injured.

There was never any doubt as to the perpetrators of this massacre of young men who, despite being in the armed forces, were strictly non-combatants, their role in any conflict being that of stretcher bearers and first-aiders. The IRA issued a statement, saying: 'Mrs Thatcher visited occupied Ireland with a message of war at a time when we want peace. Now we, in turn, have visited the Royal Marines in Kent, but we still want peace and we want the British Government to leave our country.' This statement, couched in the normal form for an authentic claim by the IRA, was signed by P O'Neill, Irish Republican Publicity Bureau, Dublin.

In the days that followed this outrage, the people of Deal arrived at the gates of the barracks in their hundreds, laying bunches of flowers and bowing their heads in silent respect. One of the most poignant sights that quiet Sunday afternoon was a lone Marine, limping to face the entrance and sobbing as he stood to attention for his comrades.

Once the first shock had worn off, there were vociferous demands to know how, at a time when IRA activities were at a peak, such an outrage could have occurred. Most of the anger was directed at the lack of security at the school and there were claims that the unarmed civilian security guards were lax and often asleep on the job. To what extent these allegations were true and may have contributed to the disaster is not known but the security was very quickly placed in the hands of armed Royal Marines.

Meanwhile, the police and intelligence services began a hunt for the perpetrators. They soon found that three Irishmen had taken a holiday lease on a house just behind the barracks and had been seen in the area. The evening before the explosion one of them had attracted attention to himself by pacing the floor of the nearby Green Beret public house, where the Marines were accustomed to meet up when off duty. The landlady, Suzanne Glidden, told the press as she comforted the girlfriend of one of the victims after the outrage, 'He stood out because we seldom get outsiders here. He seemed to be twitchy and was constantly looking at his watch. He kept rushing out, saying he was looking for a friend who was a security guard at the barracks.'

There was the usual Thursday night disco at the barracks that night and it is suspected that the three IRA plotters sent in a female associate to actually place the time-bomb. The use of young girls to infiltrate discos and other social events at military installations was one of the IRA's tried and tested tactics. 'Suitable' girls were always welcome at these discos at the School of Music and their suitability does not always seem to have been properly checked. A perusal of the guest book showed that visitors had signed themselves in, using a variety of aliases, such as Mr and Mrs Mickey Mouse. 'That's how good the security was,' said Kathleen Roe, whose husband was one of the lucky survivors.

The then Defence Secretary, Tom King, visited the scene on the day of the explosion and agreed that security was not all it should have been. 'Obviously, I am not coming here today to say I could be satisfied with security arrangements.' As he passed on messages of sympathy and condolence from the Queen and Mrs Thatcher, he added:

> What I find so appalling is that the real evil of these murderers and the godfathers who send them is that they know atrocities like this will achieve nothing. These Marine bandsmen were well-loved in this community. They provided employment for millions across the country and the world.
>
> We shall find whomever is responsible for this outrage, make no mistake about that, just as we have done with previous outrages. We will get these evil men. Twenty years on they will not win. What they want is an end to democracy and freedom.

But for the memory of those who died, we will never surrender to the killers. These people command no respect. They are just evil men whose only trade is killing. They have no respect in the Republic and little in Northern Ireland. In the end they will be brought to justice.

Despite these brave and robust words, no one was ever brought to justice for the killing and some fifteen years later, all the members of the Provisional IRA then in prison were released under the terms of the Belfast Agreement and the Northern Ireland Peace Accord.

But Tom King was right about the deep-seated affection the town felt for the band. One week after the bombing the entire personnel of the School of Music exercised their right as freemen of the town to march through the crowded streets of Deal with drums beating and colours flying. This gesture of defiance was met with enormous applause, especially when it was realised that spaces had been left in the ranks where the eleven victims should have been. One spectator, Sean White, told the BBC some years later,

I will never forget the day that our town was devastated by the IRA. At the time I was working in the town centre. We all knew we had to be strong for those who had lost loved ones and in true Deal spirit, thousands lined the street seven days later when our brave bandsmen marched through the town, leaving spaces where the murdered lads would have been.

The incident had repercussions well beyond the town of Deal, especially among other members of the Royal Marines bands, most of whom knew everybody else in that small, closed community of musicians. One of these, Sid Bratley, recalled,

I had left the Royal Marines School of Music eighteen months earlier and was serving in Scotland at HMS *Cochrane* at Rosyth. On that day I heard the news in a minibus full of my colleagues while travelling in Northern Ireland. That evening we were due to beat retreat on board a ship in Belfast. The end of the ceremony was marked by a rendition of *Sunset*. This was by far the hardest version of *Sunset* I was ever asked to play. Myself and many of my colleagues found it impossible to play continuously from the first to last note, our thoughts being elsewhere at the time.

It is a matter of deep regret to the Deal townsfolk that, only a few years after, the School of Music moved away to a new home in Portsmouth. A quarter of a century later, the incident is still remembered each year with a special service of remembrance and concerts by the Royal Marines in Deal.

Chapter 8

Plague and Pestilence

The Demise of Dode

The county of Kent has not been spared the diseases and illnesses that have afflicted the rest of the country – and indeed the world in some cases. The earliest, reliably recorded incident of these was perhaps what was then described as 'The Great Pestilence' and became known as the Black Death, which raged across Europe from the East in the fourteenth century.

Although generally regarded as a single, virulent disease, the Black Death came in three closely related forms. The most common and basic form of these was bubonic plague, so-called because of the swellings or 'buboes' (swollen lymph nodes) that appeared in the victim's armpits or groin, and which was spread by fleas that had feasted on infected rats. A complication of this was the pneumonic plague which involved the respiratory system and could be spread by simply inhaling the breath of a sufferer. Although less common than the bubonic type, the pneumonic variant was much more virulent and life expectancy was only a day or two as compared with a week or so in the case of the bubonic plague. There was also a much rarer version of the disease which affected the blood system causing septicaemia.

Although now treatable with antibiotics, there was no cure for the plague in the Middle Ages and few persons who were infected survived. Without knowledge of how the disease was spread, it was impossible for people to protect themselves from it, although many believed it to be contagious and that avoidance of the victims and their clothing and possessions was the answer. Consequently the sick were often simply abandoned to their fate. Some people believed the disease was spread by Jews, lepers and other minority groups and so these were frequently burnt alive as scapegoats. Few, if any, correctly traced the disease to rats and their fleas.

According to Giovanni Boccaccio in his *The Decameron*, the populace in Italy generally divided itself into two groups. One believed that moderate living, partaking of only the best food and wine, and avoidance of any sick person was the answer. They formed small communities apart, shutting themselves in houses where there were no ill persons and tried to ignore the phenomenon. Another group took the opposite view and adopted a 'live for today, for tomorrow we die' attitude, drinking and carousing in the taverns and taking over any of the abandoned houses that they fancied. But these, too, avoided the sick as far as possible. It may be assumed that something similar occurred in other countries affected by the plague, including Britain.

In June 1348, a fleet of ships from Bordeaux arrived at the port of Melcombe Regis in Dorset, carrying a cargo of wine – and plague-infested rats. Having raged through continental Europe, the disease had now reached the shores of Britain and soon it had spread as far as Kent. Coming as it did from the west, the plague affected the western half of the county more than the east and completely wiped out a number of villages, some of which were permanently deserted and never again occupied. One such village was Dode, in Luddesdown parish near Snodland. The precise location of this lost village is uncertain, although Dode church still remains and the village is presumed to have been nearby.

The plague spread like wildfire throughout the county with peasants dropping dead in the fields and with the streets of the town being littered with corpses, which few dared to move for fear of catching the disease. Mediaeval towns were ideal places for the disease to spread, with their filthy streets and open gutters into which the townsfolk threw all their rubbish. The Victorian historian, Dr Gasquet, described the spread of the disease in the following terms:

> One example may be given here of the rapidity with which, during the great sickness, members of a family followed one another to the grave. Sir Thomas Dene, of Ospring [sic], about three miles from Faversham, in the northern part of the Diocese of Rochester, died on May the 18th, 1349. At the time of his death he had four daughters – Benedicta, five years old, Margaret, four years, and Martha and Joan, younger still. By July the 8th, Martha, the wife of Sir Thomas, had also died, and from the inquisition (inquest) taken on Monday, the 3rd of August, 1349, it appears that of the children, the two youngest were then also dead. Thus, out of a family of six, the father, mother and two children had been carried off by the disease.

Sir Thomas's namesake (and possible relative), Brother William Dene, a monk in Rochester at the time of the plague, wrote:

> A plague such as never before had been heard of ravaged England in this year. The Bishop of Rochester (Hamo de Hythe), out of his

small household lost four priests, five gentlemen, ten serving men, seven young clerks and six pages, so that not a soul remained who might serve him in any office.

At the Malling Benedictine nunnery he blessed two Abbesses upon their appointment and both quickly died and there were left there only four professional nuns and four novices. To one of these the Bishop committed the charge of the temporals, to another that of the spirituals, because no proper person for Abbess could be found.

. . . Alas, for our sorrow, this mortality swept away so vast a multitude of both sexes that none could be found to carry the corpses to the grave. Men and women bore their own offspring on their shoulders to the church, and cast them into a common pit. From these there proceeded so great a stench that hardly anyone dared to cross the cemeteries.

In fact, enticed by the sums of money offered, a few hardy souls did volunteer to collect the bodies but the graveyards were soon full and mass burials took place in the fields or anywhere else that was remotely suitable. The population of Kent at this time was probably little more than 100,000, of whom around one-third lost their lives through the Black Death within the space of a year. Brother Dene's account continued:

So great was the deficiency of labourers and workmen of every kind in those days that more than a third of the land over the whole kingdom remained uncultivated. The labourers and skilled workmen were imbued with such a spirit of rebellion that neither king, law nor justice could curb them. The whole people for the greater part ever became more depraved, more prone to every vice, and more inclined than before to evil and wickedness.

Although the plague that swept Britain in 1348/9 was the worst and most widespread manifestation of this dreadful disease, further outbreaks were to occur during the next 300 years or so. Some scattered attempts were made to improve sanitation and a law in 1388 decreed that anyone depositing filth and dung into streams and rivers could be fined £20 but, despite this, in places like Hythe, the 'blood of swine, steers and sheep' continued to contaminate the town's springs and thence flow into the wells from which the townsfolk drew their water.

A further outbreak occurred in 1563 on the south coast and, in Maidstone, householders were ordered to throw down a pail containing at least 2 gallons of water into the gutters each day from March to September.

Although scarcely effective against this rat-borne disease, it was probably more beneficial than the King's exhortation to the bishops to encourage the saying of prayers.

In 1603 the plague was rampant again in London where dogs believed to be carrying the disease were summarily slaughtered. This example was followed in Dover two years later, when a man was paid 2*d* for every stray dog destroyed. Later, the same (or another) man was paid 8*s* for 'knocking of dogs on the head'. By 1610, 193 households in the small town of Sandwich were affected by the plague.

Folkestone was another town that was to suffer. In 1624 the town warden was unable to collect the rates and the town virtually shut down. Then it was the turn of Dover again and King Charles I, who was travelling from plague-ridden London to Dover to meet his queen, Henrietta Maria, from France, ordered that nobody who was not a member of the court was to follow his party or come within 12 miles of them.

But it was London, the great metropolis, that was the worst affected and the death rate there was 5,000 a week. As a result, the Corporation of Maidstone decreed that 'no hoy, nor foot or horse post [was] to carry any goods to London' and, similarly, no goods could be received from London unless they were already on their way, in which case they were to be opened by the hoy boatmen and dried in the fields for two weeks before being delivered. In addition, no visitors from London were to be entertained in any house in Maidstone. To enforce this, the town employed seven watchmen and seven wardmen to be posted to various places to prevent the entry of suspect goods or persons into the town. With the war against the Dutch in full swing in 1665, the Commissioner for the Sick and Wounded, John Evelyn, was having great difficulty in finding refuge for such persons. Maidstone, in keeping with its previous practice, was strongly opposed to receiving any more casualties, fearing they might bring the plague with them. Similarly, Dover continued its war against 'hogs, dogs and cats' running free and followed Maidstone's example of forbidding the sheltering of Londoners. In the 1-year period between September 1665 and September 1666, it is estimated that 352 people in Kent died from the plague.

Partly at least because of the Great Fire of London in 1666, the plague abated and the country was never again to be afflicted by this dreadful disease. Cholera, smallpox and typhus were the new scourges, but improved sanitation and better medical knowledge meant that even these would never equal the dreadful toll of the Black Death.

Death of the 'Strangers'

For over a thousand years, people in Asia had been dying from a terrible illness that brought on severe diarrhoea which in turn resulted in dehydration and, in most cases, a painful death. It was not only the peoples indigenous to that continent who suffered; the British Army in India lost many of its officers and men from this disease, which was no respecter of rank or social status. The name given to this scourge was cholera.

For most of this time cholera was confined to the Far East but, by the beginning of the nineteenth century it had made its presence known in England and Kent was not to be spared. In 1808, according to the *The Times*, the Ashford parish register recorded that:

> In the course of 37 days, 47 men in the seriously overcrowded barracks had been buried. The symptoms were fever and the appearance of a slight cold. Death occurred after two or three days.
>
> The disorder, we are sorry to add, is not in the least abated, though, happily for the inhabitants, it is by no means infectious, not a soldier or person living in the town having died of the same complaint – a positive proof that the malady is entirely owing to the unhealthy situation and construction of the barracks. But what shall we say of the criminality of those who, knowing the cause of this mortality and possessing the power to terminate it, by removing the men, still permit the evil to continue! . . . If a remedy be not instantly applied, we shall not be deterred, by any consideration whatever, from holding up to merited execration and contempt those who can be so criminally callous as to turn a deaf ear, for a single hour longer, to the imperious call of duty and humanity.

(Small wonder that the nickname of *The Times* was 'The Thunderer')

Less than a decade later, in 1817, the first of seven cholera pandemics occurred in Europe. In 1832 it was reported that there were more than eighty cases in the convict hulks anchored off Chatham, with sixteen people having died, including a nurse and Dr Conway who had been attending the sick men.

Out of ignorance, most public authorities gave advice that would have had very little real effect. At the beginning of the 1832 epidemic, in which 512 townsfolk died, the Dundee Board of Health, for example, advised that 'people of all ranks go out as little as possible at night, and to clothe themselves more warmly. During the prevalence of an epidemic, all assemblages of large bodies of the working classes, unless at church, should be avoided.' The same authority also published a pamphlet that stated that 'attacks of cholera are uniformly found to be most frequent and virulent in low-lying districts, on the banks of rivers, and where there are large collections of refuse, particularly amidst human dwellings'.

In fact, the cause of the disease – which had not yet been fully identified – was the drinking of polluted water, and the insanitary living conditions, in the towns and cities in particular, were perfect for the its spread. One of the worst epidemics was in the summer of 1849 when over 33,000 people died of cholera in Britain – 13,000 of whom were in London. The larger towns were smelly and crowded, with open-air markets and open sewers. Butchers and fishmongers would throw their offal and putrid flesh into the gutters to rot; refuse from dwellings was simply thrown into the street; an outdoor toilet would be used by several families – all of these unhygienic practices adding to the likelihood of the drinking water from the public wells and pumps being contaminated.

But some people seemed to have an inkling about where the problem really lay. Henry Mayhew, writing in the *Morning Chronicle* on 24 September 1849, described a typical scene:

We then journeyed on to London Street, down which the tidal ditch continues its course. In No 1 of this street the cholera first appeared seventeen years ago and spread up it with fearful virulence; but this year it appeared at the opposite end and ran down it with like severity. As we passed along the reeking banks of the sewer the sun shone upon a narrow slip of the water. In the bright light it appeared the colour of strong green tea, and positively looked as solid as black marble in the shadow – indeed it was more like watery mud than muddy water; and yet we were assured that this was the only water the wretched inhabitants had to drink.

As we gazed in horror at it, we saw drains and sewers emptying their filthy contents into it; we saw a whole tier of doorless privies in the open road, common to men and women, built over it; we heard bucket after bucket of filth splash into it, and the limbs of the vagrant boys bathing in it seemed by pure force of contrast, white as Parian marble.

In this wretched place we were taken to a house where an infant lay dead of the cholera. We asked if they really did drink the water? The answer was, 'They were obliged to drink the ditch, without they could beg or thieve a pail-full of water.'

'But have you spoken to your landlord about having it laid on for you?'

'Yes, Sir and he says he will do it, and do it, but we know him better than to believe him.'

Although the crowded towns were obviously where cholera was most virulent and spread most rapidly, the *Maidstone and Kentish Journal* in September 1849 took 'much pleasure in stating that there have been no cases of cholera in Maidstone for the last week or ten days!'.

However, inhabitants of the tranquil Kent countryside were not entirely immune from this disease. On 23 September 1849, the Revd Henry Wilberforce, the vicar of East Farleigh, buried forty-three 'strangers' in a mass grave in the churchyard. They had all died of cholera in what was to be one of the worst outbreaks of this disease that the country had ever experienced. In addition to these victims, around 300 workers on the farm suffered from the disease but recovered.

Why strangers? Because they were not locals and their true identity was never ascertained. These unfortunate souls were working in the hop fields at Court Lodge Farm, Barming and it seems probable that they had arrived from Ireland. The farmer, Mr Ellis, had no reason to enquire as to their identity; such people simply arrived at the farm and were taken on as seasonal workers. They were paid in cash on a piecework basis and, as there was no income tax or National Insurance deduction to be made, no questions were asked of those seeking work, whether they were locals, gypsies, Londoners or, as in this case, from further afield. In any event, this was one of the largest hop farms in the county and a huge number of hop pickers arrived there each year. By the end of the nineteenth century it was estimated that there were more than ¼ million hop pickers working in Kent, about 70,000 of whom came from the capital.

Pickers who did not live locally were mostly housed in poor, insanitary and infested shacks, hopper huts or simply in tents. The water supply was from wells or streams, or even the River Medway itself, which, contaminated by raw sewage coming down the river from Tonbridge and other places upstream, encouraged the spread of this bacterial infection. It is noticeable that those local workers who returned home each night were spared, which confirmed the contemporary view that it was the conditions endured in these temporary lodgings that were to blame.

But the outbreak was not confined to just this one farm; other hop gardens in nearby Yalding and Loose were similarly affected and a further thirty workers died there. The first signs of the disease were noted in East Farleigh on 12 September and a doctor was summoned from Maidstone. He arrived four days later and was met by a shocking scene. In his report, Dr Plomley recorded that: 'Sixty-two persons were suffering more or less from the disease. Four were in the agonies of death and eight more in the most profound collapse, all of whom died before the following morning. The melancholy was much heightened by the almost incessant wailings of the Irish in "waking" their lost friends.'

He added that:

Cholera is linked to the accommodation with which the 'strangers' were provided . . . The disease arose entirely from causes which are remediable and removable; namely impure air arising from overcrowded and ill-ventilated apartments, impure water derived from wells containing the soakage of cow yards and human filth and impure food sold at a cheap rate by unprincipled itinerant vendors of putrid fish and adulterated bread.

In response to this shocking report, other doctors quickly arrived on the scene from as far afield as Guy's Hospital and the local school was brought into use as an isolation hospital, as was part of the nearby workhouse. Nursing was provided by a handful of brave local ladies, including the wife of the vicar.

The Registrar General's Quarterly Return of Births, Death and Marriages in England, published in November 1849, reported that:

In Kent, the districts on the Thames, the Medway and the coast from Gravesend, Milton, Rochester and Chatham suffered severely. The deaths in Gravesend are on an average 127 in this quarter: they were in the last quarter 340, of which 193 were by cholera. There are no available sewers and the drainage falls into rudely constructed cesspools . . . Maidstone, on the Medway, suffered; but of 43 deaths from cholera in Loose . . . all except two or three were among vagrants, chiefly Irish, who came into the parish of East Farleigh to pick hops.

Five years later, Kent had scarcely recovered from the effects of the 1849 cholera outbreak when yet another arrived on the scene. This dreadful disease, for which there was no cure known at the time, had already struck down innumerable soldiers in the Crimea and now it was prevalent in Maidstone, Sevenoaks, Tunbridge Wells, Canterbury and many other parts of Kent, especially Sandgate, where, despite many improvements to the water supply and the drainage system, the disease still made its presence known. It later transpired that the new drainage system was faulty and prone to leaks and blockages, polluting all the private water supplies.

The symptoms of diarrhoea and cases of dysentery were treated by the much-harassed doctors and nurses and some more robust patients survived but for 50 per cent, mainly the very old and the very young, the disease proved fatal.

Barges plying their trade from London to Faversham, Sittingbourne, Maidstone, Sheerness and Aylesford were responsible for further outbreaks in October 1866. From these towns it quickly spread once more to the fertile breeding grounds of the hop fields in Yalding, Hunton, Nettlestead, Teston, Marden, Staplehurst, Otham, Bearsted and Barming.

In an effort to prevent the spread of the disease, the authorities in Maidstone arranged in September for the South Eastern Railway to convey the hop pickers direct to the hop gardens from London to safeguard the town but to no avail. Bad weather prevented any picking for several days and the pickers were confined to their insanitary huts or tents. Others, who had arrived without any prior arrangements, were sleeping under hedges or on doorsteps. In Gravesend alone, 1,200 prospective workers slept rough in Gravesend town centre each night and the Coxheath workhouse took in 600 or 700 each night. And with the rain came the disease.

Deadly Diseases

By the end of the nineteenth century, the prevalence of cholera seems to have subsided, only to have been replaced by typhoid fever and smallpox. Typhoid is caused by bacteria transmitted by the ingestion of food or water contaminated with human faeces and results in a high fever, headache and a cough. It is not always fatal and the use of modern antibiotics means that the mortality rate is nowadays negligible. But this has not always been the case; a number of famous people have succumbed to the disease, including Queen Victoria's husband, Prince Albert, and Major Gonville Bromhead VC, whose exploits at Rorke's Drift were chronicled in the film *Zulu* in which he was played by Michael Caine.

More locally and on a more mundane level, in September 1897 there was a serious typhoid epidemic in the Maidstone area which lasted all of four months. In total, there were over 1,800 cases reported in the borough which prompted the local government inspectors to write in their official report:

> We have no hesitation in coming to the conclusion that the epidemic was caused by the pollution of water by the Maidstone [Water] Company from their Farleigh sources . . . grave sanitary defects exist in the construction of some of the sewers and of many house drains and water closets . . . But the responsibility for the existence of these insanitary conditions lies with the town council whose duty it was to take steps that would lead to the effective remedy of these defects.

Every house in which a case of typhoid fever had been confirmed was thoroughly disinfected and fumigated, under the direction of the delightfully named Inspector of Nuisances, once the patient or patients had either died, recovered or been removed to hospital. The walls, floors and ceilings of the affected rooms were sprayed with water and then sulphur was burned in the sealed room for 24 hours. The ceilings were then given a fresh coat of whitewash, the walls and woodwork washed with carbolic and any soiled wallpaper removed. Bedding was taken to the laundry and disinfecting station for attention.

For at least six months, the town suffered a serious loss of trade as outsiders shunned the town. The shops were doing very little business and the two railway companies reported few passengers using their services. Only one school, St Stephen's in Tovil, remained open; the Assize Court moved to Canterbury and the Quarter Sessions to Westminster; most public gatherings were cancelled, although a very much reduced Michaelmas Fair was held in October 1897.

The pollution of the water at a hop pickers' encampment just outside the town – from the same source as that supplying Maidstone – claimed further victims in that autumn. In all, 132 people died from the disease in the 4 months it raged throughout the county town. During just one weekend, thirty victims were buried in Maidstone cemetery, prompting the *Kent Messenger* to write in its issue of 16 October 1897: 'All through Sunday afternoon, Stone Street witnessed a long, irregular procession of people bound for "God's Acre." The day of rest brought no rest to the grave digger.'

While the polluted water supply was the principal cause of the typhoid and other epidemics, the disgusting conditions in which some of the poorer classes were obliged to live did not help matters and other possible sources of contamination were faulty drains and sewers that produced 'air pollution and disease provoking vapours'. Maidstone's Medical Officer of Health, Matthew A Adams, campaigned for many years for the houses in certain parts of Maidstone to be demolished. Grove Court and Bonny's Yard by the River Len were among the oldest premises in the town and were found to be overcrowded and lacking in ventilation. In December, 1898, Mr Adams reported that, in Grove Court:

> There are nine closets about twelve feet in front of the houses with very foul hopper pans, unprovided with any means for flushing. The service channelling and pavement are defective and water finds its way readily into the basements of the dwellings . . . at No. 3 there are six inhabitants . . . [who] sleep in an attic affording only 127 cubic feet of air space per head. At No 40 Ebenezer Place the roof leaks and the wall is green from constant wet . . . the closets are wooden

structures, very dark, out of repair . . . pans very foul and unflushed.

Socially, as one might expect, they are occupied by the lowest class of the people, day labourers and costers for the most part. Sometimes bargemen and waterside loafers: such people as belong to a distinct class and who as a matter of choice gravitate to the most squalid slums they can find . . . if turned out from one place as a matter of course they emigrate to the next dirtiest and cheapest they can discover . . . In the ten years from 1 July 1888 . . . there have been fifty-two deaths upon this area, constituting a death rate 25.2 per thousand per annum which is little short of double the rate for the town generally. The mean age of death I find to be seventeen years . . . Without doubt, damp, dirt and squalor are accountable.

In fact, nearly half the houses in Maidstone had water closets with no mechanical means of flushing and the closets in two-thirds of all the houses in the town were connected to imperfectly flushed drains. The townsfolk were therefore advised to keep all food away from flies, sink waste pipes and household drains. In the event of an attack, usually indicated by diarrhoea, vomiting, headache, stomach pains and loss of appetite, they were advised to seek medical advice. A team of medical officers and doctors visited all reported cases and decided whether or not the patient should be hospitalised. As there were only thirty beds available at the West Kent Hospital, emergency hospitals or treatment centres were set up, making use of schools and mission halls. All the centres were provided with the latest innovation: a telephone. Most patients were, however, treated at home by one of the district nurses, many of whom had been brought in especially from the London hospitals. One probationer nurse who came to Maidstone from London to assist was Edith Cavell, who was to be shot by the Germans in 1915.

Only three years later, in 1900, another 132 people died from typhoid fever in the Maidstone area, this also being caused by the spring water in Farleigh being contaminated by the insanitary arrangements provided for hop pickers. And so, the poor, unfortunate hop pickers, the same kind of people who had suffered in the earlier cholera outbreaks, were now facing yet another deadly disease.

As late as 1928, Dr Alfred Greenwood, the County Medical Officer of Health, was reporting to the Royal Sanitary Institute that, the previous summer (1927), he had found that many similar sources of pollution still existed but, fortunately, they had not included the typhoid virus. He maintained that there ought to be an adequate water supply within reach of the pickers and that the use of streams for drinking water should be forbidden. There should also be adequate and suitable lavatories, there sometimes being just 1 for 200 workers.

Around the same time as typhoid fever was taking its toll, other people in Kent were falling victim to smallpox. Smallpox is an infectious disease unique to humans and the name was first coined in the fifteenth century to distinguish it from great pox (syphilis). The virus was usually passed on through breathing in airborne droplets from the nose or mouth of an infected person, although it could also be spread through infected bedding or clothing. The disease made its appearance in the form of blisters or pustules (pocks) which, when they burst, leave characteristic scars, particularly on the face, which was described as 'pock-marked'.

The disease was widespread in the eighteenth century, when it killed around 400,000 people in Europe each year, the death rate being up to 50 per cent for adults and more than 80 per cent in the case of children. There were two pandemics in 1824–29 and 1837–40, the latter claiming 30,000 victims in England. Many famous people contracted the disease, which was no respecter of rank or wealth. King Louis XV of France succumbed, as did Edward VI of England. Queen Elizabeth I contracted smallpox but survived, as did the composers Mozart and Beethoven, Presidents Washington and Lincoln of America and Joseph Stalin of the USSR. All these were scarred for the rest of their life and Queen Elizabeth endeavoured to hide the pock marks by heavy make-up. Stalin often had photographs touched up to disguise the marks.

The British scientist, Edward Jenner, had discovered a vaccination more than a century earlier but the application of this vaccine was far from universally adopted. It was reported that in towns such as Maidstone, Dartford and Gravesend, the public were completely indifferent to the protection offered by vaccination and so were highly susceptible to contracting the disease. However, this may have been due in no small measure to the cost. A few items from the Chiddingstone area that Gerald Davey found and quoted in an article in *Bygone Kent* included:

> November 1788: Mary Parson's child a smallpox inoculation, 7/6d
> 1799: Joseph Hider paid 7/6d 'for Smalpocks.'

> February 1806: Towards the inoculating of Jo Wites family of the Cow-Pox: 24/-.

Given that the weekly wage of a farm worker at this time would have been between 10s and 15s, the cost of inoculation would have been beyond the means of many families, although many such payments were in fact made by the parish Overseers of the Poor. Names, dates and costs do not mean much in themselves so to gain a little insight into just what this disease meant to at least one family, Gerald Davey supplied a typical example.

On a cold winter's day in February 1810, John Maynard, a 31-year-old shoemaker, married 17-year-old Sarah Longley in Chiddingstone parish church. They set up home in Chiddingstone Hoath where, in due course, first one and then another son was born and christened John and Thomas respectively. In October 1813, when John was about 2½ and Thomas was but a couple of months old, smallpox hit the area. The local doctor, Dr Creasey, drove over from Edenbridge and inoculated Sarah and the two infants, together with some other local residents, at a cost of *2s 6d* per person. Whether Sarah had already contracted the disease prior to being inoculated or whether she caught it despite the precautions, she very soon developed the dreaded symptoms and Dr Creasey was recalled. He examined her and confirmed that she had smallpox and so he inoculated John Maynard and fifteen other people at the parish's expense.

Sarah's condition deteriorated and now baby Thomas was also infected so the doctor rode over every day to apply a course of treatment which seemed to have had little effect. By the end of October, Sarah was seriously ill with an acute infectious fever, sickness and delirium, her normally pretty young features bloated and swollen, disfigured by the weeping, pus-filled blisters which characterise this disease. Blister powders were applied and draughts of medication given but to no avail; on 2 November 1813, Sarah died at the age of 20, to be followed to the grave by baby Thomas just four days later.

Many more of the inhabitants of this small, rural parish were infected, although most survived. When Sarah was buried three days later, the funeral service was conducted by the curate from nearby Hever as it appears the vicar of Chiddingstone and his curate were themselves, or their families, affected by the outbreak.

John Maynard's finances were insufficient to cover the cost of the funerals of his wife and son and this was paid by the parish – a total of *9s* for the two.

Even the making of vaccination compulsory in 1853 failed to resolve the problem. In fact, there was strong resistance to the idea of vaccination in certain quarters, people believing that the immunisation offered was itself responsible for other maladies or even the spread of smallpox itself. When the Prime Minister, William Ewart Gladstone, was scheduled to speak at Greenwich in 1871, posters were displayed and handbills circulated, couched in the following terms:

Mr GLADSTONE at Greenwich

VACCINATION

PEOPLE of GREENWICH, –

Mr GLADSTONE is going to address you. Now remember that, so long as the blood-poisoning produced by Vaccination, continues, other matters are of little importance. By Vaccination, the Government is spreading a pestilence throughout the land, which keeps up a sickly and diseased population.

Will you allow such a thing to continue? Surely not. Then we conjure you to ask the following questions of the Prime Minister; and mind you get an answer.

Yours &c,

A MEMBER OF THE ANTI-VACCINATION LEAGUE

October 13th 1871

1. Will you suspend the vaccination laws, which are nothing else than a system of blood-poisoning?
2. If vaccination be proved to be wrong, will you not be poisoning thousands of children before the meeting of Parliament in February next?
3. Has not the Queen suffered from her re-vaccination in the spring of this year – and do not the symptoms clearly prove that she has?
4. Do you think it right that honest citizens should be sent to prison because they refuse to poison their children by vaccination?
5. Is not vaccination a worse dogma than that of the infallibility of the Pope?
6. Does not the Report of the Select Committee of the House of Commons on the vaccination question prove that the former legislation had been wrong?
7. Assuming vaccination to be wrong, are you not from day to day producing the most fearful results as regards the population?
8. If you believe vaccination to be right, state your reasons.
9. Does not the late amount of small-pox, both in England and France, clearly prove that the more vaccination there is, the more small-pox we have?
10. Did not the late Sir Robert Peel, when in office, protest against compulsory vaccination, as being contrary to the constitution of the country?
11. Did not Sir William Jenner say before the Select Committee of the House of Commons that he was 'no authority' on vaccination? And if not, who is an authority?
12. Although you are not a Doctor, do you agree in the evidence given before the Select committee by Sir Dominic Corrigan MD & MP, that unvaccinated children are bags of petroleum or barrels of Gunpowder? And further, do you agree with Sir William Jenner, and Dr. Gull, that it is immaterial whether we vaccinate from healthy or unhealthy subjects?

Sir William Jenner – not to be confused with Edward Jenner, the pioneer of the vaccination for smallpox – was a native of Chatham and was, at the time of this dispute, the physician in ordinary to Queen Victoria and the Prince of Wales and consequently a very highly regarded doctor.

In April 1878, a Chatham watchmaker by the name of Charles Nye was sentenced to one month's imprisonment for refusing to have his children inoculated and failing to pay the fine imposed at a previous hearing. The Secretary of the local Anti-Vaccination Society, he had previously served several terms of imprisonment for similar offences.

Smallpox contamination was widespread near the Thames and Medway rivers, and it was in places along the banks of these waterways that most cases were reported. Being known to be highly infectious, the Victorians very properly resorted to isolating sufferers, using hospital ships and isolation hospitals in places like Dartford, where the Joyce Green, River and Orchard hospitals were given over to this use. By January 1903, there were more than 800 patients being treated on board hospital ships, moored in the Thames Estuary off Gravesend in what was described as the worst smallpox epidemic in British medical history.

It is sad that, although a completely safe and effective vaccination was available, so many Kentish Men and Men of Kent needlessly lost their lives through their fear of this procedure. Fortunately, as time went on, opposition to vaccination waned and the practice became routine. In 1979, the disease was declared to have been completely eradicated throughout the world.

Select Bibliography

Bignell, Alan. *Kent Headlines*, Newbury: Countryside Books, 1989

Bignell, Alan. *Kent Shipwrecks*, Newbury: Countryside Books, 2001

Byegone Kent (various articles)

Carlile, J C. *Folkestone During the War, 1914–1919*, Folkestone: F J Parsons, 1920

Coxon, Lt Cdr Stanley W. *Dover During the Dark Days*, London: John Lane, 1919

Crampton, Paul. *The Blitz of Canterbury*, Rainham: Meresborough Books, 1989

Easdown, Martin. *Victoria's Golden Pier*, Kent: Marling Publications, 1998

Easdown, Martin. *A Glint in the Sky*, Barnsley: Pen & Sword Books, 2004

Easdown, Martin and Sage, Linda. *Cries from a Deep Blue Sea*, Hythe: Marlinova, 2004

Johnson, W H. *A Grim Almanac of Kent*, Stroud: Sutton Publishing, 2008

Lane, Anthony. *Shipwrecks of Kent*, Stroud: Tempus, 1999

Moore, W G. *Early Bird*, London: Putnam, 1963

New York Times, 'Log of the Steamer Bywell Castle', 6 September 1878

Ogley, Bob. *Kent at War*, Westerham: Froglets Publications, 1994

Ogley, Bob. *Kent: A Chronicle of the Century* (vols 1–4), Westerham: Froglets Publications, 1996

Ogley, Bob. *Kent 1800 – 1899: A Chronicle of the Nineteenth Century*, Westerham: Froglets Publications, 2003

Percival, Arthur. 'The Great Explosion at Faversham, 2 April 1916', *Archaeologia Cantiana*, Vol. C (1985)

Vincent, W T. *The Records of the Woolwich District*, Woolwich: J P Jackson, 1878

White, Jerry. *London in the 19th century*, London: Vintage, 2007

Index